"Southern Baptist history is as rich as it is complicated. Only by reckoning with our history can we fulfill the promises of a brighter future for the denomination. The work and witness of T. B. Maston is part of this history that needs to be recovered and remembered. Southern Baptists and the church as a whole have much to learn from Maston's pioneering efforts in Christian ethics and racial reconciliation. His legacy is ours."

—Karen Swallow Prior
Southeastern Baptist Theological Seminary

"In this masterfully written analysis of Maston's theological project, Morrison provides much-needed insight into the theology and historical context of one of the most unsung heroes in Baptist life. Morrison . . . highlights how this towering figure shaped Southern Baptist views on race for generations to come. Morrison's work here is a gift for the church, and one that should not be ignored in the present context."

—Rhyne Putman
New Orleans Baptist Theological Seminary

"Through a critical analysis of Maston's work, Morrison provides for us today a blueprint for tackling the issues that undergird racism, prejudice, and discrimination in Christian institutions. Those who have the courage, confidence, and commitment to aggressively and proactively confront the racial problems inherent in denominational, ecclesiastical, and personal spaces will benefit and be blessed by reading and implementing the strategies put forward in this book."

—William Dwight McKissic
Author of *Beyond Roots: In Search of Blacks in the Bible*

"Those unfamiliar with T. B. Maston now have Paul Morrison to give us an insightful encounter with the theology and ethics of a brave leader who provides both an example and catalyst for our ongoing engagement on questions of race. This volume invites us to understand and utilize an approach to Christian ethics that is properly holistic and helps us think about what it means to be Christian. . . . This is a book for all Christians, not just Baptists."

—Vincent Bacote
Wheaton College

"Paul Morrison joins T. B. Maston's hope to go beyond desegregation to full integration—all races not only eating in the same restaurant but at the same table and in each other's homes. Morrison argues for racial reconciliation within the framework of inerrancy. His excitement and expertise lend to a thoroughly readable commentary on Gen 1, Acts 17, and Maston's ethics."

—Katie Frugé
Director, Center for Cultural Engagement and the Christian Life Commission

Integration

Monographs in Baptist History

VOLUME 23

Ours is a day in which not only the gaze of western culture but also increasingly that of Evangelicals is riveted to the present. The past seems to be nowhere in view and hence it is disparagingly dismissed as being of little value for our rapidly changing world. Such historical amnesia is fatal for any culture, but particularly so for Christian communities whose identity is profoundly bound up with their history. The goal of this new series of monographs, Studies in Baptist History, seeks to provide one of these Christian communities, that of evangelical Baptists, with reasons and resources for remembering the past. The editors are deeply convinced that Baptist history contains rich resources of theological reflection, praxis and spirituality that can help Baptists, as well as other Christians, live more Christianly in the present. The monographs in this series will therefore aim at illuminating various aspects of the Baptist tradition and in the process provide Baptists with a usable past.

Integration

Race, T. B. Maston, and Hope
for the Desegregated Church

Paul J. Morrison

Foreword by Malcolm B. Yarnell III

PICKWICK *Publications* · Eugene, Oregon

INTEGRATION
Race, T. B. Maston, and Hope for the Desegregated Church

Monographs in Baptist History 23

Pickwick Publications
An Imprint of Wipf and Stock Publishers
199 W. 8th Ave., Suite 3
Eugene, OR 97401

www.wipfandstock.com

PAPERBACK ISBN: 978-1-6667-3461-4
HARDCOVER ISBN: 978-1-6667-9066-5
EBOOK ISBN: 978-1-6667-9067-2

Cataloguing-in-Publication data:

Names: Morrison, Paul J., author. | Yarnell, Malcolm B., III, foreword.

Title: Integration : race, T. B. Maston, and hope for the desgregated church / by Paul J. Morrison; foreword by Malcolm B. Yarnell III.

Description: Eugene, OR: Pickwick Publications, 2022 | Series: Monographs in Baptist History | Includes bibliographical references and index.

Identifiers: ISBN 978-1-6667-3461-4 (paperback) | ISBN 978-1-6667-9066-5 (hardcover) | ISBN 978-1-6667-9067-2 (ebook)

Subjects: LCSH: Maston, T. B. (Thomas Buford), 1897–. | Segregation—United States. | Racism—Religious aspects—Christianity. | United States—Church history—20th century.

Classification: BX6237 M67 2022 (paperback) | BX6237 (ebook)

VERSION NUMBER 062022

For Sarah,

My beloved wife and friend.

Contents

Foreword

"White Supremacy." "Critical Race Theory." "Alt-Right." "Social Justice." "Patriarchy." "Reparations." "Humble Slaveholder." "Black Lives Matter." The watchwords which currently dominate conversations between American Christians on social media platforms, in church offices, and at the venues of denominational meetings may be new, but the underlying problems were long ago confronted by Christian leaders with prescient insight. Among those who tried to deal properly with the vices of racism and slavery were important African American theologians like Frederick Douglass and Martin Luther King Jr. It is more difficult to name white theologians who made significant contributions to solving the moral curse of American history. However, one of the most prophetic theological voices was that of a prominent Southern Baptist, an academic ethicist, Thomas Buford Maston (1897–1988).

Maston's life mirrored the biblical ethics he taught and the Lord he followed. The son of a poor Tennessee sharecropper, Thomas converted to Jesus Christ in 1914 and surrendered to follow his Lord as a foreign missionary. However, the severely handicapped child born to Maston and his wife, Essie Mae MacDonald, required their lifelong care. He fulfilled his call by inspiring students to go on mission.[1] Maston's influence upon the Southern Baptist academy was profound. Completing his terminal degree with H. Richard Niebuhr at Yale University in 1939, he established Ethics as a standing department at Southwestern Baptist Theological Seminary. The other Southern Baptist seminaries followed suit and invited him often to address their students. Maston's personal efforts culminated in the creation of the Texas Christian Life Commission in 1950. The Southern Baptist Convention trailed Texas Baptists in 1953 with their own Christian Life Commission, now known as the Ethics and Religious Liberty Commission.

---

1. Martin, *Passport to Servanthood.*

ix

Maston actively challenged America's dominant racism with his advocacy of social desegregation well before the United States Congress and the Supreme Court of the United States began to dismantle the malevolent Jim Crow system with effective laws and judicial rulings. He led Gambrell Street Baptist Church to become one of the first to integrate and his seminary to educate African Americans in fits and starts. Alas, however, Maston's writings on race in the church created such an uproar that resolutions were written against him. His school bowed to political pressure from the denomination, and Maston was driven into retirement in 1963. In recognition of his long service, however, he was allowed space to write in the library. From there, he continued to advocate for Christian churches and denominations to integrate and provide full opportunity for equal leadership by African Americans. Integration was, according to Maston's words and Maston's deeds, the revealed will of God.

Paul Morrison explores and extends Maston's development of a Christian ethic of race relations in this helpful book. He explains how Maston arrived at his advanced social ethics as a conservative theologian. The word of God inspired by the Holy Spirit was his supreme authority, even as he affirmed general revelation in conscience and nature. The author of a popular volume on biblical ethics still in use,[2] Maston supported his moral system in Scripture's presentation of the perfections of God. Theology proper grounds Christian ethics because human beings are made in the image of God. Morrison proceeds to show how Maston effectively exposed and corrected the culturally captive interpretations of certain Bible passages by American racists. Appreciative but not uncritical, Morrison translates the approaches of Maston for contemporary scholars by demonstrating his interpretation of Scripture was characterized by a principled hermeneutic and his moral system by a type of virtue ethics.

Although any review of this great man's legacy rightly emphasizes his work on race and Christianity, Maston was by no means a "one-issue" thinker.[3] He considered everything from personal sexuality to social ethics to political theology to discipline in home and church. If I might add my own two cents to Morrison's fine review of this great theological ethicist, I would point out that Maston provides an axiom requiring recovery today: "[O]ne's right relation to God is naturally and inevitably followed with a 'therefore' of responsibility" to one's fellow human beings.[4] Orthodox theology must

2. Maston, *Biblical Ethics*.
3. Maston, *Conscience of a Christian*, 135–36.
4. Maston, *Conscience of a Christian*, 52.

display itself in orthodox ethics. The gospel changes individual persons, who live out the gospel in society.

The believer in Jesus must follow Jesus not merely with Christian words but with Christian deeds. "Another way of expressing the same concept is to say that the real Christian is one who lets the resurrected Christ live in him and express himself through him. In other words, we are real Christians to the degree that we are Christlike."[5] The wise Christian thus rightly withholds laudation from any unrepentant leader who defended slavery, advocated racial superiority, or traded in or retained ownership of their fellow human beings. Christians are called to obey Jesus with veracity of performance, not merely chatter about Him with poetic platitudes.

Please allow me to conclude with a personal confession. T. B. Maston delivered the first theological lecture I ever heard, and it remains cherished. I was visiting the campus of Southwestern Seminary in Fort Worth, Texas, and chose to attend one of the breakout sessions, apparently by chance but certainly by providence. Soon, an assistant guided a frail professor of whom I had never heard into the Truett Conference Room. The retired professor's voice was weak, so they laboriously attached his throat to the sound system with special equipment.

Although his body was failing, the unbroken spiritual power with which T. B. Maston spoke still shakes me to the core of my being. This godly man was apprehended by the word of God, and through him the Spirit of God palpably settled upon our assembly. His extemporaneous lecture began slowly with careful biblical exegesis then proceeded apace to faithful theological interpretation and concluded with profound ethical application. I had never heard anyone speak with such astonishing intellectual and moral ease. He blended biblical piety with theological depth and practical advice in ways I never dreamed possible.

When Maston finished, the audience sat briefly in rapt silence before rising to a standing ovation. In that moment I was impressed to forget all the other seminaries and attend this school, where I was first shaped as a theologian and have now served more than two decades as administrator and full-time professor. Maston's single extraordinary lecture, delivered in human weakness, provided a magnificent standard with which to craft a theological career. I was blessed by Southwestern President Russell Dilday's decision to rehabilitate T. B. Maston and place him front and center before prospective students.

T. B. Maston brought me to Southwestern Baptist Theological Seminary. I pray I will be faithful to his courageous legacy and help the ministers

5. Maston, *Conscience of a Christian*, 32.

who come here become convicted that Christ must be presented freely to every human being, for all are equal before God. Truth without love is falsehood, evangelism without ethics is hypocrisy, and theology without integrity is idolatry, for Scripture's God is without partiality.

Malcolm B. Yarnell III
Research Professor of Theology, Southwestern Baptist Theological Seminary
Teaching Pastor, Lakeside Baptist Church of Granbury
August 26, 2021

Preface

WHEN I WAS 17 years old, I was a sarcastic white kid at a predominately African American high school in East Texas. I played whatever sport was in season and I went to church. There wasn't much else to do in my town. My classes were diverse. My teams were diverse. My friend group was diverse. My church was white.

When I was 17 years old, I also knew I was going to seminary. My friends knew I was going to seminary, and a few of my teachers knew as well, including my economics teacher, a middle-aged white woman, who did not much care for me, or Jesus. I can still remember her probing and scolding me in front of our class for believing in a faith that condoned and supported slavery and segregation. I didn't have an answer. The apologetics class of my youth group Sunday School had not prepared me for this question.

T. B. Maston helped me wrestle with this question. A man who died before I was born gave me hope and consolation in how the church can be consistent with the gospel and winsome with the world. He did not offer a white solution, but a biblical one. His words and life showed me how to engage the culture you are in for the good. T. B. Maston was a reformer of the church. I believe that his words still hold hope for homogenous churches amid diverse communities. I believe that his ideas can still reform the church. This work intends to show how.[1]

---

1. This work is an adaptation of the dissertation: "Segregation, Desegregation, and Integration: The Legacy of Thomas Buford Maston On Race Relations," Southwestern Baptist Theological Seminary, 2018.

Acknowledgments

ANY ENDEAVOR OF THIS scale is impossible to do alone, and I owe my deepest thanks to many I can never repay. I trust they will see the fullness of their rewards in heaven for their faithfulness, but I also hope these words honor their work and prayers for the kingdom and their help in my life.

First, I thank the three men who paneled the defense of my dissertation. Evan Lenow supervised this project in its dissertation form and counseled me through both my graduate and doctoral programs with great wisdom, patience, and humor. Evan made special efforts to work with my timeline and the constraints of living more than a thousand miles away for the final stages of my program. I am grateful for his patience, counsel, and care through this process and in my own ministry. William Goff was a constant source of encouragement and information as one of the last students to sit under the tutelage of T. B. Maston. He consented to a personal interview which was greatly beneficial to this project. I am thankful for his concern and prayers. Ethan Jones encouraged me to pursue doctoral studies and served as my minor supervisor as well as my friend. He offered honest encouragement as well as critique and held my feet to the fire when I needed it. I am grateful for his commitment to excellence and godliness as we cantered through this task.

Even before I formally entered the PhD program, Jack MacGorman and his wife Ruth welcomed me into their home for a personal interview. Ruth served as Maston's secretary and adopted daughter of sorts, even making Jack ask for Maston's permission for her to travel with him to meet his family before they were to be married. Their memories and hospitality were greatly appreciated.

From my undergraduate through my doctoral work, Bill Jones and the Dauphin Foundation provided an incredibly generous scholarship which opened doors that may have otherwise been closed in my academic career. For their prayers and provision, I am exceedingly thankful.

Southwestern Baptist Theological Seminary's Roberts Library staff was instrumental in the research stages of my dissertation. I am thankful especially to Robert Burgess, Jill Botticelli, Charles Huckaby, Jeffrey Bullens, and Beth Sieberhagen for gathering, scanning, and sending me copious amounts of articles, letters, and books from the Maston Archives. I am also grateful for additional research helps from the *Baptist Press*, the Southern Baptist Historical Library and Archives, and the Ethics and Religious Liberty Commission.

As Malcolm Yarnell and I shared an interest and admiration of Maston, Malcolm was one that continually encouraged me to seek to publish this work and was instrumental in the process. Malcolm typifies the work of the pastor theologian and was gracious to write the foreword for this work. I am grateful for his generosity, encouragement, and example.

Pastors Cory Wilson, Oleh Zhakunets, and Stephen Owens each agreed to read this manuscript in its dissertation form to offer sound feedback from diverse pastoral perspectives to help form the present work. I am so grateful not just for their wisdom and insight, but also to serve alongside men who love the Lord and his church and desire to see the kingdom grow across the city of Cleveland.

I am also thankful to the members and friends at The Church at West Creek and City Church. There are too many to list, but I am indebted to the many prayers and friendships I have found as their pastor and friend. To my students and coworkers at Ohio Theological Institute, you challenge and edify me to work well unto the Lord. To my friends and fellows at the Center for Pastor Theologians, you embody the calling to which I aspire, and I am grateful for your encouragement in the work.

There are countless friends and family members to whom I owe my deepest gratitude. My parents, Ray and Pam, were a constant source of encouragement and prayer line and have always served as incredible examples to me. My brother, Robert, proofread much of my dissertation and offered his editing services freely. My grandmother, Frankie, has always been my most ardent supporter and one of my greatest heroes. My wife's parents, Craig and Sheri, have been faithful encouragers. Rodrick Sweet was a helpful editor and a thoughtful critic. As was Walt Blanchard. For my countless friends that have encouraged me in this task, I am thankful. I know this will not exhaust them all, but I do want to thank Tyler and Michelle Yates, Daniel Stone, Carlton Shartle, Ryan Renfrow, Joe Rogers, Tony and Beth Loseto, Madison Grace, Austin Shaw, Matt and Kendra Shantz, Jesse and Kelly Chaney, Joel Negus, and Nick Abraham.

There is no person I should thank more than my wife, Sarah. Sarah has stood with me through every stage of our marriage and has faithfully cared for me through it all. Even before this was a dissertation, she helped me think through arguments and structure and heard me babble through research leads that would at times amount to nothing. She encouraged me to finish what I started and to balance what God has tasked us. She read and edited much of this work patiently and carefully. She has borne witness to my greatest pains and joys, and I, hers. She is a gifted writer and caring mother. I am exceedingly grateful to call her my wife and my friend.

Ultimately, I owe everything to the Lord and his faithfulness. This work's good is all the work of God and its failings are all the work of myself. God has faithfully provided at every step of this journey and his grace has never come up short. I am so grateful for so many that God has sent to come alongside me. I know that they have halved my griefs and doubled my joys. I hope this work will serve as some measure of joy in their lives as well.

Paul J. Morrison, PhD
Cleveland, Ohio
August 2021

Chapter 1

Introduction

THE SOUTHERN BAPTIST CONVENTION's legacy regarding, in part, race relations in the United States and its unbiblical past are often tragically ignored, regretfully forgotten, or wholly condemned.[1] However, such sweeping reductions fail to see the complexity and diversity of thought represented under the auspices of the Southern Baptist Convention (SBC). Every past—personal or corporate—contains both pride and shame: moments remembered with joyful nostalgia, and actions which stir up pain and regret. This is true not only of the Convention's history in totality but also as it particularly regards race relations. In 1845, the SBC formed through its departure from the Triennial Convention. The conflict at hand being a question of racial concern—namely whether slaveholders could serve as missionaries—setting a tone of moral apathy towards the mistreatment of other races that would endure for generations.[2] Further, the SBC was critically behind the social curve set in motion by the leaders of the Civil Rights Movement.[3] This was not unique to the SBC as a denomination for "[in] reality the church set the pace, established the pattern, and provided for segregation in this country. For this the church must bow its head in shame."[4] Even as recent history has had proponents within the Convention and outside of it reflect

1. See "Black Baptist Rejects Apology by SBC," 879.

2. Southern Baptist Historical Library and Archives, *1845 Proceedings of the Southern Baptist Convention*, 12–18.

3. See Williams and Jones, *Removing the Stain of Racism from the Southern Baptist Convention*; and "Resolution on Racial Reconciliation on the 150th Anniversary of the Southern Baptist Convention."

4. Thomas, "Achieving Racial Reconciliation in the Twenty-First Century," 561. See also Tisby, *Color of Compromise*.

upon this troubled history, the generalization is often of total error.[5] While
many of these accusations would be fitting to describe the majority of the
Convention's history concerning race, there was still light shining in the
darkness: a group of biblically faithful men and women who both recognized and fought for their racially marginalized brothers and sisters. Chief
among these men and women was Thomas Buford Maston. T. B. Maston,
often called "the conscience of Southern Baptists,"[6] served as Professor of
Christian Ethics at Southwestern Baptist Theological Seminary from 1922
to 1963. Beyond a stellar academic career, Maston's legacy finds its weight
through the impact he had on his students, his colleagues, and his church.
His reputation is one of a "superior teacher, dedicated Christian, involved
churchman, devoted family member, understanding friend, prolific author,
disciplined human being, friend of students, outstanding scholar, [and a]
servant of Jesus Christ."[7] This reputation was not easily attained and often
cost him severely to retain among those looking on, to the displeasure of
many. His convictions on race would cost him future promotion and, eventually, his professorship.[8] Yet he writes, "If Christians do not attempt honestly to apply the Christian spirit and Christian principles to race relations,
how can they expect others to respect their Christian claims or to hear and
accept the message they proclaim?"[9] Maston's voice was not merely one of
dissent, but one of reforming action and hope.

Racial tensions exhibit both historically and anthropologically. This
friction remains one of the most pivotal discussion points within a search
for unity in the church today. Gone are the days of legal slavery and segregation in the United States, and, as a result, some believe racism followed
suit.[10] However, the sentiment of racism as a departed struggle is carried
predominately by White evangelicals unable to recognize the pain of their
brothers and sisters in the minority—primarily because of an ignorance
surrounding the reality of their fight.[11] Further, there can be difficulty in

5. For an example of this generalization, see Newman, *Getting Right with God.* For
examples countering this claim, see Pennington, "Blueprint for Change," and Roach,
"Southern Baptist Convention and Civil Rights.

6. Maston and Tillman, *Perspectives on Applied Christianity,* 1.

7. Pinson, *Approach to Christian Ethics,* 29.

8. MacGorman and MacGorman, personal interview, October 22, 2015. The Mac-
Gormans specifically recall that Maston was to be named president of his alma mater,
Carson-Newman, but that the offer was withdrawn as a result of his stand on race.

9. Maston, *Bible and Race,* 95.

10. Yancy, *White Self-Criticality Beyond Anti-Racism,* 30.

11. Emerson and Smith, *Divided by Faith,* 18. "Evangelical" here is in the traditional vein of protestant conservatism which can be several clearly seen in Bebbington's

moving the conversation forward as "evangelicals have a tendency to define problems in simple terms and look for simple solutions."[12] However, the race conversation is anything but simple. The answer is neither found in pretending that it is unneeded nor in dismissing the task as unattainable.

Maston's work offers a pattern that may help to address the questions of the race issue. Read in a post-twentieth century context, Maston's works may not, at first glance, seem exceptionally revolutionary or worth noting until the reader sees the copyright date. Maston was writing on racial equality well before the Civil Rights movement, on desegregation before *Brown v. Board of Education*, and continued to be years ahead of his contemporaries throughout his life. In the end, the hope is that this development would lend a hand to the present conversation and problems, as Maston says, "Spiritual maturity on the part of God's people of all races would go a long way toward finding a solution for our present problems."[13] To move to this maturity, this book will offer an historical-ethical sketch of the life and works of Maston. This sketch will give a foundation for better understanding the past of the SBC, as well as offer an answer to contemporary questions of racial integration.

This book examines the writings of T. B. Maston in his efforts to reform the racially misguided interpretations of Scripture in the church and their subsequent prejudices. This is to say that these interpretations were racially misguided insofar as racial preconceptions and perceptions influenced the ways biblical texts were understood. Many historians hold that the SBC's eventual position on race was one thrust upon it by the shifting of the culture outside of the church, rather than the result of men and women working within the denomination.[14] Maston is not merely a visionary who foreshadowed the eventual position of the Convention but is one who directly caused legitimate change through his impact on both readers of his work, and more notably, the students that sat under his instruction. Maston's influence upon his students shaped a generation of leaders in the Convention that fought for racial progress even after his death. Though he is often painted as a liberal scholar to dismiss his work as social rather than biblical and limit the application of his blueprint in a distinctly more conservative Convention today.[15] This relegation of social intent over biblical truth would

---

quadrilateral of conversionism, biblicism, crucicentrism, and activism in Bebbington, *Evangelicalism in Modern Britain*, 3.

12. Hays, *From Every People and Nation*, 18.

13. Maston, "Biblical Teachings and Race Relations," 242.

14. See Newman, *Getting Right with God*, or Stricklin, *Genealogy of Dissent*.

15. For an errant depiction of Maston as a liberal who relied more upon sociological and cultural progression instead of theological and biblical motivations see Gin Lum

set issues of race as a tertiary discussion of the church. This book argues that Maston's work towards and through desegregation used theologically and biblically coherent argumentation to effect eventual change in race relations within the Southern Baptist Convention. Further, Maston's work gives a blueprint for future racial reconciliation through integration in the church. This book will follow the structure of Maston's assessment of race relations in the pattern of segregation, desegregation, and integration. This inward mobility is more than a simple historical observation as it represents Maston's more profound argument towards biblical racial reconciliation.

This work is both historical and conceptual. The endeavor is a deep evaluation and application of Maston's racial ethics.[16] However, Maston's arguments and assessment of racial ethics necessarily move through the historical cycle of segregation, desegregation, and integration. The historical setting in which Maston lives and writes must set the context to evaluate the coherence and blueprint of his racial ethics. This historical-ethical presentation demonstrates the coherence of Maston's method as well as the first two components of the blueprint through segregation and desegregation. The third component consists of the most significant contribution to the field and will thereby receive weightier treatment.

Foundational Terms

Strained conversations are often broken by participants using the same language but meaning different things. It would help to avoid this as much as possible by defining key terms that either are used frequently or carry loaded connotations. Chief among these is the definition of race or ethnicity, used here interchangeably.[17] Definitions and concepts of race fluctuate through-

and Harvey, *Oxford Handbook of Religion*, 496; Jones, "T. B. Maston: The Man, His Family, and His Ministry," 6; and Spain, "Oral Memoirs of T. B. Maston," 128.

16. Racial ethics and ethics concerning race are to be understood here as synonymous descriptions of the concept of race explored ethically, rather than a modifier of action. This is the conceptual aspect of this work. The conceptual recognizes the underlying truth explored here exists apart from time. This especially relates to the assertion of coherence and evidence for the acceptance of Maston's blueprint. However, this truth also operates historically through Maston's work in the SBC. This is directly tied to the cause of eventual change. Both aspects reveal the fullness of Maston's racial ethics.

17. While some sociologists and anthropologists, such as García, draw distinctions between these terms, the absence of consistency and genetic support of physical traits or skin color leaves an exclusively physical or biological definition, as is generally given to race, lacking. Further complexity is seen in definitions which emphasize language, which may be a clear mark between places like Norway and Vietnam but is more muddled in a place like Burkina Faso which has several languages and dialects represented

out history. It is helpful to consider that categories are traditionally and primarily constructed around physical appearance and language.[18] However, as biologists have gained a better understanding of the genetic makeup which would shape this physical appearance,

> the term "race" is currently believed to have little biological meaning, in great part because of advances in genetic research. Studies have revealed that a person's genes cannot define their ethnic heritage and that no gene exists exclusively within one race/ethnocultural group.[19]

J. Daniel Hays posits that subcategories of race often include "geographical location, ancestry (real or mythic), dress, diet, or numerous combinations" of social boundaries.[20] Race, as used in this book, is meant as a "socially defined manner of identifying and categorizing individuals into groups on the basis of actual or perceived differences . . . [the] basis for defining similarities and differences, and subsequently establishing collective group identities [being a combination of] physical/biological traits and social/cultural traits."[21] As a reflection of "folk conceptions" of race,[22] it is generally an overstatement to reduce entire ethnic groupings to such terms as "White" or "Black." Yet, this is the most often named racial divide in the United States from the nineteenth century to today.

This division has taken several terms over the years, generally due to shifting connotations of terminology. For example, in his discussion of racial groups, Maston would employ the terms "White" and "Negro" or "Colored." While the latter terms carry an obviously pejorative connotation today, at the time of Maston's writing, the terms were standard across racial lines. Accordingly, these should not be read as derogatory statements or as a sign of prejudice on the part of Maston. Further shift can be seen today in many

in its peoples.

18. For a deeper reading of historical-racial divisions constructed biblically, see Hays, *From Every People and Nation*.

19. Chismark et al., "Race." Even from a biological standpoint, declarations of the fact that there is only one race—the human race—are often unhelpful. These assertions are ultimately dismissive of the problem at hand. There is, of course, a common source and aligned identity in the image of God (each explored in ch. 4), but the social connotations and language of race speak more to ethnic identity than the class of humanity over against the rest of Animalia. To use race in the narrowest sense often comes across as a co-opting of colorblindness.

20. Hays, *From Every People and Nation*, 28–29.

21. García, "Ethnicity."

22. See the entry for "Race" in Atkinson et al., *New Dictionary of Christian Ethics*, 716.

circles to include "Black" or "African American" within a larger grouping of "People of Color."[23] These divisions and nuances should not be overlooked as what some may deem political language but viewed as using the nuances of language to convey respect and concern consistent with the Spirit of Christ. For this reason, much of the conversation surrounding shifts in terminology from "Colored" and "Negro" to "Black" or "People of Color," marks a shift in the terminology from a deriding imposition to an empowering willful implementation. This book then will consider the primary racial divide as between White and Black Americans within the context of the United States while affirming that said divisions are social constructs that extend beyond any particular stereotypes. This divide will offer a narrower focus, which subsequent universals may then apply to other racial groups or struggles. This is also the primary division referenced by Maston. The racial concerns of this test case necessarily extend to any discussion of racial interaction or racism. Racism is any action or belief that holds one or more racial or ethnic groups as categorically superior or inferior to another. This perception is a false estimation of reality. Racism presents subtly and overtly, and a biblical ethic of race repudiates either expression.

Turning to the concepts of segregation, desegregation, and integration, Maston's definitions here are most helpful. Maston affirms the classic definition of segregation posited by Liston Pope in 1957 as "the enforced separation of racial groups, either in regard to a few areas of life or in regard to many or all."[24] Maston notes further that this enforcement is most often maintained legally, but may also be seen as compulsory in social customs and economic practices.[25] Segregation is the physical expression of the sin of partiality and should itself be considered as sinful. In consideration of segregation, the ideal response is not simply one of undoing, but of uniting. A proper theology of God necessarily dismantles the improper view of his creation.

> Segregation that is maintained by law can be repealed by law, although as a real achievement desegregation requires more than the mere passing of a law. A law or the repeal of the law, however, may provide the basis for and give support to moral action. It may maintain pressure toward a desired end. After all, desegregation as such is not directly concerned with inner attitudes and purposes. It cannot and does not attempt to eliminate prejudice. It is concerned with the removal of injustice.

23. Goto, "Beyond the Black-White Binary of U.S. Race Relations," 35.
24. Pope, *Kingdom Beyond Caste*, 80.
25. Maston, *Segregation and Desegregation*, 44.

Prejudice is a problem for the school and the church. Injustice is a legal matter, and hence its correction is the responsibility of the state.[26]

Desegregation concerns the removal of barriers, legal or social, that have served injustices on the basis of one's race.

> Desegregation with a minimum of disturbance depends primarily on the following: (1) A clear and unequivocal statement of policy by leaders with prestige and authority. (2) A firm enforcement of the changed policy by the authorities even in the face of initial resistance. (3) A willingness to resort to law and strong enforcement policies when necessary to deal with actual or attempted violations or incitement to violation of the new policy. (4) And appeal to the individuals concerned in terms of the religious convictions and their acceptance of American ideals.[27]

The next term which needs to be defined is integration. Maston describes integration as the ultimate goal for the church regarding race. In his work, *Segregation and Desegregation*, Maston responds to the desegregation marked by *Brown v. Board of Education* and the ecclesial response to the ruling. Desegregation and integration are both responses to segregation but are necessarily distinct. Maston notes the differences between the two saying that "integration involves more than the removal of barriers and the elimination of compulsory segregation. This may be accomplished by desegregation. The latter is legal and more or less formal. Integration is voluntary and social."[28] He then notes this process as far lengthier than desegregation. The concern of integration is full acceptance and reconciliation in community. Martin Luther King Jr. describes it in this way,

> we do not have to look very far to see the pernicious effects of a desegregated society that is not integrated . . . a society where men are physically desegregated and spiritually segregated, where elbows are together and hearts are apart. . . . it leaves us with a stagnant equality of sameness rather than a constructive equality of oneness.[29]

Integration consists of the full amalgamation and reconciliation of previously segregated groups in a single community. This integration is not an

26. Maston, *Segregation and Desegregation*, 64.

27. Maston, *Segregation and Desegregation*, 71.

28. Maston, *Segregation and Desegregation*, 62.

29. King, *Testament of Hope*, 118.

artificial measurement of diversity from wide-sweeping demographics but should reflect the immediate community racially.[30]

Integration is not simply a cultural goal amid racial divisions in the American church. It is a biblical goal of the global church. King's prediction has come true. We are the same, but we are not one. To be one, requires intentionality. The unity presented in the New Testament church is not a heavenly unity. It is difficult, and can be painful, but it is worthy of pursuit. To be satisfied with desegregation is to be satisfied with spiritual stagnancy. Holiness demands more. Christlikeness demands integration.

Methodology and Hermeneutic

Maston understood the need for integration. He saw the SBC where it was in segregation and made great strides to desegregate. He died with hope that the church, and specifically the SBC, would integrate again. Maston's arguments were theologically sound and biblically coherent and are evident in the full measure of his worldview—including his theology, anthropology, and ethics. Each of these three facets aligns itself to assess the patterns of segregation, desegregation, and integration. This threefold pattern is seen most clearly in *Segregation and Desegregation* but is also evident in his racial works at large.

Maston drew each facet of his worldview from the text of Scripture. Before moving to any such texts, it is necessary to outline in detail the hermeneutic that is utilized herein. This includes the interpretation of Scripture and its subsequent assumptions.[31] Maston's work on race deals firsthand with texts both in the Old and New Testament. With any biblical text, it is necessary to understand first the original context of each passage. This includes, but is not limited to, the author, audience, and circumstance of the passage and the book as a whole. The Bible is not merely a record of wisdom void of time or space but stands as a historical record, written and compiled over more than 1,600 years. Each book has a unique purpose and intentionality with its inclusion. Within the realm of Christian ethics, there can arise a tendency to simplify and reduce portions of Scripture, specifically the Old Testament, to a single imperative. But it must be remembered, as

30. A comprehensive examination of the immediate community would need to assess historical and sociological causes for the present community, such as shaped by slavery or red-lining policies. See Rothstein, *Color of Law*.

31. To be clear, this is the hermeneutic implemented by the present author in order to evaluate Maston. To see and understand the fuller hermeneutic of T. B. Maston, see McCullough, "Evaluation of the Biblical Hermeneutic of T. B. Maston."

Hays writes, that "the Law is not presented by itself, as some sort of disconnected but timeless universal code of behavior. Rather it is presented as part of the theological narrative that describes how God delivered Israel from Egypt and then established them in the Promised Land as His people."[32] Understanding the fullness of context in the Law, Prophets, and other types of Scripture helps to avoid this dissonance. This question of context is the chief determinant of the biblical coherence, which is being tested in this work. When a text is described as hermeneutically accurate or appropriately interpreted, the assertion is that the history of interpretation being presented has rightly considered aspects of right textual interpretation—rather than a wider allegorical or imposed reading of the text.[33]

After understanding the passage's original context, it is then helpful to note the modern culture, context, and the differences between modernity and what is written to apply the text appropriately. To this end, many propose methods of simplifying or unifying ethics within the testaments.[34] Traditional approaches such as the threefold distinction of moral, civil, and ceremonial laws, initially put forth by Justin Martyr, can be helpful for the layman to overcome an initial panic over how to understand the scope of the Law's application.[35] To be sure, Martyr's division is a helpful tool in every pastor and believer's toolbelt to dissuade the sweeping doubt towards Scripture by the young believer and the bold refute of the atheist alike. However, as a proper hermeneutical strategy, there can arise a tendency towards the

> inconsistent and arbitrary, and the Old Testament gives no hint of such distinctions. This approach errs in two ways. On the one hand it dismisses the civil and ceremonial laws as inapplicable. On the other hand it applies the so-called moral laws as direct law. In addition the traditional approach tends to ignore the narrative context and the covenant context of the Old Testament legal material. Principlism, an alternative approach, seeks to find universal principles in the Old Testament legal material and to apply these principles to believers today. This approach is

32. Hays, "Applying the Old Testament Law Today," 24.

33. More detailed scholastic interpretation might include the processes employed in Goldsworthy, *Christ-Centered Biblical Theology*, and Mead, *Biblical Theology*. The history of interpretation taken up here is consistent with the history of conservative exegesis generally aligned with the assumptions stated in this chapter.

34. Examples of this simplified reduction can be seen in such ranging ideas as Immanuel Kant's "kategorischer Imperativ" (Kant, *Metaphysics of Morals*), or Joseph Fletcher's "service of love" (Fletcher, *Situation Ethics*).

35. Martyr, *Dialogue with Trypho*, 37–46.

more consistent than the traditional one, and it is more reflective of sound hermeneutical method.[36]

Principlism seeks to find the truth of the passage before it finds the imperative of that truth.

The issue of this terminology, of course, must be addressed, as one might argue that Principlism rightly describes methodology rather than hermeneutic. However, Maston used Principlism to describe his hermeneutic and his ethics, no doubt highlighting how closely what Scripture taught and how Scripture should be applied were related in his mind. Further clarification requires delineation between Principlism as a hermeneutic and Principlism as a system of ethics. The former can remain titled as such, as it aligns with both current terminology and reflects Maston's work. Guy Greenfield, a student of Maston's who would later assume his post at Southwestern, writes in Maston's *festschrift* that Maston's colleague, H. E. Dana, shaped this hermeneutic and described it as "the principlist approach."[37] In his own words, Maston writes that "[principles] will not only help us to know the will of God, they also will deepen our desire to walk in his will. They will even provide a basis for the proper interpretation of the specific teachings of the Bible."[38] This approach grounds itself as more teleologically balanced than the simple deontology to which Martyr's threefold approach inclines itself. This question of deontology versus teleology pertains to the foundational understanding of ethical motivation. To understand the fullness of this motivation, it is necessary to briefly delineate the two broad systems to see their weight on the present hermeneutic.

Deontology, from the Greek *deon* (δεόν: what is due, duty, or obligation), asserts objective rules or duties that dictate moral procedure. David W. Jones describes this process as a system in which "moral praise or blame is assigned based on the conformity (or lack thereof) of specific actions to prescribed morals. As such, deontological theories are usually described as action-based ethical systems."[39] To help illustrate the systems that fit this category, Steve Wilkens helpfully summarizes ethical theories with short maxims, small enough to fit on a bumper sticker.[40] For example, he describes Divine Command Theory, one of the most common deontological systems, as "God said it, I believe it, that settles it," and Situation Ethics as

36. Hays, "Applying the Old Testament Law Today," 35.

37. Greenfield, "Hermeneutics of T. B. Maston," in *Perspectives on Applied Christianity*, edited by Tillman, 39–40.

38. Maston, *God's Will and Your Life*, 65.

39. Jones, *Introduction to Biblical Ethics*, 11.

40. Wilkens, *Beyond Bumper Sticker Ethics*.

"All you need is love."[41] Deontologies simply elevate the action itself in their considerations of right and wrong.

Teleology on the other hand, from the Greek *telos* (τελός: goal or end), instead holds "that the ultimate criterion or standard of right and wrong is ends or results."[42] C. D. Broad, one of the earliest to distinguish between these theories, summarizes them saying,

> Deontological theories hold that there are ethical propositions of the form: 'Such and such a kind of action would always be right (or wrong) in such and such circumstances, no matter what its consequences might be.' . . . Teleological theories hold that the rightness or wrongness of an action is always determined by its tendency to produce certain consequences which are intrinsically good or bad.[43]

Again, Wilkens is helpful in illustration. He describes the teleology Ethical Egoism with the aphorism, "Look out for number one," and the rampant Cultural Relativism with, "When in Rome, do as the Romans do."[44] Where Deontologies consider the action, Teleologies consider the end result, no matter what means may be required to get there. The ends justify the means. Deontology and Teleology may be new ten-dollar words, but their thought processes undergird questions of morality people have seen in their lives, in literature, and in television and film. Even errant expressions have some understanding of this foundation, as *The Office*'s bumbling manager, Michael Scott remarks, "This seems mean . . . but sometimes the ends justify the mean."[45]

Every ethical system will consider action or result in a manner that falls somewhere along the deontological or teleological spectrum. A balance of the two elevates both the truth and the subsequent imperative, and that balance will be the endeavor of this book hermeneutically. Namely, this is a move towards Deontological Virtue Ethics. While Principlism generally describes the hermeneutic—and was even the word Maston used to term his system—Deontological Virtue Ethics focuses on the specific virtues exuded magnanimously by the Godhead and is a clearer term for his system that will not conflict with his hermeneutic discussed above. At large,

---

41. Wilkens, *Beyond Bumper Sticker Ethics*.

42. Hollinger, *Choosing the Good*, 27.

43. Broad, *Five Types of Ethical Theory*, 206–7.

44. Wilkens, *Beyond Bumper Sticker Ethics*.

45. Reitman, *The Office*, Season 5, episode 8, "Frame Toby."

virtue ethics argues that the traditional approaches of conse-
quentialism and principle ethics are not only wrongheaded
in their foundations and methodologies, but they also ask the
wrong question about ethics and the moral life. The key issue
is not What ought we to do? but rather What ought we to be?
The kind of people we are as evidenced by our virtues, firmly
implanted within, is the heart and essence of ethics.[46]

This is to say that the generalizations of Maston's Principlism find clarity in
Deontological Virtue Ethics, which chapter 4 discusses at greater length.

This hermeneutic makes several assumptions. Chief among these is
the assumption and conviction that Scripture is the inerrant word of God
and is totally relevant and authoritative for man, regardless of time or place.
This is to say that the authors of Scripture have been divinely inspired by
the Holy Spirit to record the words of narrative, poetry, and instruction as
the standard measurement for all action and thought common to the human experience across any time, culture, or location because these words
are inspired and breathed out by an unchanging God. This is particularly
relevant in the case that Maston used theologically and biblically coherent
argumentation as the crux of his argument. Further, this work assumes
that Scripture is comprised of the sixty-six canonical books of the Old and
New Testaments. This full canon is not merely a historical record of Israel
in the Old Testament followed by the instruction of Jesus and his apostles
in the New Testament as the normative commands of Christianity today
but should be understood as the fullness of God's counsel fulfilled in Christ
and for the benefit of the church in perpetuity. This canon does not negate
the historicity or truthfulness of extrabiblical sources or materials but holds
that no other words achieve the level of faultlessness and apartness that the
biblical canon does. This implies that context must necessarily include the
totality of Scripture rather than draw a perceived or apparent observation
from a limited pericope.

Finally, this work assumes faith on the part of the reader. The message
of Christ for the church is only as accepted and imperative as the reader is
submissive to Christ as Savior and Lord. While desegregation has no necessary ties to faith, a theological or moral argument offers the best objectively
centered case against segregation.[47] Culture faces racism and prejudices in
the world around it and within the heart of every individual. As it does, it
becomes clear that the source of these injustices is not limited to the worst
of humanity scattered intermittently around the world but is found in the

---

46. Wilkens, *Beyond Bumper Sticker Ethics,* 45.

47. This claim will be discussed in ch. 4.

fallen condition of man. However bleak this estate, the image of God, which chapter 3 discusses at length, remains intact and redeemable by the grace of God through faith in Christ alone. This faith is paramount to progress.

Outline of Chapters

Chapters 2 and 3 summarize the context for Maston's work by outlining the SBC's history of race relations through the lens of Maston. Maston's theology offers a proper evaluation of segregation. These chapters introduce Maston in greater depth, describe the context of the SBC at the time of his work concerning race and segregation specifically, and offer five combatants to segregation in the character of God put forth by Maston. By exploring and evaluating Mastonian theology, these chapters set the groundwork for understanding Maston's thought. In their conclusion, these chapters discuss the full circle of integration from the New Testament church through the United States as the subsequent goal to return to integration using Maston's framework.

Chapters 4, 5, and 6 examine the work and legacy of T. B. Maston within race relations on both the written and anecdotal level, especially as desegregation meets a proper anthropology. These chapters examine Genesis 1:26–28, Acts 17:24–31, and Genesis 9:20–27 to address the cultural misconceptions surrounding the race issue within the biblical context according to the apt interpretation of T. B. Maston. The lasting impact is recognition of what Maston foresaw as a lingering problem insufficient in itself. This is the measure of what Maston saw accomplished in his lifetime. Yet, there is a sense in which Maston's legacy is still bearing fruit, being shaped, and impacting the kingdom.

Chapters 7 and 8 apply the work of Maston to the continued task of unity within the church racially through integration. This is the application of Maston's ethics as a blueprint for racial reconciliation. Focusing first on the principle of Maston's ethics, these chapters argue that Deontological Virtue Ethics best describes Maston's Principlism.

Chapter 9 applies the principles of Maston's ethics into Maston's levels of integration. Integration, as a consequence of Maston's ethical system, offers some proposed actions from integrating the individual, the local church, seminaries, and the convention at large as the realization of Maston's work.

Chapter 10 provides a summary of the work, as well as gives an address of potential issues and critiques. Most notably, Maston posited that interracial marriage is, at times, unwise for the Christian and raised greater issues with Scripture as inerrant. Each of these issues weakens his arguments for integration and requires an answer. Additional critiques concerning the proposed system of integration will also be discussed here before concluding the work.

Conclusion

This work traces the overall coherence, results, and blueprint of Maston's work in the field of racial ethics. In doing so, it is hoped that this will be of great benefit to the bride of Christ represented in the Southern Baptist Convention. Integration in the church is not a lofty ideal that is reserved only for the new creation. Rather, it is the discipline of unity and purity that the church is able to display as a city on a hill. T. B. Maston is no longer a household name in the SBC, but his work has an opportunity to continue to bear fruit. By examining Maston's theology, anthropology, and ethics as they square with the sequence of segregation, desegregation, and integration, this work demonstrates the fullness of this fruit.

Chapter 2

Segregation and the SBC

Introduction

THE ISSUE OF RACE has a complex and tragic history. A touting of errant racial superiority has often led to great injustices and pain. Whether from the extremes of Nazi Aryanism and the attempted genocide of the Jewish people or the supposedly more tolerable discriminations of Jim Crow and the segregation and subjugation of People of Color, the twentieth century saw its fair share of racial prejudice. While these events are tragic in and of themselves, it is even more disconcerting that many supporters of such discriminatory patterns did so in the name of faith and, specifically, the God of the Bible. The SBC at large, while standing adamantly against Nazi Germany and anti-Semitism, overlooked, and in many regards, supported the racial prejudices in the United States during the same period.[1] However, this is not to say that the Convention in its entirety misstepped.

During his time at Southwestern Baptist Theological Seminary, Maston taught and wrote of his convictions without compromise. This posture eventually led to his dismissal from the teaching faculty of Southwestern.

---

1. For SBC resolutions concerning Nazism and anti-Semitism see such statements as the 1972 resolution, "Therefore, be it RESOLVED, That this Convention go on record as opposed to any and all forms of anti-Semitism; that it declare anti-Semitism unchristian; that we messengers to this Convention pledge ourselves to combat anti-Semitism in every honorable, Christian way." which can be found at http://www.sbc.net/resolutions/653/resolution-on-antisemitism as well as the 1948 resolution, "RESOLVED, That communism, fascism, political ecclesiasticism, and anti-Semitism are utterly contrary to the genius of our Baptist concept of freedom and spiritual values," which can be found at http://www.sbc.net/resolutions/932/resolution-on-protestants-and-other-americans-united-for-separation-of-church-and-state.

Following the publication of his major works on race, *Segregation and Desegregation* and *The Bible and Race*, in 1959, Southwestern leadership began to be pressured for Maston to be fired by donors and church leaders offended by Maston's arguments.[2] When his contract expired, Southwestern president, Robert Naylor, bent to these pressures to force Maston into retirement in 1963.[3] This unseasonable retirement served as a compromise to pacify Maston's most zealous opponents, while he continued to serve his students in an advisory role. Though he was no longer an active professor, Maston was still able to retain an office in the library on campus and continue his writing.

Many of these new writings continued to carry his great concern for racial reconciliation. While much of Maston's arguments regarding race obviously concerned anthropological and sociological facets, at their core, there was a theological concern. This chapter shows that the beginnings of change in Maston's work, as a response to the historical segregation of the United States, were deeply rooted in a concern for proper theology. This argument examines the biblical theology of God in relation to the race issue expressed by T. B. Maston as a combatant of segregation. Primarily, this focuses on God as 1) Moral Person, 2) Creator, 3) Ruler, 4) Sovereign, and 5) Father. These five aspects are explicitly implemented by Maston within his arguments in *Segregation and Desegregation* regarding race but also reveal significant themes across his corpus at large.[4] This argument includes an historical-ethical framework in its approach. Beginning with an introduction to Maston, the chapter presents the historical backgrounds of both segregation and the SBC's specific history of race. Next, it discusses the necessity of proper theology in this area over against a simple anthropology,[5] and addresses liberation theology, among other answers to the issue, and subsequent departures and distortions of biblical theology. Then, the chapter turns to discuss each of the five characteristics of God mentioned above, respectively. Finally, it offers a relative summary of church history regarding race in the cycle of segregation, desegregation, and integration. This summary points to a solution through the implementation of a right view of God as presented to move towards integration in the church once again. Noting that

---

2. Examples of this pressure can be seen in the files included under the subheadings, "Letters Against," in the T. B. Maston Collection, A. Webb Roberts Library. Southwestern Baptist Theological Seminary, (Fort Worth, TX), Box 44: 2453–54.

3. William Goff, personal phone interview, April 10, 2018.

4. Maston, *Segregation and Desegregation*, 82–86.

5. The Mastonian Anthropology is addressed in depth in ch. 6.

So long as the promises of integration remain unfulfilled, it is premature to inquire after segregation as if it were over. If anything, it's the former whose time may have passed, for these promises, in all their deliberate speed, are rarely encountered these days outside the refuge of a museum.[6]

This chapter seeks to aid the church in this fulfillment.

Thomas Buford Maston: A Biographical Introduction

Thomas Buford Maston was born in 1897 in Jefferson County, Tennessee, into a Christian family on a rural farm.[7] From an early age, Maston had some idea of his future in the life of the church. In 1914, the sixteen-year-old Tom Maston was baptized into the Smithwood Baptist Church before expressing a felt call into ministry.[8] Two years later, before starting college, he was licensed to preach. After graduating from Carson-Newman College (now Carson-Newman University) in 1920, Maston moved to Fort Worth, Texas, to begin work on a Master of Religious Education degree at Southwestern Baptist Theological Seminary. A year later, he married his college sweetheart, Essie Mae McDonald, whom he would affectionately call "Mommie." They would have two sons, Thomas McDonald "Tom Mac" (1925) and Harold Eugene "Gene" (1928). Tom Mac was left physically and mentally disabled as an effect of "something that probably happened during birth."[9] The Mastons cared for him for his entire life in ways that were always described as patient, loving, and dear. It is no wonder then that Maston would say that "the home is God's first institution: first in time and first in importance."[10] This was a balance Maston carried from his earliest days at Southwestern, first as a student and later as a professor.

By 1922, he was teaching in the seminary, and in 1925 he completed a Doctor of Religious Education at Southwestern, as well as an additional master's degree in sociology from Texas Christian University. Desiring to expand his education even further, Maston entered a second doctoral program at Yale in 1932, to study under renowned ethicist H. Richard Niebuhr. After completing his PhD in Christian Ethics in 1939, Maston expanded Southwestern's ethical prowess, by establishing the Department of Christian

6. Schleitwiler, "Into a Burning House," 149.

7. For a full timeline of Maston's life see Maston et al., *Perspectives on Applied Christianity*, 5–6.

8. Maston et al., *Perspectives on Applied Christianity*, 5–6.

9. Maston et al., *Perspectives on Applied Christianity*, 12.

10. Maston and Tillman, *Bible and Family Relations*, 56.

Social Ethics and developing a course of study for a ThD in Christian Ethics. He further influenced the development and normalcy of ethics across the denomination by establishing it as an independent field of study in SBC seminaries. In addition to his post at Southwestern, Maston was a guest professor at Southern Baptist Theological Seminary, Southeastern Baptist Theological Seminary, Golden Gate Baptist Theological Seminary (now Gateway Seminary), Midwestern Baptist Theological Seminary, and even spent time on the mission field teaching at Arab Baptist Theological Seminary in Beirut, Lebanon. Maston is revered today for his contributions to the field of ethics at large, and specifically among Southern Baptists. Maston wrote no less than twenty-seven books, more than two-hundred-seventy-five publications for the Baptist Sunday School Board (now Lifeway Christian Resources), and hundreds of articles, pamphlets, and lectures. Most notable among these contributions include his 1967 seminal work *Biblical Ethics*, his 1974 work *Why Live the Christian Life?*, and most obviously explored here, his works on the issue of race.[11]

Unlike many ethicists, "[Maston's] expression of Christian ethics did not begin with a faddish issuism but rather was based solidly on theological precepts he drew from the Bible."[12] These precepts for Maston were ultimately rooted in the character of God. While they manifest through commands and obligations, they shine best in the principles of virtue found in the person of Christ. Theology and ethics are closely related for Maston especially as, "they have similar goals: knowledge of God and His will and purpose. . . . [But] they do have some distinctive phases and functions. To a degree they supplement one another. Ethics looks back to theology; theology looks forward to ethics."[13] Concerning race, Maston was a consistent advocate across racial lines in his words, actions, and academic contributions. In addition to a plethora of articles and monographs, the earliest being a 1927 pamphlet titled *Racial Revelations*, Maston "initiated a course on race relations in 1944, which he continued through the rest of his teaching time at Southwestern."[14]

In 1946, Maston wrote his first full work on race, *"Of One" A Study of Christian Principles and Race Relations*, for the Home Mission Board (now North American Mission Board) as part of a series of books on race and missions in the American South. Barely more than one-hundred pages, *Of*

11. "[Maston, Thomas Buford] Bibliography," 7–8.

12. Maston et al., *Both-And*, 59. For issue-based ethics, see such works as Clark and Rakestraw, *Readings in Christian Ethics*, and Davis, *Evangelical Ethics*, among others.

13. Maston et al., *Both-And*, 97.

14. Tillman, "T. B. Maston (1897–1988)," 78.

One offers a cursory look at the issue of race. Maston would say later that the "book was prepared as a study guide on the race problem, for use primarily by Church women."[15] This guide addresses just a handful of key biblical passages which relate to race, but also offers his strategy in a brief section titled "The Christian Program for Social Change." Here, his three points of regeneration, education, and demonstration all point to the weight of proper theology.[16] He writes, "the Christian goal for race relations, and for every other area of social life, will become clear and meaningful to the world only to the degree that [the ideals of Christ] are embodied in the lives of individual Christians and Christian groups."[17]

Then in 1959, as racial tensions rose, Maston published two new works through Broadman and MacMillan, respectively, each speaking to a unique audience. *The Bible and Race* produced for the layman an expansion and replacement of the more limited 1946 work, *"Of One"*. He states in the preface that, "while the Bible has very little to say directly on race, it does contain some basic concepts that are relevant to the problem. The present volume is an attempt to state and to interpret some of these concepts."[18] Simultaneously, Maston was developing a more academic response to the reception and consequences of the 1954 Supreme Court ruling in *Brown v. Board of Education*. His MacMillan work, *Segregation and Desegregation*, was an idealistic approach to evaluate "segregation and desegregation from the Christian perspective."[19] These works together reveal Maston's primary thought on the segregation of the SBC into which he arrived.

Segregation's Beginnings

Segregation, like any sin, has been prevalent in varying degrees, depending on the time and culture examined. In the ministry of Jesus, there appears to be a socially enforced segregation between Jews and Samaritans. This is, of course, confronted by Christ speaking to the Samaritan woman in John 4, among other places. From this point, there is ample teaching and, at times, rebuke concerning the broader division of Jews and gentiles in the first-century church (Acts 20:21; Rom 3:9; Gal 3:11). As the church developed, the race issue saw a full range of segregation, desegregation, and integration.

15. Maston, *Bible and Race*, vii.

16. Maston, *"Of One"*, 104–7. These three points will be revisited and explicated in ch. 9.

17. Maston, *"Of One"*, 106.

18. Maston, *Bible and Race*, vii.

19. Maston, *Segregation and Desegregation*, vii.

In the United States, particularly, the primary racial divide obviously began with slavery—which was already well established on the continent by the time the new nation formed. John Quincy Adams, the statesman and closeted abolitionist, writes, "it is among the evils of slavery that it taints the very sources of moral principle. It establishes false estimates of virtue and vice: for what can be more false and heartless than this doctrine which makes the first and holiest rights of humanity to depend upon the color of the skin?"[20] Slave owners often feigned interest in the salvation of their slaves, allowing or forcing them to go to church with them. Emerson and Smith explain that, "for many Anglos, 'Christianizing' slaves came to be seen as a Christian responsibility."[21] However, noting Maston's distinctions between the terms defined in the first chapter, this could only be described at best as desegregation, as there was a clear pattern of superiority and privilege.

This justification of privilege led to an excusal of sin. David Theo Goldberg notes that, "For political theology, authority and power are shaped and animated by conviction, conviction reified, recast, resisted, and redirected by power."[22] Following the Emancipation Proclamation in 1863, and the subsequent end of the American Civil War in 1865, slavery was abolished in the United States. While there was some assimilation of former slaves and people of color into newly freed society, such as the Civil Rights Act of 1875, genuine equality was never realized.[23] In its place came the phrase "separate but equal"; a response to complaints that the former legislation's call for equality could still maintain separation, handed down from the Supreme Court in the infamous 1896 case, *Plessy v. Ferguson*, marking the beginning of the Jim Crow Era.[24]

While legal segregation came to fruition in the late 1800s, it was beginning to take root in the churches of the United States more than a century earlier. "By 1750, about 20 percent of the American population was African or of African descent (compared to about 13 percent today). The slaves' growing presence in and importance for 'the American way of life' led to . . . the new call to Christianize slaves and, fearful of revolts, an increased emphasis on order."[25] This order maintained a desegregated society in which both White and Black Christians would occupy a single church building, but in separate pews and with distant hearts. Eventually,

---

20. Adams, "Washington, March 2, 1820," 83.

21. Emerson and Smith, *Divided by Faith*, 22.

22. Goldberg, "Political Theology of Race," 534.

23. Gillette, *Retreat from Reconstruction*, 259.

24. Groves, "Separate but Equal," 66–72.

25. Emerson and Smith, *Divided by Faith*, 22.

independent churches formed altogether. Maston notes that "Negroes took the initiative [during the Reconstruction period] in a large-scale separation or withdrawal from the White churches. One reason for their separation was they are inferior status within those churches."[26] Specific examples of this initiative are seen in the historic formation of The African Methodist Episcopal Church in 1816, The National Baptist Convention in 1880, and The Church of God in Christ in 1907. This shift went hand in hand with segregation in the schools as former slaves rarely, if ever, previously had the opportunity even to attend. For some years, formal segregation in the schools was not yet a concern to many as few of the newly freed slaves were receiving any formal education, "hence, there was neither segregation nor integration in the schools."[27]

Even after the Supreme Court abolished segregation in the schools in 1954 with *Brown v. Board of Education*, there was a still a mindset of intolerance and even defiance in the face of the law.[28] Of course, this only addressed the schools, as public segregation would persist formally in most other areas of life for another decade until The Civil Rights Act of 1964. During this span of nearly ten years, there were varying degrees of intolerance among Southern Baptists as some promoted selected Bible verses to argue that their racism was justified. Moderates on the issue argued that their "support for the separation of the races derived from custom and an acceptance of the existing social order, believing that the Bible neither advocated nor condemned segregation."[29] While moderates would wane from one side or another, strict segregationists fixed their arguments in the very character of God in their theology.

God as Segregator

In the eyes of the segregationist, segregation was not only what they saw as best for themselves, but they would further argue that segregation is also best for the racial minority and ultimately right in the sight of God. One piece of evidence for their argument is the simple fact that races existed. Their argument posited that because God had created the nations and races, he intended for them to remain as distinct as they were created and not

26. Maston, *Segregation and Desegregation*, 47.

27. Maston, *Segregation and Desegregation*, 44.

28. For example, many of the nation's private schools were founded in order to maintain segregation. See Tatum, *"Why Are All the Black Kids Sitting Together in the Cafeteria?"*, 14.

29. Newman, *Getting Right with God*, 21.

intermingle. Segregationists would cite such Old Testament passages that condemned Israel for taking wives and giving their daughters as wives with the people around them, and further, the tower of Babel as God separated the nations to fill the earth.[30] If God were the initial segregator, then continuing segregation would be in keeping with his purpose and plan. Others even went as far as to say that those promoting the mixing of the races did so as the work of Satan.[31] Some in the SBC feared that interracial marriages would naturally yield children of a mixed-race. Formal complaints and appeals were made at the SBC Meeting in 1954 in an attempt to scare or anger those present, saying, "some of you who sit in this audience today will have grandchildren with mixed blood."[32]

Concerning the New Testament, segregationists would use such passages as Acts 17:26 in which Paul says to those in Athens, "And he made from one every nation of mankind to live on all the face of the earth, having determined allotted periods and the boundaries of their dwelling place."[33] They would argue that Paul's point in this verse is that God's determining of times and boundaries extended to racial segregation. This passage would serve as the biblical basis for holding God as segregator in the eyes of the segregationist. Many would even say that since Jesus never personally addressed integration or segregation, he must have condoned the path taken, and further upheld the separation of Israel from the surrounding nations.[34] However, in every case, the presenter of each argument would never give the full context of whatever proof-text they would offer, nor would they interpret Scripture in its entirety to have a full understanding of God's counsel.[35] These arguments continued during Reconstruction. Schools began to

30. Killingsworth, "Here I Am, Stuck in the Middle with You," 88.

31. Killingsworth, "Here I Am, Stuck in the Middle with You," 53.

32. Thomas, "Achieving Racial Reconciliation in the Twenty-First Century," 562.

33. Unless otherwise noted, all translations of Scripture will be the author's personal translation of the original languages which aims to reflect the fullness of meaning, especially in regard to the subsequent implications explored in this book. Though many translations impose an object to ἑνὸς (henos) here, usually "man," the author has chosen to leave the direct translation "from one." This is particularly significant to the two interpretations which Maston explores in the options of the one being either a common ancestor or an allusion to God's creation and the image. This is explored in greater depth in ch. 4.

34. See Dailey, "Sex, Segregation, and the Sacred after Brown," 119–44, and Rouse, "Role of Segregation in Southern Baptist Polity," 19–38.

35. It should be noted that even as the present reader may be quick to brand these men as racists and question their love of the Lord, that they were also adamant about evangelism and stated often that winning the lost was their primary concern. History is not compiled of purely evil or righteous men. Sin affects all men, even those that believe they are carrying out the work of God expressed in Scripture. It should further

segregate around the time churches began to separate.[36] Rather than moving forward together, racial groups moved further apart, spurred on by Jim Crow and other discriminatory policies.

> The appeal to authoritative reason, the god of race, was to be replaced by the appeal to secular reason, to the racial equivalent of laicization. The arbitrariness of racial appeal was supposed to give way to the refusal to judge or assess people and their worth on the basis of morally inappropriate or irrelevant categories like race.[37]

Secularization, however, was not the only factor in play. Greater injustices arguably came by the hands of those in the church who should have known better.

In his book *The Bible and Race*, Maston argues that segregationists can only achieve their supposed evangelistic motive through the abolition of segregation. He then addresses each argument for segregation from the biblical perspective. Beginning with the idea of God creating the nations, Maston notes that all nations still had a common origin, not only to Adam but further in the image of God, which strips any concept of the superiority of any group.[38] He continues by addressing Israel's separation from the other nations and explains this was by no means in response to racial distinctions, but rather religious ones. Maston takes each verse in its fuller context and explains the full aspect with which it should be considered, even in the face of what is culturally uncomfortable. He uses winsome and simple arguments while supplementing academic depth and support of every fact.

Maston's greatest emphasis of *The Bible and Race* did not merely dismantle segregationist arguments but instead showed what Christ requires. Two of his chapters address Christ's most well-known commands concerning people; to love one's neighbor and the Great Commission. Noting the closest comparison to segregation in Jesus's day, Maston points out Jesus's use of Samaritans in both his parables and the ways that he ministered (Luke 10:25–37; John 4:1–40). He notes that not only is there no separation,

---

be noted that some of the men used by God held deeply racial prejudices, such as Jonah and Peter. In these cases, it is likely that their consciences have been malformed by the social norms of their surrounding cultures. This is no excuse for these prejudices, but an opportunity for saving grace to renew minds with truth. See Mattison, *Introducing Moral Theology*, 107–8.

36. For a survey of educational development for African Americans, see Du Bois, *Souls of Black Folk*, 9–21.

37. Goldberg, "Political Theology of Race," 526.

38. A full discussion of these texts will be offered in the following chapters.

but Jesus makes it a point to go beyond the cultural norm. This crescendos in the story of the good Samaritan, as the traditional men who would be respected and viewed as righteous, all pass by the beaten man, but the despised and outcast Samaritan shows grace and favor. Jesus then asks which was the better neighbor, the answer, of course, coming as the result of action rather than proximity or similarity.

Further, in examining the Great Commission, Maston takes note of the importance of taking the gospel to all nations. Christians do not have the luxury to pick and choose who they see fit to enter the kingdom but must take the gospel to all people. "If Christians do not attempt honestly to apply the Christian spirit and Christian principles to race relations, how can they expect others to respect their Christian claims or to hear and accept the message they proclaim?"[39] While many resented Maston's claims, there was no argument concerning their truthfulness.

Maston did not simply stop at showing the truths of Scripture in response to the ideas of race as a whole, but further wrote specifically concerning segregation. In his work, *Segregation and Desegregation: A Christian Approach*, Maston takes the truths of Scripture and molds his opinions and convictions around those truths. This was quite the opposite approach from his opponents, who instead sought to justify their prejudices with Scripture. In short, he concluded that, "[the] Christian ideal would demand the elimination of all segregation, by law or custom, based on class or color. This is true because segregation, which inevitably means discrimination, is contrary to the spirit and teachings of Christ."[40]

Maston saw the reality of segregation, as did so many who led the charge against it, namely that "separate but equal" was never truly equal. Even when segregation stood legal, Maston did what he could to operate within the law. He and a handful of other select faculty members of Southwestern Seminary trained African Americans during night classes before *Brown v. Board of Education*, equipping them for the work of ministry. The waves caused by his work in racial ethics forced his retirement in 1963 only a year before the Civil Rights Act. Though his teaching career was already more than forty years long, he still had much to give. He would continue to teach for nearly twenty more years at various institutions, as well as write some of his greatest contributions to the field of Christian ethics.[41] Maston is even credited by some with the number of African American churches today in the SBC. Working for the Home Mission Board, Gary Farley writes

39. Maston, *Bible and Race*, 95.
40. Maston, *Segregation and Desegregation*, 163.
41. Pinson, *Approach to Christian Ethics*, 27.

that it "is probable that the current growth of Southern Baptist churches and adherents among African-Americans in the United States builds on the foundation that T. B. Maston laid in the hard days of the 1950s."[42] That current growth would have been, in many ways, unfathomable to those who created the Convention more than one-hundred years prior.

The SBC and Race

It is no secret that the SBC has a painful history surrounding race. As noted earlier, the Convention formed as a departure from the Triennial Convention in 1845 over contention concerning the ability of a slave owner to serve as a missionary. This new convention soon confirmed its first president, William B. Johnson, an adamant slave owner, and White supremacist. Timothy George notes, "It is important to recognize that Johnson and his peers of the time represented the best, not the worst, of Southern culture and religion."[43] The Convention showed great regard for the cause of Christ in missions abroad, yet failed to grasp the weight of the cause of Christ before them. The Convention passed several resolutions, even from its earliest days, to show missional regard for the "colored population" among them, but failed to recognize the injustices of their own relationship towards them.[44] Following the Emancipation Proclamation in 1863, newly freed slaves began their mass exodus from the convention of their former owners. By 1890, there were more than one million Southern Baptists, and not a single one was Black.[45] This dark shadow loomed over the convention through Reconstruction and raised its head once more during the height of segregation and racial prejudice. As Maston asserts, "racial prejudice is both a cause and an effect of segregation."[46]

In Maston's earliest years in SBC life and at Southwestern, prejudice continued to grip formal and informal facets of the church. Racial prejudice became so common that even some Southwestern professors were members of the Ku Klux Klan. As one example of such involvement, Maston was warmly invited to a Klan meeting in 1923 or 1924 by W. T. Conner, Southwestern's founding professor of systematic theology.[47]

42. Farley, "T. B. Maston," 31.

43. George, "Southern Baptists' Long Journey," 16.

44. Williams and Jones, *Removing the Stain of Racism from the Southern Baptist Convention*, xxxv.

45. Maxwell, "Black Southern Baptists," 27.

46. Maston, *Segregation and Desegregation*, 49.

47. Spain, "Oral Memoirs of T. B. Maston", 57.

In the same year Maston began teaching at Southwestern, P. I. Lipsey described the Black race as "unsuspecting and credulous sons of Africa."[48] Lipsey espoused the larger view of Baptists and White Americans as they viewed Black men and women as inferior and childlike compared with their White counterparts. Paternalism then became the most common response in race relations. The White SBC saw African Americans as incapable and spoke of them in a general fashion, rarely recognizing the identity or personality of individuals.[49] Nominal regard was the norm. Southern Baptists viewed any overt care for African Americans as suspect. During the presidential election in 1928, for example, Southern Baptists in Mississippi published their endorsement for Herbert Hoover over Al Smith because Smith employed African Americans and regarded those employees well.[50] Only a year prior, in 1927, Maston saw the need for a Baptist statement on race and consequently published his first short pamphlet for the Women's Missionary Union entitled *Racial Revelations*.[51] This short pamphlet briefly covers the Christian attitude towards those of other races and marks the distinct progress in Maston's thought over against the norm of the SBC.

As Maston progressed through his academic career in the next decade, finishing his PhD in Christian ethics under H. Richard Niebuhr and establishing the Department of Christian Social Ethics at Southwestern, prejudice and racism in the SBC marched on. Foy Valentine notes an overwhelming "attitude of paternalistic condescension" that characterized SBC leaders' perception of Black churches and their membership.[52] Baptist articles of the day notably evidenced this in their possessive language, referring to "our Negro Baptists,"[53] and "our colored people."[54] This unshifting regard once again caused Maston to dig deeper into Scripture and respond how he was able. Moving beyond minute applications, by 1938, Maston taught an entire course entitled "Social Problems in the South," and regularly wrote on the topic of race in his monthly series for the Training Union.[55]

Into the 1940s, the SBC continued its pattern of paternalism and disregard. Tensions, if there were any, were supposed to be merely the fault of "racial rabble rousers . . . [and that all would] continue to live together in

48. Lipsey, "Anti-Lynching Bill," 4.

49. Valentine, "Historical Study of Southern Baptists and Race Relations," 44.

50. "Who Loves the Negro?," 2.

51. Maston, *Racial Revelations*.

52. Valentine, "Historical Study of Southern Baptists and Race Relations," 104.

53. Alexander, "Evangelistic Conference for Negro Baptists," 4.

54. Farmer, "Our Colored People," 6.

55. Jones, "Race Relations," in *An Approach to Christian Ethics* edited by Pinson, 62.

peace . . . if outside agitators [would quit] meddling."[56] But Maston was no outside agitator. A year later, Maston published his first comprehensive work on race relations in *Of One* through the Home Mission Board of the SBC.

Following school desegregation, the Convention publicly praised the Supreme Court for its ruling in *Brown v. Board of Education.* Yet, as Jane Dailey notes, the Convention's leadership held that

> the Supreme Court decision was "a purely civic matter" and thus an inappropriate topic for the Christian Life Commission in the first place. . . . Hudgins echoed SBC president J. W. Storer, who endorsed the Brown decision on civic rather than theological grounds. Public schools belonged to Caesar. Racial purity belonged to God.[57]

Further, it would be helpful to consider the widely accepted and promoted statement by G. T. Gillespie, who writes,

> While the Bible contains no clear mandate for or against segregation as between the White and Negro races, it does furnish considerable data from which valid inferences may be drawn in support of the general principle of segregation as an important feature of the Divine purpose and Providence throughout the ages. . . . [To] summarize the interpretation of the passages above considered, the following conclusions would seem to be warranted (a) Since for two thousand years the practice of segregation was imposed upon the Hebrew people by divine authority and expressed command, and infractions of the command were punished with extreme severity, there's certainly no ground for the charge that racial segregation is displeasing to God, unjust to man, or inherently wrong; (b) Since Christ and the Apostles taught the love of God for all mankind, the oneness of believers in Christ, and demonstrated that the principles of Christian brotherhood and charity could be made operative in all violations of life without demanding revolutionary changes in the natural or social order, there would appear to be no reason for concluding that segregation is in conflict with the spirit and the teachings of Christ and the apostles and therefore unchristian.[58]

56. Gardner, "Racial Rabble Rousers," 3.

57. Dailey, "Sex, Segregation, and the Sacred after Brown," 132.

58. Gillespie, *Christian View on Segregation*, 8–13. Gillespie was president of Belhaven College, a Presbyterian school in Jackson, Mississippi, but he carried influence with Baptists and this argument was circulated widely in the SBC, as noted by Dailey. See Dailey, "Sex, Segregation, and the Sacred after Brown," 123.

During the early part of the 1950s, Maston served on a committee of the SBC to determine the denominational calendar. At one such meeting of the committee, Maston advocated "that the Convention observe a race relations Sunday—a suggestion that was squelched somewhat quickly and rudely."[59] Only a few years later, in 1956, the Advisory Council for the Southern Baptists for Work with Negroes asked Maston to produce a pamphlet for the Christian Life Commission entitled *Integration*.[60] This work shaped Maston's major works on race, *The Bible and Race* and *Segregation and Desegregation*, which were published only three years later. As noted earlier, these works faced considerable opposition. Formal resolutions and protests of the pamphlet published by First Baptist Church of Mansfield, Louisiana as well as The Selma Baptist Association of Alabama state that,

> The positive stand taken in this pamphlet favoring integration of the races does not represent the views of the majority of the members of our Southern Baptist churches. We feel that this is an improper use of funds from the Cooperative Program in publishing this type of material. If this practice is not discontinued it will endanger the support of the Cooperative Program in our church and in many other churches with which we are familiar.[61]

Maston's writings were not the sole efforts of his fight. Though not subject to the *Brown v. Board* decision as a private seminary, Maston continued to lead the fight for racial equality on Southwestern's campus. "In 1956, Maston led the faculty to forward a recommendation . . . to admit blacks to the dormitories and all of the boarding facilities."[62] Full desegregation on Southwestern's campus was a huge victory in itself, but it did not change the wider mindset of the SBC that was still profoundly racist.

It is not surprising then that "Opinion polls taken in the 1950s and early 1960s consistently found that approximately 64 to 70 percent of southern Whites favored 'strict segregation.'"[63] Craig Mitchell notes, "for many years the SBC was located only in the South, and it held strongly to the racism endemic in that region. With few exceptions, the SBC supported racism

59. Pinson, *Approach to Christian Ethics*, 24.

60. Maston, *Integration*.

61. "Protest Pamphlet on Integration," 3; and "Selma Association Adopts Resolution on Integration," 1.

62. Martin, *Passport to Servanthood*, 67.

63. Newman, *Getting Right with God*, 20.

and Jim Crow laws."[64] This is the culture to which Maston speaks, and the heart of his response is a return to proper theology.

Segregation and the prejudices of the SBC have at their heart a distorted perception about the nature and character of God. The history of segregation in the SBC is not simply one of economic or social justification. H. H. Weatherspoon writes that strictly preserving racial distinctions "would be in harmony with the teachings of Jesus."[65] Segregationists in the SBC consistently superimposed the teachings and character of God to support their prejudices.[66] Maston's arguments step into this historical framework, and more often than not, begin with the nature of God as the first combatant of segregation. Maston recognized that the character of God, understood through a proper theology, leaves no room for racial prejudice or segregation.

64. Mitchell, "Role of Ethics in Removing the Stain of Racism from the Southern Baptist Convention," in Williams and Jones, *Removing the Stain of Racism from the Southern Baptist Convention*, 62.

65. Weatherspoon, "Christ and Human Brotherhood," 10.

66. For a more comprehensive historical examination of the SBC and race, see Valentine, "Historical Study of Southern Baptists and Race Relations"; Pennington, "Blueprint for Change"; and Porter, "Southern Baptists and Race Relations."

Chapter 3

Segregation and Mastonian Theology

Competing Theologies or a Distorted Anthropology?

SOME MIGHT ARGUE THAT the concern of segregation is primarily a question of anthropology. If the division is between men, the solution should ultimately be found in a better understanding of who or what man is. This point is true to a degree, but primarily in that man is the image of God. While the subsequent chapter explores a full discussion of the content and being of this image, the key at this point is to place the proper focus on the character and person of the God of this image. This is to say that, "Anything that threatens this value and importance will therefore be seen as threatening God's image; anything that leads to the abuse of people will be an affront to God . . . and can thus only be understood as heresy."[1] Racism is not the unforgivable sin, but has often been the plank in the eye of the Baptist, as the same Baptists who would have great concern for the African to be saved had far less concern for the African American down the street.

Racism is as heretical as any distortion of the character and creation of God. The full response to racism begins with establishing ethics in theology. A focus on ethics rooted in theology can be seen explicitly in the works of Maston's mentor, H. Richard Niebuhr. Niebuhr writes that ethics moves to the "more important concerns of theology, that is, faiths about the nature of God and man which lie behind human actions as their source and sanction."[2] However, the particular theology implemented varies from circle to circle.

1. Holder, "Issue of Race," 46.
2. Beach and Niebuhr, *Christian Ethics*, 3.

The most common response to racial injustice from a theological standpoint comes in liberation theology.[3] Liberation theology has several expressions and variations but is generally seen as a special regard by God for the oppressed towards liberation. Liberation theology developed concurrent with the Civil Rights movement and, therefore, alongside Maston's most influential racial ethics. James Cone, arguably the most prominent Black liberation theologian, writes that "Christ is not a proposition, not a theological concept which exists merely in our heads. He is an event of liberation, a happening in the lives of oppressed people struggling for political freedom. He is the eternal event of liberation in the divine person who makes freedom a constituent of human existence."[4] For the liberation theologian, participation with God becomes a social process towards an event of liberation. Consequently, God is made impersonal, a concept and framework to an end replacing orthodoxy with community. This is not to call the proposed ends of liberation theology into question, but rather to measure the costs at which they come.

Walter Strickland, in his dissertation "Liberation and Black Theological Method: A Historical Analysis," notes that the "Courthouse" roots of Cone's interpretations, compared with the more theologically driven "Church House" approach of Deotis Roberts, naturally form a varied range within Black Theology. He explains that, "Roberts and Cone agree upon the centrality of Jesus in the Christian faith, but Roberts's position focused upon Christ in priority over outside influences, and Cone's criteria for inclusion in the theological process welcomed other ideologies to reshape the essence of the Christian faith."[5] By imposing the limitations of Cone's liberation theology upon God, there is an objectification and appropriation of doctrine in place of God's communicative revelation of objective truth. The question then is raised of how to approach the end goals while still maintaining the revealed nature of God in theology proper.[6]

Here, biblical theology offers an answer. By searching for a text's intended message rather than imposing dogmatics or presupposed conclusions upon it, a greater picture of the reality of God is understood. Maston explains that, "The proper beginning place for a study of the teachings of the Bible on segregation, or on any other issue, is its teachings concerning

3. For a full history of Liberation Theology, see Coffey, *Exodus and Liberation.*

4. Cone, *God of the Oppressed,* 32.

5. Strickland, "Liberation and Black Theological Method," 129.

6. Strickland notes this movement in the work of Deotis Roberts as uniting liberation to Christian reconciliation rather than Black Power—a similar source and end to the one proposed here, expressed through the history of the black church. Strickland, "Liberation and Black Theological Method," 164–65.

God. He is the point of reference in the Christian religion. He is the source of authority in Christian theology and in Christian ethics."[7] Maston's focus on the God of Scripture simultaneously shifted focus away from the improper theologies of his segregationist contemporaries. It is helpful at this point to note the differences and purposes between a biblical theology and theology proper. The former represents the field and approach which seeks in one regard to trace "the major themes and overarching structural ideas through the whole of Scripture."[8] The latter is a description of the person of God. Both coalesce in this task to explore Maston's theology proper through a cogent biblical theology. As the focus is shifted from a simple relationship between men to right relationship and understanding of God as he reveals himself, there is reached a greater depth and richness of relationship and a betterment of those consequent relations. Reinhard Feldmeier and Hermann Spieckermann write that "the doctrine of God in the mode of theological argumentation must communicate knowledge of God with its objective being the insight that human beings can appreciate their lives only when they recognize God as the source and Savior of their lives and acknowledge God as Lord of their lives."[9] This biblical presentation of the character of God also adds a level of congruency with the task of ethics. "The Biblical doctrine of God intersects with presentations of Biblical anthropology and ethics because a doctrine of God is not an undertaking that disregards human beings and their existential and behavioral orientation but that, in fact, integrates the two."[10] This congruency then leads to a discussion of Maston's first facet of the nature of God in God as moral person.

God as Moral Person

Scripture often describes God anthropomorphically. His qualities are regularly tied to an expression of physical presence that extends beyond corporeal reality. Whether it is an outstretched arm or a description of sight, it is generally held to be description for the purposes of human understanding.[11] Yet, at the same time, there also exists in Scripture a clear personhood of God. This personhood is not an anthropomorphic expression of a spiritual God, but characteristics which are separate from a bodily presence. Maston explains that "God has all the qualities that are essential to personality: the

7. Maston, *Segregation and Desegregation*, 82.

8. Klink and Lockett, *Understanding Biblical Theology*, 59.

9. Feldmeier and Spieckermann, *God of the Living*, 7.

10. Feldmeier and Spieckermann, *God of the Living*, 8.

11. See Culver, *Anthropomorphism, Analogy and Impassibility of God*, 1.

power to think, to judge, to feel, to will, to communicate. We discover that he is not only a Person but that he is a moral person. . . . His moral character is portrayed in the Bible as dependable, as a constant among the uncertainties in human life and history."[12] Leviticus 19:2 reads, "Speak to all the congregation of the sons of Israel and say to them, 'Be holy, because I the Lord your God am holy.'"

This is the constancy of God's virtue, both in his unchanging nature and his purity. David Stern remarks on the rabbinic understanding of God's personhood, saying, "the advantage of reviewing God as a character is both methodological and substantive: it opens up a new perspective from which to consider an old question—namely, how the rabbis represent God in their literature—and it promises as well to make visible, from this perspective, new aspects of the rabbinic representation."[13] Each facet of God's character points to the greater personhood of God. This moral personhood speaks to the issue of race as this imitation of holiness extends the spirit and attitude of God towards all men created in his image. This is an imitation of the divine person of God, an uncompromising and perfect moral person. This moral person is further a unified person. The unity of the Trinitarian God is expressed distinctly by each person, yet all maintain equality of glory and majesty. The moral personhood of God is such a distinction. Each person of the Trinity possesses moral personhood as an undivided essence and character of the Triune God. The division of morality and images is the division of God himself. This division is beyond orthodox Trinitarianism. It is a polytheism and fracturing of the Godhead, which in turn gives a fractured anthropology. To hold a unified theology necessitates a unified moral person, which dismantles segregation as a distortion of proper theology itself. Maston presents God as a moral person to show the moral conflict in segregating his creation.

God as Creator

The second facet of the nature of God Maston emphasizes is God's identity as creator. His creative action is a reminder of the superiority and greatness of God over man. Herbert McCabe and Brian Davies explain that even the terminology for God builds upon an understanding of his creative character. They state, "We can use the word 'God' correctly or incorrectly, but the criterion for correct and incorrect use is not something we know about the nature of God. It is something that is thought to be true of our world. In

12. Maston, *Segregation and Desegregation*, 82.

13. Stern, "*Imitatio Hominis*," 157.

other words, God's being creator of the world is what gives us our meaning for the word 'God.'"[14] The word for the creative "make" is the same as a simple human action of "make" regardless of its subject. McCabe and Davies state that, "It follows from this, of course, that you cannot deduce the activity of the Creator from the fact that things have the property of being created. There is no such property as the property of being created."[15] The quality of the creation of God is often described and emphasized in Scripture and finds a particular emphasis in Isa 42:5, "Thus says God the Lord, who created the heavens and stretched them out, who spread out the earth and its offspring, who gives breath to the people over it and life to those who walk in it." This is a revelation of God as creator of all things. There is no limit to his glory in creation, as Paul says in Col 1:16 that "all things were created through him and for him." John Webster explains,

> God loves, and in providence and reconciliation acts towards, that which he causes to be. Rather, a double assertion is being made. First, the creator is radically incomposite [sic]. As the cause of finite being, God is not one term or agent in a set of interactions, not a "coeval, co-finite being", but unqualifiedly simple and in himself replete. Second, to deny that God bears a "real" relation to created things is to characterise [sic] the kind of relation which he has to creatures, one in which God is "in himself his own beatitude . . . all-sufficient to himself and needing not the things he made."[16]

For Maston, God's creative nature comes with a reminder that the children of God ought to view all of creation as a part of the plan of God. This inescapably determines that "his sons and his daughters from the east and the west, from the north and the south have been created by him for his glory."[17] The creative order of God necessarily dictates the outcome and purposes of his creation. Creation is unable to impose its purposes upon the creator, as the creator determines its intended purpose. Race as a part of creation then serves the created purposes of God as revealed by God. Maston presents God as creator to display the created purpose that is violated in segregation.

14. McCabe and Davies, "God and Creation," 386.
15. McCabe and Davies, "God and Creation," 390.
16. Webster, "'Love Is Also a Lover of Life,'" 165.
17. Maston, *Segregation and Desegregation*, 84.

God as Ruler

Maston extends these initial purposes of creation to God's ongoing purposes. He posits that the creation of all naturally encompasses the right and ability to rule over that creation.[18] God's rule is illustrated especially in God's presence on the throne. Specifically, regarding race, God's expression through creation is a picture of the coming reign of himself before all people. Revelation 7:9–10 reads that, "After this I looked, and behold, a great multitude which no one was able to number, from every nation and all tribes and peoples and tongues, standing before the throne and before the Lamb, clothed in white robes, with palm branches in their hands; and they cry out with a great voice, saying, 'Salvation to our God who sits on the throne, and to the Lamb.'" Hays explains that, "The fourfold formula [of tribe, language, people, and nation] stresses the ethnic and cultural diversity of the people gathered around the throne of God."[19] This diversity is the ultimate picture of integration before God; all peoples united before the throne in praise of him. This is not to say that true diversity in unity is a lofty goal, only possible in the coming of Christ, but rather is an ideal to be strived for while in community on earth. It is also a reminder that man's ability does not determine God's rule. Maston states that "man's activity or inactivity will not condition or determine whether or not God will be ultimately triumphant."[20] God is already on the throne, and he will not abdicate his rule. Maston also says that the throne should remind the child of God that regardless of opposition because God is on his throne, his child will also be victorious in the end. Maston presents God as ruler to demonstrate segregation's conflict with God's continual rule and authority.

God as Sovereign

An understanding of God as ruler is tied closely with God's sovereignty. This is particularly expressed in the will of God. God's sovereignty leaves nothing outside of his concern, interest, or activity. Concerning race then, God's sovereignty means that "racialization or racial division in the Church thwarts the plan of God and is in direct disobedience to this central Biblical

18. While the discussion of this point may require a more expansive study on the philosophical requirements of authority, the acceptance of Maston's connection is sufficient here to determine the biblical and theological coherence. For a deeper discussion of the types of authority see Tutt, "Notion of Authority," 43–45.

19. Hays, *From Every People and Nation*, 197.

20. Maston, *Segregation and Desegregation*, 84–85.

theme [of unity as the people of God]. Racial segregation among the people of God is a movement away from following God's redemptive plan."[21] Sovereignty is the expression of omniscience in planning and omnipotence in carrying out that plan. God's will is made known to man in revelation as well as in prayer through the Spirit. Romans 8:26–27 states, "Likewise the Spirit also helps our weakness; for we do not know how to pray as we should, but the Spirit himself intercedes for us with unspoken groanings; and he who searches the hearts knows what the mind of the Spirit is, because according to the will of God he intercedes for the saints." Maston explains that the specific will of God concerns every area of human relations, including race. At this point, many liberation theologians impose an interpretation of that specific will, which ultimately bolsters their case for God as Liberator. However, the will of God will not bend to the religious leader, layman, or king. Maston presents God as sovereign to illustrate the foolishness in opposing his revealed will to support the benefits of segregation in the mind of the segregationist.

God as Father

Turning finally to God as Father, the conversation examines the most common and significant implication of proper theology to Maston. God as Father is the most consistent facet of theology implemented by Maston throughout his works. God as Father is the only point of biblical theology regarding the character of God that is found in *Of One*, *The Bible and Race*, and *Segregation and Desegregation*. Gregory Cochran explains that,

> Whatever we go on to say about the familiarity we have with our Father, we must begin such statements of familiarity with the startling reality that he alone is set apart in holiness. The Father must be allowed to stand alone in holiness. Such holiness in the Lord's Prayer is an indication that our approach to the Father is more about honoring and revering him than it is asking for goods and services to be rendered by him.[22]

Christ's ministry emphasizes God as Father, especially. From his instructions to the disciples concerning prayer to the Father in Luke 11 to his own entreaties before God, Jesus elevated the importance of coming to God as his children. Deuteronomy 32:6 records, "Is He not your Father who bought you? He has made you and established you." This specific emphasis of God

21. Hays, *From Every People and Nation*, 63.
22. Cochran, "Remembering the Father in Fatherhood," 18.

as "Our Father" is paramount for Maston. He writes, "my relation to him as my father will not be most meaningful unless I equally recognize him as your father . . . just as God reveals the fatherly attitudes toward all, even those outside his spiritual family, so we his children should show the brotherly attitude toward all."[23] The relationship of God as Father before man has vast implications on the segregation of those made in his image. The pain of separation and isolation finds its solution in coming before a father faithful to forgive and give good gifts to his children. Maston concludes,

> If all of us had a proper understanding of our relation to God as Creator and ruler we would see how foolish and irrelevant is the whole discussion of the supposed innate superiority and inferiority of races. In the presence of God, the creator and sustainer of all, there is no room either for haughty egotism or for a cringing sense of inferiority and defeat. In God's presence all are equal. All of this is doubly true of those who have come into the family of God through union with Christ. They are children of the King. There is no partiality in his family.[24]

Maston presents God as Father to show the clear failure of segregation to view the Father as Father of all races.

A Full Circle of Integration

The application of the principles of a proper theology and the distinct nature of God offers a chance for the church to return once again to the integration it once knew. The picture of the New Testament church is one of integration and concern across racial lines. This includes both the full picture of the achieved integration displayed in Revelation as well as the atmosphere of intentional integration in the New Testament church. An ecclesial atmosphere that repudiates racism's subtle and overt forms and seeks intentional unity in Christ. This is, in part, an overcoming of those false estimations and perceptions of superiority or inferiority based upon race. Paul expresses this concern in the unity of God rather than the unity of man. In Gal 3:28 Paul writes, "There is neither Jew nor Greek, there is neither slave nor free, there is neither male nor female; for you are all one in Christ Jesus." Paul's words are not in a dissolution of the diversity of God's creation through dismissing the intricacies of creation. He instead focuses on finding unity in the moral person of Christ. But even the integration portrayed here was

23. Maston, *Bible and Race*, 19–22.
24. Maston, "Biblical Teachings and Race Relations," 239.

not immediate. As Christ confronted the social segregation of Jews and Samaritans, he called his church to break the world's patterns (John 17:11–19). These patterns, at times, resurface. Maston notes that

> organized Christianity tends to go through a regular cycle in its relation to the world. There is a period of withdrawal for revival and renewal, followed by a gradual adaptation to the world, which means an infiltration by the world. The world so completely permeates and dominates the church that another period of withdrawal from the world for renewal is necessary.[25]

Even the early church struggled to move from segregation to desegregation. Specifically, in Acts 6:1–6, the church selected the first deacons out of a neglect of widows stemming from a racial divide between Hellenistic and Hebraic Jews. Stephen and the other six men handled the daily distribution so that there would be equal treatment before the people. I. Howard Marshall posits that these men were selected, not only by their reputations in the community but also in the racial representation of the church, indicated by their names and descriptions.[26] That is, the first seven deacons represented the diversity of those whom they served. The church countered racialized exclusion by subverting its response in racial inclusion. Christ himself broke the pattern of segregation in his time and commissioned the disciples to the nations. The church then fought desegregation as a false unity within the body of Christ and moved towards integration. Integration's ideal is expressed clearly in Paul's rebuke of Peter in Gal 2:11 for showing partiality. When the church seeks to apply the ethics of Christ to the issue of race, racial superiority and divisions are rooted out of the body of Christ.

When the church loses focus of the implications of Christ's ethic, it becomes susceptible to fall back into the cycle from integration back to segregation. In the present focus, the integrated church moved back towards desegregation during slavery, segregation during Jim Crow, and once again finds itself in a desegregated society. Peter Kreeft notes that part of this shift is simply surface level. He writes, "a merely political abolition of slavery, desirable as it obviously is, would destroy only slavery's flower, not its root in the human heart, the desire to enslave, and that root would grow new flowers of evil."[27] There is hope in the application of proper theology that integration will once again prevail. Maston writes, "in the deepest sense, integration has taken place only when those of another race or class are accepted as full and equal partners in a common task. It is based on mutual

25. Maston, *Christianity and World Issues*, 10.
26. Marshall, *Acts*, 136.
27. Kreeft, *Back to Virtue*, 150–51.

respect and on a sense of the dignity and worth of the human person. There must be a sharing with one another in the life of the community."[28]

Conclusion

This task is one requiring patience and constant reflection. The church finds great hope in the fact that God is a moral person, a divine creator, a powerful ruler with a sovereign will, and that all men across all nations may come to him as Father. Maston asserted and reminded segregationists of these facets of God's character, even as the SBC at times seemed to forget the full implications of the character of God.[29] Thankfully, in times of blindness, God in his sovereignty sends prophetic voices to his people. Thomas Buford Maston was such a voice. Maston argued for and implemented a distinctly biblical theology to combat segregation. This reasoned theological pursuit helped shift the SBC over time. Following Maston's example, the present church can take such reflections on the character of God as expressed in Scripture and apply their implications to the solution of the present race issue to the glory of God. Proper theology dismantles segregation. However, the task remains to move to the next point of progress in desegregation. To this end, a deeper examination of Maston's anthropology should be discussed.

28. Maston, *Segregation and Desegregation*, 63.

29. See especially correspondence concerning Maston's racial works, T. B. Maston Collection, Box 44.

Chapter 4

Desegregation and the Image of God

Introduction

Turning from the character of God to the image bearer of God, this chapter begins to examine Gen 1:26–28, Acts 17:24–31, and Gen 9:20–27. These key passages address the cultural misconceptions surrounding the race issue within the biblical context per the apt interpretation of a Mastonian anthropology. These verses were a point of vigorous debate in the church during the years of racial inequality in the United States surrounding the Civil Rights Movement. Further, they were vital to T. B. Maston's arguments towards desegregation. Genesis 1:26–28 sets the immediate context of an understanding of biblical equality among every nation and tribe as rooted in the image of God at creation. This argument seeks first to define the image of God, address the influence of the fall on this image, and finally offer an understanding of race from this image.

Historically, the *imago Dei* has been understood in one of three ways: structural, functional, and relational.[1] In the examination of each of these three positions, this chapter shows, as Maston first argued, that taking a single interpretation void of the others' complement is to hold a limited and insufficient understanding of the image. Instead, it is hermeneutically accurate, and culturally practical, to unite the positions for a full understanding and to trace this understanding's implications.[2] Genesis 1:26–28, rightly

---

1. These terms of interpretations have also been referred to by various camps as substantial (structural) and vocational (functional). While there may be subtle differences between them on the part of individual authors (see Sands), this book will use the terms interchangeably.

2. Hermeneutical accuracy, here, pertains to the adherence to the text's original

understood, is the strongest biblical argument towards progressing to total racial reconciliation in the first step of desegregation.

Acts 17:24–31, on the other hand, has been used by both segregationists and desegregationists alike.[3] Consequently, this section discusses the text's original context and conception before implementing it towards a modern application. The text does not set a precedent for segregation as much as it shows the sovereignty of God over all peoples and the unity of those peoples in a common origin. A proper understanding of the image of God, and a common origin for all peoples, dismantles any argument for the persistence of segregation according to racial categories. This accordingly compelled Maston and his counterparts to fight for desegregation in the United States at large as well as in the SBC.

The final passage explored in this section, Gen 9:20–27, is arguably the most significant in the mind of the segregationist. It has historically been used as biblical justification for slavery and racism.[4] This passage records the events surrounding Noah's son Ham uncovering his father's nakedness and the subsequent curse upon Ham's son, Canaan. This "Curse of Ham," or "Curse of Canaan" as Maston prefers, is a chief concern of Maston's in the discussion of supposed inferiority of the races. This section offers the various interpretations of the implications of this curse, including most notably the appropriation of the passage as it relates to the Black/White divide. Next, it turns to Maston's assessment and response to the curse. This section concludes by tracing Maston's fight for desegregation and the lasting effects of his work upon today's desegregated society.

Proper Anthropology

Anthropology is that category that would seem most apparent in an evaluation of race relations. Yet for Maston, the fullness of the doctrine was too weighty a task for him to offer a comprehensive study on the matter.[5] Instead, he offered more extensive works he felt offered a fuller discussion, and highlighted the key components he determined to be the most significant.[6]

context and intent. This is an extension of the hermeneutic laid out in ch. 1.

3. See Dailey, "Sex, Segregation, and the Sacred after Brown," 122–26.

4. Valentine, "Historical Study of Southern Baptists and Race Relations," 214–15.

5. Maston, *Christianity and World Issues*, 30.

6. Maston, *Christianity and World Issues*, 30. As comprehensive and diverse approaches to a "complete doctrine of man," Maston offers Niebuhr, *Nature and Destiny of Man*; Brunner, *Man in Revolt*; Berdiaev, *Destiny of Man*; and Wright, *Biblical Doctrine of Man in Society*. Maston's key components include the image of God, Sin and the image, Equal Yet Unequal (giftings and experiences, not rooted in race), and the Christian

While his anthropology can be seen in most his works in piecemeal, two works explicitly develop Maston's conception of humanity. In his chapter "Christianity and the Individual," in *Christianity and World Issues*, Maston develops what he describes as "the Christian View of Man."[7] Maston's view of man is set on the image of God foundationally and unambiguously. To be sure, Maston is so convinced of the biblical anthropology he considers surging movements such as humanism or Marxism as errant, not simply because of their conclusions, but on a deeper level because of their faulty anthropologies.[8] In *Why Live the Christian Life?* Maston devotes an entire chapter to the nature of man.[9] Here, Maston offers a fuller discussion of such concepts as community, responsibility, and freedom but ultimately hinges his argument on the image of God and the wholeness that man finds in it. He writes, "No concept concerning man is more significant for human relations and for the Christian life in general than the fact that man was created in the image or likeness of God."[10] In every case, Maston's primary reliance is on the word of God. He reflects that "the study of scripture was what influenced me the most in race relations."[11]

The question of anthropology for Maston is beyond asking the content of man as he is and to explore further that which man is intended to be. To say it another way, proper anthropology understands both the image of God and the effects of sin on that image. Maston writes,

> The end or goal of the Christian's knowledge, which is being constantly renewed, is the full realization or restoration of the image of the Creator. . . . As we grow in our likeness to the One who gave his life to restore the image in us, we will grow in our likeness to the One who originally created us in his image. . . . The rapidity of the change depends on our co-operation with him. He will mold us more and more into his image or likeness, if we will let him.[12]

As the full representation of Maston's anthropology, this image must be clearly defined and its implications discussed. For this definition, Maston turns to the beginning.

View of Man Versus the Classical View of Man (internal vs. external).

7. Maston, *Christianity and World Issues*, 30–46.
8. Maston, *Christianity and World Issues*, 54.
9. Maston, *Why Live the Christian Life?*, 31-46.
10. Maston, *Why Live the Christian Life?*, 33.
11. Moore, *His Heart Is Black*, 52.
12. Maston, "Biblical Teachings and Race Relations," 241.

The Image of God in Gen 1:26–28

The first pages of Genesis, and by extension the Bible, contain the record of God's creation work. These pages detail the progression of this world's conception from a declaration of light to the formation of land and sea and the animals that would fill them. Each part of creation was good and complete in the eyes of God, but one thing was created intentionally different from the rest: man. Genesis 1:26–28 says,

> Then God said, "Let us make man in our image, as our likeness; and let them rule over the fish of the sea and over the birds of the sky and over the beast and over all the earth, and over every creeping thing that creeps on the earth." And God created man in his image, in the image of God He created him; male and female He created them. And God blessed them; and God said to them, "Be fruitful and multiply, and fill the earth, and subdue it; and rule over the fish of the sea and over the birds of the heavens and over every living thing that crawls on the earth."

Beginning with the passage's context, it is helpful to be reminded that this passage is not only the origin of man but also the beginning of the Pentateuch, the standard instruction for Israel written by Moses to remind Israel of not only its history of salvation out of Egypt but of the full nature, ability, and sovereignty of the Lord.[13] The creation account itself was given in many regards to show God's close relationship to man. As Israel receives the words of creation from Moses, they are reminded of God's strong regard for man and shown the distinct uniqueness of creation contrasted by the surrounding cultural milieu.[14] Man is distinct in creation from other accounts, as well as other created things. Man's creation is clearly different from that of the other animals created on the sixth day for several reasons. First is the specific and separate nature of its mention in the creation sequence as something apart from the other created beings. Secondly, the very nature of the author's language shows a distinction as "'Let us make'

---

13. Gen 1:26–27 records the first instance of the image of God in Scripture and is explicitly tied to the point of creation. The image is also seen or alluded to in Gen 5:1–3, Gen 9:5–6, Ps 8, Rom 8:28–30, 1 Cor 15:49, 2 Cor 4:4, Col 1:15, Col 3:9–10, Phil 2:5–8, Jas 3:9, and Heb 1:3. While the concern in this chapter is uniquely surrounding the creation instance, the full range of verses are helpful to this study. Namely, in the New Testament uses, the image is most often referring to the person of Christ as the image of God. This usage seems to imply in its context that Christ is the perfect image of God and that man's image has been marred by sin to some degree and is in need of Christ's restoration of this image.

14. Wenham et al., *Genesis 1–15*, 58.

stands in tacit contrast with 'Let the earth bring forth' (24); the note of self-communing and the impressive plural proclaim it a momentous step; and this done, the whole creation is complete."[15] The most obvious distinction here, which must be explored, is that man is made in the "image of God."

This concept, often referred to as the image of God, the *imago Dei*, or simply the image,[16] is historically one of the most significant phrases to be found in Scripture. In it can be found questions of anthropology, theology, soteriology, and practically any field of study within the realm of thought. Thousands of scholars, theologians, and believers through the ages have wrestled with this simple phrase. Historically, three understandings of the image have risen: the structural image, the relational image, and the functional image.[17] These three levels of understanding were first formally noted by Millard Erickson in his classic *Christian Theology* but have essentially existed in one form or another for millennia.[18] To have a full understanding of the truth that moves to application, each of these positions must be examined in depth. As each position is presented, it is assessed to address the impact of the fall upon the image and evaluated to determine where it may be lacking or overreaching.

Structural Image

The first and most common understanding of the image of God is that it describes a structural aspect unique to man, generally including either his moral capacity, his ability to reason, or both intellectual and moral components. The structural image has been espoused by such prolific theologians as Augustine, Aquinas, and John Calvin.[19] James Orr defines this conception of the image as

> a mental and moral image. It is to be sought for in the fact that man is a person—a spiritual, self-conscious being; and in the attributes of that personality—his rationality and capacity for

---

15. Kidner, *Genesis*, 55.

16. Maston favors variations of the English image of God, Likeness of God, or image more so than the Latin, *imago Dei*. He also implements the Likeness as synonymous.

17. For a fuller history of the doctrine, see Barth, *Church Dogmatics*, III.1, 191–206.

18. Erickson, *Christian Theology*, 498–510. Noted as the first proponent by Grenz in *The Social God and the Relational Self*. While the first formal presentation of the categories came in 1983, they can clearly be seen in any classical discussion of the image as is demonstrated here in an evaluation of Maston.

19. Augustine, *Confessions*, 13.11.12; Aquinas, *Summa Theologica*, 1.92.1–93.4; and Calvin, *Institutes of the Christian Religion*, 1.3.1.

moral life, including in the latter knowledge of the moral law, self-determining freedom, and social affections.[20]

Though written more than a century ago, in the scope of history, Orr's definition is one of the more recent examples of structural thought. A structural concept of image is nearly as old as Western thought itself finding its initial discussion in the works of Philo, who posited that the *nous* (νοῦς: mind) was itself the unique structure of the image.[21] This uniqueness is an obvious distinction of man. From technological and medical advances to the ability to quantify modal logic, man is intellectually superior and different from even the cleverest of animals. Concerning this structural image, Vern Poythress explains, "Our experience of thinking, reasoning, and forming arguments imitates God and reflects the mind of God. Our logic reflects God's logic. Logic, then, is an aspect of God's mind. Logic is universal among all human beings in all cultures, because there is only one God, and we are all made in the image of God."[22] Concentration on man's rational capacity is traditionally elevated above other qualities or components of man by those who ascribe to the structural image.[23]

The structural interpretation also centers on the moral capacity of man. This is to say that morality is something beyond a Darwinistic understanding of a perceived standard, which is nothing more than the adaptation within culture to facilitate survival. It was through subjective relativism that Charles Darwin was able to excuse even genocide from his deeply rooted racism, writing in his work *The Descent of Man*, "The Western nations of Europe . . . now so immeasurably surpass their former savage progenitors [that they] stand at the summit of civilization. . . . The civilized races of man will almost certainly exterminate and replace the savage races through the world."[24] However, if man possesses intrinsic moral values, there are clear objectively moral wrongs that cannot be excused by individuals or cultures at large regardless of their power or influence.

Concerning the effects of sin on the image, there is some variation within the structural view. For those who hold structure to be primarily built of reason and intellect, the image is mostly intact, as reason leads to

20. Orr, *God's Image in Man*, 56–57.

21. Krause, "Keeping It Real," 363.

22. Poythress, *Logic*, 64.

23. It should also be noted that this conception of the image is the most compatible with secular thought. Those who ascribe to a structural view of man do not necessarily have to found that structure in the image of God. For this reason, the structural view is often presumed as the foundational anthropology of most secular humanists or those working separate from a theological perspective.

24. Darwin, *Descent of Man*, 133–34.

the grasp of general revelation and allows for men to approach the truths of God from the point of the observation of general revelation alone. This is demonstrated through the observations of Plato, Aristotle, et al. The ability is not as tarnished as the usage becomes when "fallen beings inevitably use their rational capacities in sinful ways. Substantialist views distinguish, therefore, between the formal possession of rational capacities and the material realization of godlikeness. Human beings retain the *imago* . . . in spite of sin, but human beings no longer resemble God because of sin."[25] Aquinas considers the fall's impact upon the image as making it "imperfect, and to a certain extent destroyed, in the wicked; because in them the natural inclination to virtue is corrupted by vicious habits, and, moreover, the natural knowledge of good is darkened by passions and habits of sin."[26] Martin Luther represents the furthest extreme as he posits that the image is lost entirely in sin until it is retrieved by Christ.[27] Regardless of the level of sin, Harold DeWolf offers "that [man] is sinful we know all too well, but sinner though he is, he bears upon his person the stamp of his maker . . . in four persistent qualities of human life . . . [1] spiritual being . . . [2] the sense of moral obligation . . . [3] longing for union with God . . . [and 4] aspiration to goodness."[28]

The structural image has dominated the history of Western thought but is not without its flaws. Most notably among them is that its elevation of rationalism "establishes a mind-body dualism inconsistent with a biblical view of humanity."[29] This rationalistic dualism is a primarily Hellenistic concept which elevates the mind above the body in a way that is like Paul's warnings against Gnosticism in his letter to the Colossians (Col 2:8). Not only can it tend to lead to an improper promotion of knowledge above the physical, but it also totally disregards the traditional Hebraic understanding of the image, which covers the whole person rather than just his aptitude intellectually or even morally. In fact, "we never encounter in the Bible an independently existing abstract, ontological, structural interest in man."[30] This is, at its root, a hermeneutical issue that ignores the original context of the term. Maston expresses this same critique stating that "[the] claim that man is like God because he has the capacity to judge or to reason . . . may

25. Sands, "Imago Dei as Vocation," 32.

26. Aquinas, *Summa Theologica*, 2-1.93.6.

27. Luther, *Disputation Concerning Man*.

28. DeWolf, *Theology of the Living Church*, 205.

29. Sands, "Imago Dei as Vocation," 33.

30. Berkouwer, *Man*, 196.

be correct as far as it goes, but it is too narrow and restrictive."[31] He goes on to say that the contemplation of God is a logical good of man, but it is not in itself the image. The rational nature of man expressed in the structural image is simply an instrument for Maston.[32]

Concerning race then, the structural image seems at first glance to have little concern or bearing on the issue. As the image consists of non-physical faculties, differences of race tied to the image would need to find root in a mental or moral source. But the race issue is instead generally demarcated by physical distinctions. This is not to say that segregationists throughout the ages have not held other races as intellectually or mentally inferior as an effect of hereditary distinctions.[33] Rather, the assertion is that the primary distinction of the image is external.[34] The weight of the fall on the structural image concerning race begins to explain racial prejudice when considering a moral corruption in place of a mental one. Those holding to a structural view can easily see that a moral decay in the image is responsible for subsequent racial discrimination and mistreatment.[35] Even still, a structural image confronts divisions of race because of the common mental and moral capacities of all men.

Relational Image

The second category of interpretation is the relational image. This view posits that the image is related not to a unique quality within man as much as it is a unique ability to commune with God. "If man is the image of God . . . then we have to conceive of an image that is capable of responding to its creator; an image capable of approaching God in prayer, worship and sacrifice that come from its own creative powers, from its wisdom and from its deep devotion to what is made in its own likeness: a fellow human being made of flesh and blood."[36] This view gained prominence in the writings of

---

31. Maston, *Christianity and World Issues*, 32.

32. Maston, *Christianity and World Issues*, 32.

33. Kendi, *Stamped from the Beginning*, 456–58.

34. See Kaplan, "Race, IQ, and the Search for Statistical Signals," 1–17.

35. See Joustra, "Embodied Imago Dei," 9–23. Joustra specifically draws on Bavinck's use of an "organic motif" which expresses itself in a structural moral component. It may also be noted that a mental break would cause poor thinking which would include false conceptions of superiority and inferiority. However, moral decay is a better explanation.

36. Schüle, "Made in the 'Image of God,'" 19.

theologians like Karl Barth and Emil Brunner,[37] but has been fully realized by scholars like Stanley Grenz. Grenz writes,

> Being-in-relationship with the triune God by means of participation in the Jesus narrative and hence incorporation into Christ by the Spirit not only inherently includes but also is even comprised by being-in relationship with those who participate together in that identity-producing narrative and thereby are the ecclesial sign in the present of the eschatological new humanity. . . . The Christian identity, therefore, is more than personal; it is a shared identity. The identity is bound up with the human destiny to be the *imago Dei*, to reflect the character of, and to exemplify the pattern of life that characterizes the triune God. Because the triune life can be represented only within a relational context, the self is truly ecclesial; the self of each participant in the new humanity is constituted through the relationality of the community of those who by the Spirit are 'in Christ.'[38]

Grenz contends that this relational aspect of the image is the uniquely human aspect of man's existence. A chimpanzee uses his ingenuity to fashion tools for breaking open hard nuts and fruit, and a single honeybee can communicate complex intricacies to her entire hive through dance. Some aspects of what would seem to be structural components of image are present in animals as they are in man, but no chimp or honeybee can claim relational concern by God in the manner which man does.[39] This is the unique nature of the relational image: that the Godhead shows concern and communes with man personally beyond the sovereignty He has over the rest of creation.

Further, communion and relationship with God reveal a relational aspect of man to the rest of his fellow mankind. David Cairns explains that "It is the individual-in-the-community—rather than the community itself—that is in the image of God."[40] This is the echo of Christ when asked of all the Law, what is the greatest commandment (Matt 22:35–40; Mark 12:28–34). Christ's immediate answer of course is to love God fully. However, Christ never leaves a question at its face value as he goes on to explain that the love

37. Barth, *Church Dogmatics*, 197–98; and Brunner, *Christian Doctrine of Creation and Redemption*, 78.

38. Grenz, *Social God and the Relational Self*, 331.

39. This consideration of shared structural components, of course, does not consider the moral aspects which seem to be unique to man. The proponent of the relational image is more concerned with arguing for the relationship than detracting from alternative theories. As will shortly be shown, these positions are not mutually exclusive.

40. Cairns, *Image of God in Man*, 44.

of one's neighbor is the natural procession of this love. Kierkegaard writes that "As Christianity's glad proclamation is contained in the doctrine about man's kinship with God, so its task is man's likeness to God. But God is love; therefore we can resemble God only in loving."[41] This love of neighbor is rooted in the Godhead's love within itself as "The relational view makes much of the enigmatic plural pronouns in Genesis 1:26 and the close association of the *imago*. . . . The plural pronouns in v. 26 are interpreted as an adumbration of the Trinity and thus an early indication that God is essentially relational."[42] Man is a relational being because he has been created by a relational God.

Concerning the fall, the relational image initially follows a similar path as that of the structural image. Namely, sin damaged first and foremost man's relation to God as a severance from his holiness. Further, the way man communes with his fellow man has been damaged and finds itself harming those around him rather than fulfilling the mandate of the image within him. Sin destroys communion with God and distorts communion with man. Unlike the structural view, this conception of the image is more than the mind of man. The inclusion of the body is not an inclusion of sinful flesh as some may contend, but "the embodied nature of human existence is part of creation, not a result of the Fall. . . . [The image is reflected] in ourselves, in who we are and what we do and in the way we do it, we should reflect who God is. We—humans, uniquely—were made to do and be this."[43] It is when man fails to commune with God that the image is degraded at the earthly level.

This argument, however, does not come without its faults. Man is a relational creature, and much of this position illustrates quintessential anthropology, but this does not necessitate that this is the intention and meaning of the *imago Dei* of the biblical text. To this end, the relational image can fall short. Vitally, it hinges upon the hermeneutical understanding of Trinitarian language in Gen 1:26–28. As mentioned earlier, this work has assumed faith and canon and would not deny that the full Godhead was both preexistent and foundational to the creation account. However, to say that the enigmatic plural pronoun demands a Trinitarian reading is to disregard the original audience and context of the passage. Israel was uncompromisingly monotheistic, hence the ignorant rejection of Christ's claims of divinity (Matt 26:65; Luke 5:21; John 10:33). Instead, it is better read in one of "three different biblical traditions . . . [1 in a singular entity

41. Kierkegaard, *Works of Love*, 74.
42. Sands, "Imago Dei as Vocation," 34.
43. Roberts, "Toward a Theological Anthropology," 139–40.

expressed through] the plural of solidarity (fullness), self-deliberation, or self-exhortation . . . [2 in] the plural of majesty . . . or [3 in] the true plural [to draw the attention of the angels]."[44] In these readings then, the relational image has little textual evidence in the creation account.

The relational image has a much more incorporated view of race as it pertains to the image. First, in man's relational interaction with God, race is a non-issue to the blood of Christ. If there is any racial division present, it is between Jew and gentile as those grafted in secondarily, but even then, the New Testament is clear that the death of Christ was on behalf of the entire world (1 John 2:2). Second, the relational image's understanding of the fall also gives a definite explanation for racial divisions and prejudices between fellow men. In the same way, the sin of selfishness or pride drives a wedge between people, further severing the brokenness of relationship, and racism moves towards a further isolation of peoples. It promotes antisocial, and by extension, antirelational behavior. The relational image, therefore, sets all races on equal footing before a relational God. Maston writes, "it is man's capacity for communion with God that makes him most distinctly a being created in the image of God."[45] Undoubtedly, the relational image is the primary thrust of Maston's perspective, but it is not exclusively such.

Functional Image

The final of the three positions is the functional image. This interpretation is described best by Douglas Hall, who explains, "humanity in the intention of God—genuine, authentic, 'true' humanity (*vere Homo*)—is humanity 'in the image of God.' To use the more philosophical language with which the term eventually became associated, *essential* as distinct from *existential* humanity is humanity imaging God."[46] This verbal sense of the image is more consistent with a Hebraic understanding of being and is better aligned with the contextual reception and understanding Moses's original audience would have understood it to be.[47] Cuthbert Simpson writes, "the body in Hebraic thought is 'an outward manifestation of the reality of which it was part.'"[48]

Within the functional image, there seems to be a range of what function the image fulfills. One of the earliest examples of this is put forth by the Socinians, a Polish group of nontrinitarians, and described in their

44. Garr, *In His Own Image and Likeness*, 18–21.

45. Maston, *Bible and Race*, 5.

46. Hall, *Imaging God*, 61. Italics original to the author.

47. Hall, *Imaging God*, 61.

48. Simpson, *Interpreter's Bible*, 484.

Racovian Catechism. Here they explain the image as a functional dominion of superiority tied closely to the subsequent command to totally subdue the earth in Gen 1:28.[49] Hall, on the other hand, holds that the function is applied to a stewardship in dominion and man's relationship to God by way of his relationship to nature. He argues for general ecologically beneficial principles. Others, such as Wilma Ann Bailey, take a similar approach to Hall but with a greater push to look at the garden as evidence of the way the world should be. Bailey promotes an ecological extreme that places so much emphasis on the fall that man is reduced to the same level as the rest of creation. She writes, "We . . . fulfill our responsibilities to rule the earth and make it the kind of place where humans and animals can live . . . we honor the Creator's intention to provide habitats in which all can thrive, and we image God in doing God's work in the world"[50] Whatever function or degree of imaging is posited, the base idea is that man's likeness to God is both being and action.

In the functional view, the fall has marred the image and function of man and is only seen fully in the person of Christ. As Christ images God and invites man to commune with him, he invites him to have his function restored in pursuit of God. This view does not argue that there are no structural or relational aspects of the image, but instead offers itself as the synchronizing of all the views. For this reason, some scholars have argued that this view is less of an interpretation of its own, and more of the outworking or consequence of the image.[51] By combining each facet of the image, the functional view addresses the faults of the preceding understandings.

In the structural component, there is no longer a mind-body dualism from and elevation of Hellenistic thought. Instead, as is the hope of this chapter, the Hellenistic observation and Hebraic tradition come together to offer the full understanding of an innate quality within man that reveals the nature of God. In part, then, the image is "something within the substantial form of human nature, some faculty or capacity man possesses . . . [which distinguishes] man from nature and from other animals."[52] This demands that all men, regardless of their origin or state, reflect the nature of God and must be considered as possessing innate worth because of the constitution of their being found in the image of God. Westermann writes,

> concerning the relational aspect, this combination removes the singular reliance on one hermeneutic and allows the fullness of

49. Rees, *Racovian Catechism*, 28–44.
50. Bailey, "Way the World Is Meant to Be," 52.
51. Turretin, *Institutes of Elenctic Theology*, 466.
52. Ramsey, *Basic Christian Ethics*, 250.

the image to be expressed socially per the intention of God for man. The creation of man in God's image is directed to something happening between God and man, the creator created a creature that corresponds to him, to whom he can speak, and who can hear him. It must be noted that man in the Creation narrative is a collective. Creation in the image of God is not concerned with an individual, but with mankind, the species, man. The meaning is that mankind is created so that something can happen between God and man. Mankind is created to stand before God.[53]

This demands empathetic concern for all other image-bearers as it relates to proper communion with God.

Finally, in the verbal function of image, man images God by looking to the example and person of Christ as the complete image and form all thought and action to and within him. In this moment, the believer, structurally resembling the God with whom he communes, displays this image missionally as the ethic of his faith. Man is not merely the image in essence or relation but in action. This demands a neverending pursuit of the will of God in proper stewardship and mission. In the same way the relational view offered the greatest evidence for racial tensions, the functional image offers the greatest solution to them. The action that follows a structural mind across races and a restitution of broken relationships between races is one that images God and his character in every facet of life and being, including naturally any previous division of race. The structural component of rational and moral capacity is one applied across all races. As such, there can be no claim of one racial group being intellectually or morally inferior to another because each is made in the image of God. The relational image includes the call to commune with those made in the image of God, which breaks the pattern of the call of segregation. The functional image unites these components in the verbal sense of imitating Christ.[54] This combined approach to the image of God achieves the balance which Maston applied to life.

Maston's Use of Image

The image of God was of requisite concern in the writing of T. B. Maston. In his 1959 work, *The Bible and Race*, Maston begins with a discussion of the image of God. This section is one of the unique additions to his work surrounding race as he reworked his 1946 book, *Of One*, to include both Gen 1

53. Westermann, *Creation*, 56.
54. Clines, "Image of God in Man," 103.

and Acts 17, and to move deeper into Scripture for *The Bible and Race*. Maston notes the sheer importance of the image as it relates to the race issue and turns to deal with the text in its fullness. Maston's interpretation of the image includes direct mention of both the structural and relational views. Maston does not compare the two, nor opine that one is right and the other wrong, but utilizes each to paint a full picture of the functional image. Concerning the functional image, Maston explains that man has been created in the image to serve as God's representative.[55] Maston often speaks of the consequential obligations that man has as God's representative, saying that "the responsibility of man . . . an innate sense of oughtness, [is] an evidence and expression of the image of God within man."[56]

The chief concern Maston takes up is the effect of sin on the image and the restoration of the image. Maston argues that sin has not destroyed the image, but has rather marred it, and in one sense, man has been "re-created in the image of sin."[57] Even in this sin, the image remains as he cites Genesis 9:6, which explains that murder is wrong based upon the image of God, here clearly after the fall. Restoration of this image is only possible in Christ but remains a process that is never fully completed but is the sign of faithfulness and growth. This has an immediate impact upon race relations as he writes, "to the degree we have progressed in the likeness of our Creator, to that degree we shall be free from class and racial consciousness and discriminations . . . Our racial attitudes may be a real barometer of our spiritual maturity."[58] Maston viewed race relations as a measurement of spiritual maturity, especially as it shows an understanding of God's mission to the world. He saw great irony in missions organizations so willing to go to great ends for people of color across the globe while hating those closest to them. He writes, "the people to whom the missionaries go . . . demand that the gospel be validated by the lives of the folks who send it to them."[59] Racial concern is the sign of a mature heart that fully understands the call to love one's neighbor. It is the consistency of word and action in the life of the believer.

For Maston, a full understanding of image became the ultimate value of mankind. To hate someone made in the image of God is to hate God himself. The image is something of personal structure and relationship with lasting consequences and responsibilities. This synchronous perspective is

55. Maston, *Why Live the Christian Life?*, 34.
56. Maston, *Bible and Race*, 8.
57. Maston, *Bible and Race*, 6.
58. Maston, *Bible and Race*, 10–11.
59. Maston, *Segregation and Desegregation*, 156.

further consistent with Maston's emphasis of "Both/And," which holds that God reveals himself in balance more than polarities.[60] The image of God is for Maston the most significant component of a proper anthropology. The inversion of this image because of sin is the chief cause of prejudice and racism displayed in segregation and the mistreatment of peoples. Maston's concludes that

> surely the God who created man in his own image, who made of one all men, who is no respecter of persons, who loved all men enough to give his Son for their salvation, and who taught us to love our neighbor as ourselves did not and does not intend that any man or any segment of mankind should be kept in permanent subserviency or should be treated as innately inferior, as second-class citizens in a first-class society.[61]

The image draws man to an understanding of God's person, but for the segregationist, a distortion of His person and nature willed segregation. The faulty theology has led to a faulty anthropology. Segregationists separate the creation of God from the intent of God. Even if they were to concede the image of God in all people, they would argue that there are divisions given after the image according to the habitation argument of Acts 17.

60. Maston et al., *Both-And*, 5.

61. Maston, *Bible and Race*, 117.

Chapter 5

Desegregation and Segregationist Texts

"Of One" What? Examining Acts 17:24–31

FEW SEGREGATIONISTS USED THE *imago Dei* as part of their arguments for racial discrimination. However, Acts 17:24–31 has been taken up by both segregationists and desegregationists alike. It reads,

> The God who made the world and all things in it, he is Lord of heaven and earth and does not dwell in temples made with hands; nor is he served by human hands, as though he needed anything, he himself gives to all people life and breath and all things; and he made from one every nation of mankind to live on all the face of the earth, having determined allotted periods and the boundaries of their dwelling place, to seek God, if therefore they might reach for him and find him, and yet surely he is not far from each one of us; for in him we live and move and exist, as even some of your own poets have said, "For we also are his children." Therefore, being the children of God, we ought not suppose that the divine is like gold or silver or stone, an image formed by the art and thought of man. Therefore, having overlooked the times of ignorance, God now commands to men that all people everywhere should repent, because he has fixed a day in which he will judge the world in righteousness by a man whom he has appointed, having given proof to all men by raising Him from the dead.

This passage finds Paul in Athens' Areopagus addressing the Athenians' altar to an unknown God. Paul uses this altar as an opportunity to declare the gospel. Concerning this passage's further context, Paul's speech invokes *both* [Hellenistic Accommodation and Jewish Critique] . . . to narrate the complete incongruity between the Christian movement and Gentile religion—an incongruity exemplified by the speech's critique of Greco-Roman religiosity, anti-idolatry polemic, and its theologically exclusive claims; and to exalt the Christian movement as comprising the best features of Greco-Roman philosophical sensibilities and therefore as a superior philosophy.[1]

This pericope's primary concern is the message of the gospel coming to the Athenians, but from it has risen a verse claimed by two opposing ideologies of great weight to the issue of race. Verse 26 says, "He made from one man every nation of mankind to live on all the face of the earth, having determined their appointed times and the boundaries of their habitation." This verse has been used by both sides of the segregation debate to further each argument and shows the significance of proper hermeneutics. In the same way the section on Gen 1:26–28 explored each interpretive option, Acts 17:26 will be examined through the interpretive lenses of the segregationist and the desegregationist before finally illustrating Maston's explicit use of the passage.

Segregationist Perspective

The segregationist draws attention to the latter half of verse 26 as biblical justification for a legal separation between the races, as it was God who "determined their appointed times and the boundaries of their habitation." Initially, there is almost no concern for civility or ploy for the trite cliché "separate but equal," which became the justification for the mistreatments that came with segregation. C. R. Dickey unapologetically states that "An unholy mixing of races in defiance of God's stated command is the gravest danger now threatening Christian civilization. The patter about equality of all races, without regard to their inherent character and potentialities, is foolishness. It is not supported by the Bible nor by the facts of life."[2] Dickey argues that Acts 17:26 is one of many biblical justifications for segregation. She goes on to say that the verse had even been poorly translated because it left an opportunity for progressives to twist it towards desegregation. Her proposed translation of the first half of the verse instead reads, "He made by One [i.e., Christ] every race of men to dwell upon the whole face of the

---

1. Jipp, "Paul's Areopagus Speech of Acts 17:16–34," 568. Italics original to the author.

2. Dickey, *Bible and Segregation*.

earth."[3] By removing any common origin and instead using "one" as a clarification of means rather than source, Dickey shifts the verse's core intent and veracity to remove this verse from the arsenal of the desegregationist.

Another outspoken proponent of segregation at the time was Finis Dake, a renowned Pentecostal pastor. Dake wrote an article entitled "30 Reasons for Segregation of Races," in which he justified three reasons for segregation by citing Acts 17:26. He writes, "1. God wills all races to be as He made them. Any violation of God's original purpose manifests insubordination to Him. . . . 3. God originally determined the bounds of the habitations of nations. . . . 21. All nations will remain segregated from one another in their own parts of the earth forever."[4] He went on to say that heaven itself would be segregated.[5] Dake and Dickey are only a fraction of those making arguments of the like in the church during this epoch. Today there are supposedly Christian denominations at large which declare White supremacy to be God's intention.[6] Alex Poinsett opines that

> For the segregationist use of the Bible as an indictment against Negroes is, after all, a now-pathetic, now ludicrous spectacle of creatures recreating their Creator, The God who is the fountainhead of all values, becomes in their hands a cesspool of race prejudice. The God whose love inundates the universe, transforms into a Niagara of hate. The God who is the Poet of the world, is recast as a poison-penned propagandist. His mercy becomes malice. His justice gives way to partiality and His goodness emerges as mockery. The cosmic Spectator of all time and existence narrows his vision, stepping into human history solely to bless whites and damn Negroes.[7]

The glaring fault in the segregationist's argument is its failure to read the passage in context. When viewed in isolation, especially as Dickey translates it, verse 26 makes clear sense as the borders of the races, instilled by God for his purposes. However, this completely ignores the surrounding verses and authorial intent of the passage. The wider context deals with the commonality of all men in relation to God. He even mentions the divine

3. Dickey, *Bible and Segregation.*

4. Dake, "30 Reasons for Segregation of Races," 159.

5. Dake, "30 Reasons for Segregation of Races," 159.

6. See Kaplan, "Christian Identity," 50–53. Groups which subscribe to "Christian Identity" include Kingdom Identity Ministries, The Church of Jesus Christ Christian, The Phineas Priesthood, The Suidlanders, and the Oklahoma Constitutional Militia among others.

7. Poinsett, "What the Bible Really Says About Segregation," 73–76.

nature in verse 29 as an attack upon the idols surrounding him by revealing the image as children rather than conceivers. Further, this argument fails to consider the full argument of Scripture, especially as displayed in the Jew/ gentile controversy of the early church, which many have used as a paradigm for understanding the racial issues surrounding the United States.[8] Racialized sentiments that God ordained segregation in his creative and sustaining actions were also seen greatly in the SBC. W. A. Criswell, the pastor of First Baptist Church, Dallas and future SBC president, speaking at an evangelism conference in 1956, said he believed "in religious segregation as well as racial segregation. Those who would integrate, let them integrate . . . they are all a bunch of infidels, dying from the neck up."[9] Though Criswell would later repent of his racism,[10] this vitriolic statement drew mixed responses. Many in favor of segregation heartily affirmed, those against stood shocked, and still others found themselves in agreement with the principle yet uneasy with the attitude and insult.[11] Other Baptists like H. T. Sullivan concluded that "God considered segregation to be wise and best from the very beginning of time."[12] Many in the SBC simply saw segregation as a part of the greater plan of God for man, and used Acts 17:24–31 as an example of this revelation.

Desegregationist Perspective

The desegregationist, on the other hand, looks to Paul's speech as the unifying text of origin. This mounts in one of two ways. First, the phrase "from one" or "of one" could be referring to God as the progenitor of creation. This, of course, has direct ties to the image of God, which has been previously considered. Joshua Jipp posits that "Luke exploits the overlap between biblical and Stoic traditions: both affirm that God is one, that the human race is unified and originates in God, and that God orders the seasons and humanity's habitations."[13] Alternatively, some posit this instead is referring to a common ancestor, namely, Adam. The particular translation or interpretation has little bearing on the conclusion upon race relations. Whether all races originate spiritually or physically from the same source, there remains a unity and regard between all peoples as equal.

8. See Hays, *From Every People and Nation.*

9. "Dallas Pastor Stirs Controversy with Statements on Integration," 1.

10. Freeman, "'Never Had I Been So Blind,'" 1–12.

11. Porter, "Southern Baptists and Race Relations, 1948–1963," 96–101.

12. Sullivan, "Christian Concept of Race Relations," 1.

13. Jipp, "Paul's Areopagus Speech of Acts 17:16–34," 582.

Concerning the latter half of the verse, desegregationists posit that Paul's concern was not to display God's separation of different men on the basis of race as much as he was showing God's sovereignty over all men. Athens is a city full of idols, each thought to rule over another separate part of creation. Paul proclaims that a single God, whom they had determined to offer praise to, was the God over all nations. The Athenians stand in awe, hearing for the first time that the true diversity is not found in varied deity, but in varied peoples with a common source. This diversity of nations and peoples is not an effect of the fall, but a beauty of creation. Paul "affirms the creation of human beings by a direct act and declares that God's design was for various cultures to cover the face of the earth in a harmonious patchwork of diversity."[14] As he proclaims to them the beauty of salvation, at the same time, "it appears that the gift of life to all peoples includes a specific plan for geographical diversity, inasmuch as it was God who sent each people to inhabit a particular territory."[15]

Maston's Use of "Of One"

Maston notes the emphasis "of one" to point to a common origin. His concern is not to take a stand upon one interpretation or another regarding "one Father" or "one ancestor," but to show the unity towards which both interpretations incline man. Concerning "one Father" Maston makes his way through the numerous descriptions in Scripture of God as Father, explored in the previous chapter. Maston points out the conclusion that there is no exclusivity to God as Father and that, "He is the father of *all* who believe, regardless of class or color . . . [and that] just as God reveals the fatherly attitude toward all, even those outside his spiritual family, so we his children should show the brotherly attitude toward all, even those who may not be our spiritual brothers."[16] The same principles of "one Father" are shared in the interpretation of "one ancestor."[17] In each, there is a familial bond to be upheld. Maston continues to say this brotherly obligation is of chief concern to the Christian as Christ teaches in Matt 5:23–24 that the one bringing an offering to God must first be reconciled to his brother before any offering could be made. Maston contends that reconciliation must precede worship, and this must extend honestly to racial reconciliation.

---

14. Larkin et al., *Acts*, 257.

15. Godwin and Chol, "'God Gave This Land to Us,'" 211.

16. Maston, *Bible and Race*, 21–22. Italics original to the author.

17. Maston, *Bible and Race*, 24.

This unified origin is the second component of Maston's anthropology. Here, the familial bond in the community of man and further in the community of believers is paramount to understanding the Christian view of Man. Maston argues that the individual is both dependent and independent of the community. He writes, "Belonging to the earth [the individual] is dependent on the community; but there is a transcendental point of reference in his nature that makes him independent of the community."[18] The tension Maston strikes here is where the image of God meets the community of man. Genesis 1 and Acts 17 collide as the structural, relational, and functional being is applied to all human origin, regardless of race. Unity becomes the emphatic statement, "of one." Maston points to this unity as going beyond God's paternal nature and further into the fullness of the Trinity. He specifically notes the reconciliation of Eph 2:14 between Jews and gentiles and extends this unity to all that are in Christ.[19] Maston describes the unified origin as rooted in both creation and salvation. As the believer comes to grips with the implications of a shared ancestral line—as well as the reconciliation of previous divisions by Christ—there is no room in the faithful practice of a believer for segregation. The collective community is essential for the church to demonstrate love to a watching world. Any failure to love the whole community is a failure to embody the whole love of Christ. Desegregation is the bare minimum of a proper anthropology. Maston writes elsewhere that the church "is a shared fellowship through union with and in Christ."[20] This fellowship is the illustration of the greater kingdom of God seen in the universal church. The local church should consequently reflect the same standards of admission and practice as the kingdom. Maston's anthropology holds this as gospel. However, the segregationist's anthropology still holds one final distinction.

The Curse of Ham in Gen 9:20–27

The third passage, Gen 9:20–27, is the lynchpin for the segregationist's most direct biblical supports of racism. Maston says that the curse is used "to defend the *status quo* in race relations . . . to mean that the Negro, as a descendent of Ham, is destined by God to fill permanently a subservient place in society, that he should never be considered as an equal by the white man."[21] Setting the stage of the text in the Genesis narrative, mankind has

18. Maston, *Christianity and World Issues*, 49.

19. Maston, *Bible and Race*, 26.

20. Maston, *Segregation and Desegregation*, 123.

21. Maston, *Bible and Race*, 105.

grown exceedingly wicked to the point God decides to destroy them with a great flood and repopulate through the lineage of Noah, a righteous man who finds favor in God's sight. After the flood subsides, the Lord makes a covenant with Noah and his descendants that he would never completely flood the earth again. The reader is reminded of Noah's sons Ham, Shem, and Japheth, noting that Ham was the father of Canaan, and all people come from these three. Genesis 9:20–27 then reads,

> Noah began to be a man of the soil, and he planted a vineyard. He drank from the wine and became drunk and uncovered himself in his tent. And Ham, the father of Canaan, saw the nakedness of his father and told his two brothers outside. But Shem and Japheth took a garment, set it on both their shoulders, and walked backward and covered the nakedness of their father. Their faces were turned backward, and they did not see their father's nakedness. When Noah awoke from his wine and knew what his youngest son had done to him, he said, "Cursed be Canaan; a servant of servants he will be to his brothers." And he said, "Blessed be the Lord, the God of Shem; and let Canaan be his servant. May God enlarge Japheth, and let him dwell in the tents of Shem, and let Canaan be his servant."

It is a common trend to teach this passage's effects primarily as the result of Noah's drunkenness.[22] Perhaps if Noah had not been drunk, Ham would have never been cursed. It is not the place for today's reader to speculate the potentialities of what could have happened, but rather seek to understand what did and why. Further, while Noah's drunkenness may have been the initial cause of the situation, the text makes clear that Noah was the first to plant the vineyard. Being "unacquainted with the effects of wine," Noah could hardly be blamed for what happened with Ham.[23] However, the severity of the curse does raise the question of the nature of Ham's fault.

Ham's sin is found in verse 22 as he, "saw the nakedness of his father and told his two brothers outside." However, there is no immediately clear violation of law or culture as is understood through Scripture in an immediate reading of the text. There is a shame in nakedness, reminiscent of just three chapters earlier in the Genesis account (Gen 3:7–10), which points in part to Shem and Japheth's entrance into the tent. But the severity of the subsequent curse seems out of step with everything else the account has given. For this reason, the reader must come to understand the very core of what is being said in the verse, especially as it relates to Noah's nakedness.

22. See Cohen, *Drunkenness of Noah*, 8.
23. Driver, *Book of Genesis*, 109.

Moving from the most innocent to the most extreme, the interpretive options range from a simple and possibly accidental sight of nakedness, a lustful and intentional voyeurism, a usurping castration of Noah, and an incestuous connotation where Ham rapes either his father or mother.[24] For Maston, the question of Ham's sin goes to the wayside in light of the greater question that is the extent of the curse which follows.

Interpretive Options of Ham's Curse

The curse in this context has been widely discussed, as each interpretation is forced to wrestle with the uniqueness of this passage. One issue every interpretation must face is why it appears that Canaan and his descendants were cursed while Ham was not. Some scholars and historians have suggested that because of the repeated wording, "Ham, the father of Canaan" (Gen 9:18, 22), that the text suggests that Canaan was either present alongside Ham, or even that it was not Ham who sinned at all, but rather Canaan. As evidence of this possibility, they cite that "youngest son" in verse 24 suggests Canaan as the youngest descendant rather than a literal reading of son.[25] However, it seems more likely that the intent of "father of Canaan" is to simply remind the reader of Ham's relation to Canaan and explain the coming effect of Ham's sin onto his son. Another more likely possibility is that since God had blessed Noah and his sons in 9:1, Ham, having received that blessing, was unable to be cursed. In contrast, his brothers could receive a double blessing (Gen 9:26–27), excluding Ham and further cursing his lineage. Maston notes that to curse one that has already been blessed would be inconsistent.[26] Further, it may not even be possible. Consider the case of Balaam in Num 22–23. Balak summons Balaam to curse Israel, but in 22:12, "God said to Balaam, 'Do not walk with them; you shall not curse

24. A full examination of this question is beyond the purposes of the present endeavor as the act itself has little bearing on the implications of the curse. For this reason, it will be most helpful to simply include each interpretive option with sources for further examination. For the reading of a simple gaze see Cassuto, *Commentary on the Book of Genesis*, 151. For lustful voyeurism see Clement, *Christ the Educator*, 2.6. For castration theory see Baumgarten, "Myth and Midrash," 68. Finally, for incestuous rape see Gagnon, *Bible and Homosexual Practice*, 66–67. The present writer holds to the latter-most position of a paternal homosexual rape in an attempt at usurpation. Namely, the linguistic phrasing of "Ham, the father of Canaan, saw the nakedness of his father" in the Hebrew וַיַּרְא חָם אֲבִי כְנַעַן אֵת עֶרְוַת אָבִיו (*wayyar' ḥām 'ăbî kĕna'an 'ēt 'erwat 'ābîw*) is consistent with similar uses that suggest sexual relations or rape. See Gagnon, *Bible and Homosexual Practice*, 66. However, the interpretation of the specific action has little bearing on the curse as it is discussed here in relation to race.

25. Kugel, *Traditions of the Bible*, 223.

26. Maston, *Bible and Race*, 110.

the people, because they are blessed.'" The prophet of God was unable to curse that which had already been blessed. However, in the very next chapter, Balaam blesses Israel again. God is not a god of confusion or conflict. He will not bless and curse simultaneously. Ham, therefore, could not be the recipient of the curse, but his brothers could be blessed again, and his son could be cursed. Canaan's cursing in place of Ham is greatly significant as Canaan is not the lineage drawn to the Cushites and Black Africans by segregationists. Instead, Canaan's descendants would have been physically similar to the Israelites apart from their theology.[27]

One implication of the passage is how the text fits in the story of Genesis, as well as the full scope of Scripture. Genesis 9 presents both the corrupt nature of man as demonstrated by Ham and the subsequent punishment/reward structure of God's response. God punishes the wickedness of Ham and rewards the righteousness of Shem and Japheth. O. Palmer Robertson states that, "the Lord of the covenant will be the God of some of the descendants of Noah, bringing blessing to their lives. At the same time, others of the descendants of Noah will be cursed by this same God."[28] It is this portrayal, and subsequent split, of covenant that will carry out the redemptive story, which is eventually restored in Christ.

Ham's disobedience and sin towards, not simply the honor of his father, but to such degrees as castration or rape illustrate the very depravity of the world that had just been destroyed by the flood showing the extent of Adam's curse. The sins of fathers often leave deep repercussions "to be laid upon the children."[29] Canaan's curse was well merited considering the wickedness of his father's actions, and its effects are long-reaching in the history of Israel.[30] Many have taken this passage to explain the hostility historically shown to Black people and defend slavery.[31] Scholars have sought to give a balanced interpretation concerning the effects. Still, it is clear from the standpoint of the sin itself that whatever division was wrought, it at least divided those that would follow God and those that would follow their passions—no matter how depraved those passions might be.

Canaan's lineage sees the effects of the curse, as Canaan becomes the land that Abram sojourns in, a man following the same Lord that Canaan's fathers rejected (Gen 12:5). God calls the land of Canaan land of the wicked

27. Hays, *From Every People and Nation*, 55.

28. Robertson, "Current Critical Questions Concerning the 'Curse of Ham,'" 183.

29. Shakespeare, *Merchant of Venice*, Act 3, Scene 5.

30. This is assuming that the curse was not in response to an accidental view of his father's nakedness, which most scholars note as unlikely. See Gagnon, *Bible and Homosexual Practice*, 66.

31. Bradley, "Curse of Canaan and the American Negro," 103.

and commands Israel not to walk as Canaan did before he brings them into that land (Lev 18:3). It would be the Canaanites Joshua was to drive out and destroy to take the land promised to Abraham (Josh 3:10). It would be the Canaanites that contrast Israel during the time of the Judges, and would constantly rise to destroy them (Judg 1:1). Even following the exile, the Canaanites are a thorn in the side of Israel and the antithesis to their God's commands (Ezra 9:1). The subjugation of the land of Canaan by Israel is the fulfillment of this prophecy.[32] Even if the curse punished a single racial group, it had since been satisfied. Note the dismissal of the curse by Christ as it is a Canaanite woman in Matt 15:22–28 who cries out to Jesus only requesting the crumbs that fall to dogs, to whom Jesus says, "O woman, your faith is great; it shall be done for you as you wish." Canaan's curse was a just response to Ham's sin, and Canaan's descendants typified wickedness and disobedience in contrast to God's people. Still, Christ's work of grace and love allowed for even Canaan to become "fellow heirs and fellow members of the body, and fellow partakers of the promise in Christ Jesus through the gospel" (Eph 3:6).

Appropriation Towards Inequality

Still, it is no secret racial supremacists often employ the curse of Ham as evidence of a racial hierarchy. Josiah Priest posits that the "servitude of the race of Ham, to the latest era of mankind, is necessary to the veracity of God Himself, as by it is fulfilled one of the oldest decrees of the Scriptures, namely, that of Noah, which placed the race as servants under other races."[33] A. W. Pink's popular work, *Gleanings in Genesis*, continues to espouse the curse of Ham's racial implications. Pink specifically writes of the curse that "the whole of Africa was peopled by the descendants of Ham. . . . And, as is well-known, the negroes who were so long the slaves of Europeans and Americans, also claim him as their progenitor."[34] This statement demonstrates the understanding that the sons of Noah, through this curse, each become heads of the three major races. Hays summarizes this distinction saying that "Japheth represents the White or Caucasian race, Ham the Black race, and Shem the Semitic race."[35] From here, the curse of Canaan is used to show a permanent hierarchy of the races by the segregationist. However, even if the segregationist were to read the text as referencing all of Ham's descendants,

32. Hays, *From Every People and Nation*, 56.

33. Priest, *Bible Defence of Slavery*, 393.

34. Pink, *Gleanings in Genesis*, 126.

35. Hays, *From Every People and Nation*, 56.

there is no textual or historical connection between Ham that displays a racial heritage. The traditional tie to racial subjugation is connecting the name Ham with the Egyptian word for black. This has no more connection to race or skin color than Jacob's father-in-law Laban would be to the Hebrew word for white.[36] H. E. Ryle comments as early as 1921 that, "the application of this clause to the African races is an error of interpretation."[37]

Maston's Response

Maston addresses this interpretation further, asserting that "the curse of Canaan has no direct relevance to the contemporary racial situation. The Negro was not included in the original curse, since he was not and is not a descendent of Canaan. Even if he were a descendent of Canaan, the curse itself is no longer in force."[38] His argument points out the thriving of many descendants of Ham, the limitations of inferring a connection to racial subjugation based on faulty hermeneutics, that there is no claim that the curse is divine, and that the curse was a conditional prophecy more so than perpetual subjugation. Maston maintains throughout his work that man shares equality in every category which defines man. However, in his Both/And fashion, Maston does note a simultaneous inequality regarding each individual's function and responsibility. This is to say that he maintained Genesis 9 has no special demarcation of rankings between various races, but when all mankind came from these sons of Noah, individuality came with them. No modern sense of "Justice as fairness" will do for Maston.[39] He insists that balance is needed as

> a too exclusive emphasis on equality leads to a one-sided individualism that magnifies the rights rather than the responsibilities of the individual. On the other hand, an unbalanced emphasis on the inequality of man leads to a one-sided, extreme

---

36. Hays, *From Every People and Nation*, 57.

37. Ryle, *Book of Genesis*, 128.

38. Maston, *Bible and Race*, 116–17.

39. See Rawls, *Justice as Fairness*. Justice as fairness is not concerned with what is due as much as it is with what Rawls determines to be equality. Fairness becomes the measuring stick of all action and inaction. Unfortunately, Rawlsian justice has become one of the most widely held systems of ethics in today's culture alongside Fletcher's situation ethics which will discussed at length in ch. 7. Rawls's system fails to grapple with a biblical definition of justice and gives no comprehensive standard for what is fair beyond an appropriation of Utilitarianism, which will also be discussed in the coming chapters.

collectivism which magnifies the rights and privileges of the collective or of a "superior" segment of society.[40]

In his pursuit of a balanced anthropology, Maston disputed the claims of segregationists who sought to use Scripture to justify their prejudice in the SBC. The Curse of Ham, simply put, would not be permitted to justify perpetual hatred and sin.

The final blow against using this interpretation as a justification for racism came at the 2018 annual meeting of the Southern Baptist Convention. "Resolution 4—On Renouncing the Doctrine of the 'Curse of Ham' as a Justification for Racism,"

> RESOLVED, That the messengers to the Southern Baptist Convention meeting in Dallas, Texas, June 12–13, 2018, maintain and renew our public renunciation of racism in all its forms, including our disavowal of the "curse of Ham" doctrine and any other attempt to distort or misappropriate the Bible to justify this evil.[41]

Maston's declaration of equality between the races and his dispute of the distortions of this curse were finally formally affirmed fifty-nine years after he made his case in *The Bible and Race*. Undoubtedly, this is part of the eventual change for which Maston fought. These arguments which apply Maston's appeal for a biblical anthropology mount his greater fight for desegregation.

---

40. Maston, *Christianity and World Issues*, 39.
41. See "On Renouncing the Doctrine of the Curse of Ham."

Chapter 6

Desegregation and Mastonian Anthropology

Maston's Fight for Desegregation

MASTON'S FIGHT WAS NOT one made on the steps of congress but in the pews of the church and the hallways of the seminary. Maston's "constant instruction was to deal with the issue, not personalities. While attacking segregation from a biblical base, he did not condemn the segregationist and that is how he lived."[1] Maston's arguments and writings dealt with the current issues and climate of segregation in a way he saw to be consistent with Scripture and the will of God—displayed most clearly in his 1959 work, *Segregation and Desegregation.* This work responds to the renowned *Brown v. Board of Education* case of 1954, which, of course, deals specifically with the desegregation of schools. Maston uses this decision as the leaping point to explore the case itself and responses to it to give a Christian perspective on the issue of race and segregation. He opens with what is primarily an historical examination of what preceded the decision and the contents of the case itself, affirming that separate does not mean equal. He explains that this principle will be used to examine the existence of segregation at large and what Scripture says towards it.

Surprisingly enough, Maston records that the reception of the decision in the SBC was a positive one, though he has been credited as the driving force behind this acceptance.[2] However, there was also a great deal of vocal negative response. These dissenters came in every form, from the outspoken

1. Farley, "T. B. Maston," 31.
2. Storey, "Thomas Buford Maston," 35.

Klan member to upstanding members of the Citizen's Council, who not long before that, were the White Citizen's Council. Unfortunately, some of the most outspoken, as Maston notes, were prominent leaders of the church. He explains again that segregation in the schools developed alongside a segregation in the church following the Civil War. Segregation came at a great cost. Maston points out that the effects of segregation are seen psychologically, socially, and spiritually on the majority and the minority as well, even to quote King in saying that segregation "sears the soul of both the segregator and the segregated."[3]

Maston then turns to Scripture to draw ideals and principles relevant to the conversation of segregation, as it is not directly mentioned in Scripture. The first principle rests in the nature of God; namely, he is a moral person, creator, sovereign ruler, and Father, each explored in the third chapter. The next is in the nature of man as consistent with the previously examined aspects of having a common origin (Acts 17:26), being made in the image of God (Gen 1:26), and possessing a human equality which has been drawn out in this section. Further, the concepts of the work of Christ, God as no respecter of persons, and Scripture's address of man's relation to his fellow man each play an additional role. His greatest point is that the Bible should be utilized to challenge deficiencies and immoralities rather than to twist God's word and character to "clothe our sins in the garments of sanctity by an appeal to the Bible."[4]

The greatest ethic, then, must be an obedience to the will of God, for "to the degree that we take up a cross, to the degree we deny ourselves, to that degree and to that degree only do we really follow Christ."[5] This is chiefly and finally guided by the Holy Spirit. Maston takes this ethic and applies it to the church by way of the New Testament depiction of the body of Christ. Christ alone is the head of the church. As such, Christ alone has the right to admit or forbid any person or race from his gathering. This is true despite the signs outside of many churches in 1959 that stated otherwise.[6] "The world needs desperately a living demonstration of God's ideal or goal for human society. The church is the only institution that can give such a demonstration."[7] At the time of *Segregation and Desegregation*'s publishing, the church had yet to become that demonstration. Most dreadfully, Maston remarks,

3. Maston, *Segregation and Desegregation*, 57.
4. Maston, *Segregation and Desegregation*, 99.
5. Maston, *Segregation and Desegregation*, 114.
6. See Haynes, *Last Segregated Hour*.
7. Haynes, *Last Segregated Hour*, 130.

> How tragic it would be if the church became "the last bulwark of racial segregation!" What a paradox of secularism and the secular institutions "outchristianize Christianity!" It has frequently been said that eleven o'clock on Sunday morning is the most segregated hour of the week. This is close enough to the truth to embarrass many of our churches to give to many Christians an uneasy conscience. Segregation itself will not be so bad as long as the "uneasy conscience" or "embarrassment" remains. As long as these continue there will be hope of improvement. It is a deep tragedy, however, when a segregated church is content with that segregation. How can such a church claim to be the "church of God?" How can it claim to speak for Christ?[8]

Unfortunately, this same statement could be said of much of the church today to some degree. Thankfully, segregation no longer stands formally in the United States, and racial reconciliation has made great progress towards those cultural aspects of desegregation, and in more and more places a full integration in the Spirit of Christ.

Lasting Impact

Maston's résumé is impressive as it relates to Christian ethics and to race relations, not to mention his legacy beyond these specificities. His impact can be traced through his students to Southwestern at large as a tribute of his academic work, as well as an impact on the SBC and its entities, particularly the Christian Life Commission (now ERLC). This impact demonstrates the coherence of Maston's work as he moved the SBC through the historical pattern of segregation into desegregation. This impact is the proof of the efficacy of his work historically. Moving from the personal outward, arguably his greatest impact was upon the students that sat under his tutelage. Maston's closest students were those he supervised through doctoral studies. These forty-eight men would go on to become pastors, professors, entity heads, and denominational leaders. Their affection for their mentor is easily seen when flipping through his *festschrift*, or any of the numerous books and chapters written in his honor. The most notable student interactions in this conversation, however, are those he had with his Black students. Maston was among those few professors in the 1930s seeking to offer a course of study for Black ministers, a request granted by SWBTS president L. R. Scarborough, and carried out by Maston and others in night classes. When the school finally opened its day classes in 1951, parts of the campus remained

---

8. Maston, *Segregation and Desegregation*, 136.

segregated, including campus housing and common areas. To this end, the Mastons opened the second floor of their home to serve as a student center of sorts for the students unwelcomed elsewhere. Maston constantly instructed and demonstrated a fraternal concern for those he encountered. Harold Sanders, one of the first Black students to enroll in 1951, recalls Maston sitting beside him in chapel and with arms around each other's shoulders asking the man, "Dr. Maston, why do you want to sit by me? You are under enough fire anyway."[9] To which Maston retorted simply, "I am just doing what Christ would have me do."[10] C. B. Lucas, a 1957 Southwestern graduate, on another occasion, explained that, "At a time when I wasn't even allowed to live in the dormitories, Maston would come and talk with me. He didn't treat me like a crippled person . . . he offered some direction, then let me as a proud human being struggle with it myself. . . . I personally prefer this to any paternalism."[11] These interactions were the rule for Maston rather than the exception. His constant effort to be a brother rather than a father to all characterizes his impact. This fraternal care caused W. T. Moore to say of Maston that "his skin is white but his heart is black."[12] Further, Moore notes that Maston "more than once had blacks introduce [him] to black audiences [by this phrase as] . . . it was the highest compliment they could pay. It meant that the man—through his calling from God—had identified with the people with whom he worked."[13] This consistency and demonstrative nature demonstrated clearly Maston's anthropology. In the classroom and outside of it, Maston's work was paramount in the desegregation of Southwestern Seminary.

Maston's work further served as a litmus test for the convention's efforts. Not only was he the founding chairman of the Advisory Council on Southern Baptist Work with Negroes, but further, in 1962 that Council stated its pursuit of racial progress as following Maston's pattern. They state, "T. B. Maston expressed a belief that we 'can go much further' in our materials now than a few years ago. He indicated that he is now getting less violent reactions to his writings than in the past."[14] The great irony here is that these decreasing "violent reactions" were still common enough to force Maston into retirement not a year later. Nevertheless, Maston's presence was weighty upon the Convention. This was especially palpable in the Christian

---

9. Moore, *His Heart Is Black*, 55.

10. William Goff, personal phone interview, April 10, 2018.

11. Lucas, "T. B. Maston," 37.

12. Moore, *His Heart Is Black*, 58.

13. Moore, *His Heart Is Black*, front cover.

14. Moore, *His Heart Is Black*, 52.

Life Commission (CLC). Maston essentially founded the Texas CLC and greatly shaped the SBC level as well. Part of this influence was once again through his students. Aaron Weaver notes that "thirty professional Baptist ethicists served as full-time employees during the first thirty years of the existence of the SBC's Christian Life Commission. Maston heavily influenced seventeen of those thirty."[15] Maston further directly impacted the Commission as a consistent counselor, speaking and leading conferences, presenting papers, and publishing pamphlets for the Commission. This work through the convention even had the effect of churches clinging to segregation formally protesting these writings through a resolution concerning the "integration trend."[16] However, Maston's vision for the full circle of race relations to move once again from segregation through desegregation and finally into integration was never achieved in his lifetime. Desegregation is no small victory, but it should not bring with it a satisfaction which can only be found in integration.

The Present Desegregated Society

In 1965, only a year after the Civil Rights Act became law, Martin Luther King Jr. famously stated that "the most segregated hour of Christian America is eleven o'clock on Sunday morning."[17] Though formal segregation has passed, this appalling fact is still largely true in most churches. This is because of desegregation presents itself as a false integration. Of the 47,272 SBC churches, only 182 of them could be described as multi-ethnic.[18] There are obvious caveats which should be made to this idea, as it is likely that many of these churches are in primarily racially homogenous neighborhoods or towns. However, when the scale of those cities and towns are considered in which there is a racial diversity which is not adequately seen reflected in the local church, King's words still ring true. There are no longer any legal barriers which would keep racially diverse communities from worshipping together regularly, yet they remain distinct. As Maston and King would both say, these communities have been desegregated but not integrated. Maston writes that the very "idea of a homogenous church . . . may fall short of the New Testament ideal. That ideal is a closely knit fellowship of people of different classes, colors and cultures: all brothers and sisters in

15. Weaver, "Impact of Social Progressive T. B. Maston," 22.

16. Pennington, "Blueprint for Change," 125.

17. King, "Un-Christian Christian," 76.

18. See http://www.sbc.net/BecomingSouthernBaptist/pdf/FastFacts2018.pdf.

Christ."[19] Beyond the presence of ethnically homogeneous churches, there is one key indicator of the present desegregated society. Simply put, no comprehensive integration has yet occurred. Per the definition given in the first chapter, integration should be understood as the full amalgamation and reconciliation of previously segregated groups in a single community. While groups are no longer formally segregated, an integrated community is the exception rather than the rule. Desegregation continues. The primary cause which perpetuates of desegregation is the issue of apartness.

Apartness

Apartness is a symptom of the underlying desegregated society. This is not necessarily physical apartness, as the true implementation of desegregation removes physical barriers. Apartness is the basic idea that many of the prejudices of this world, conscious or otherwise, are due in part to an ignorance of separation. Essentially, there is no concern for a struggle that is not understood or experienced, and empathy is raised when there is a personal concern. This leads to a social indifference, not as a "total absence of feeling, positive or negative, but simply an unusually low degree of feeling, usually negative."[20] An emotional apathy of sorts casts aside any that does not look or struggle in the same way. Apartness can be seen in nearly every vice in the issue of race and is paramount for understanding the fullness of the conversation. Apartness today exists in part because of the climates that introduced them, namely in the slavery and segregation in the United States already presented. This is of course heightened in a post-civil rights era culture, but it is nothing new as it seems that,

> instinctively we tend to gravitate toward people and cultures most like us. That is a safe place. But the moral choice, the one that shows the character of Christ, who resides in us, is to act out our "go ye therefore" edict and open ourselves up to a diversity of cultures in order to reach them with the gospel and fellowship with them as our brothers and sisters.[21]

Apartness is a failure to grapple with the proper anthropology presented in Scripture and applied by Maston.

---

19. Maston, "Continuing Concerns." The question of this ideal will be taken up in a later chapter.

20. Willard, *Renovation of the Heart*, 33.

21. Lewis-Giggetts, *Integrated Church*, 85.

In many cases, those who have crossed these lines or are standing against the oppression of others do so because of a personal relationship with someone different than themselves. Whether it be growing up in a similar neighborhood or serving alongside another person in the military or workforce, the realization of equality rarely finds its footing from a Bible study or lecture but rather from the everyday life away from apartness. To this end, the most effective thing for movement from desegregation towards integration and life at large moving forward in a socially diverse society is to bridge the gap of apartness, intentionally and relationally. Maston writes, "It is sin that has broken man's fellowship with God and his fellow man. This means, among other things, that racial distinctions, racial prejudice, customs, or taboos that destroy, disturb, or make difficult our fellowship with fellow human beings and particularly with fellow Christians is sin."[22]

Conclusion

The Southern Baptist Convention has a long and complex history, but even at its most troubling times, it would be ill-fitting to call this past totally dark. One such reason for this was the light exuded by T. B. Maston in his stand against segregation. To this end this chapter examined three of Maston's arguments surrounding a biblical perspective on race. Genesis 1:26–28 contains the initial understanding that all men are created in the image of God which can be understood to consist of structural qualities, relational capacities, and functional obligations. This image compels right perspective of equal treatment of all men. Acts 17:24–31 contains a reminder, that amid God's sovereignty over a great and wonderful diversity, all men have a common origin both spiritually and ancestrally. This compels man to reconcile with his brothers in their common pursuit of God. Genesis 9:20–27 fails to support racial discrimination despite the history of an abusive hermeneutic applied to the passage. T. B. Maston understood the weight of each of these passages and used them to shape his own work and life, as well as challenge those around him who believed contrary to him. His life and writings are a testament of faithfulness, humility, and love of God and man. He leveraged his biblical anthropology to overcome segregation and to move to deseg-regate. The Mastonian anthropology demonstrates both biblical and theo-logical coherence as it combats the arguments of segregation and proposes desegregation as the first necessary step towards full racial reconciliation. Maston writes, "Let the Christian forces of the [world], white and colored, join hands in solving their pressing problem and it will be a most striking

22. Maston, "Bible and Racial Distinctions," 2.

object lesson to the world of the sufficiency and efficiency of the Christian program for social reconstruction!"[23] His biblical blueprint was unsatisfied in his life, but remains an effective path for full racial reconciliation through integration.

23. Maston, *Of One*, 123.

Chapter 7

Integration and Mastonian Ethics

Introduction

HAVING ESTABLISHED THE BIBLICAL and theological coherence of T. B. Maston's theology and anthropology from segregation through desegregation, the bulk of Maston's legacy hinges on his ethics. More than this, his ultimate contribution hinges explicitly on the conclusion of his racial ethics in integration. This chapter represents the fullness of Maston's argument and blueprint for future racial reconciliation in the church. Beginning with Maston's ethical thought, this chapter lays out the fullness of Maston's case for integration, moving from the underlying principles to proposed actions for the church to facilitate complete racial reconciliation. These arguments demonstrate the fullness of Maston's ethics.

A Case for Deontological Virtue Ethics

Maston is remembered for his distinct contributions to the development of Christian ethics in the Southern Baptist Convention. Yet, even in the copious amounts of writings and publications he composed in his lifetime, there is little which would show or describe where his thought would land amongst traditional systems of ethics.[1] This is primarily because Maston was simply not a systematician, nevertheless, there is still a framework that

---

1. Traditional theories here are those which would be categorized in sources which lay out the most common systems historically such as Sidgwick, *Methods of Ethics*; MacIntyre, *Short History of Ethics*; and, perhaps most helpful, as previously referenced, Wilkens, *Beyond Bumper Sticker Ethics*.

describes his ethical motivation and method cogently.[2] The closest sem-
blance of his system is in a discussion of what Maston calls principles or
Principlism.[3] However, this self-implemented term lacks clarity outside of
his corpus. The chief reason for this vagueness is the conflation of the term
recently in both theology and ethics. In the former, it is more indicative of
the interpretive hermeneutic,[4] which "seeks to find universal principles in
the Old Testament legal material and to apply these principles to believers
today."[5] This hermeneutic is plainly seen in Maston's use of the Scriptures,
but it is insufficient to describe an ethical system for a different reason. In
the latter, it is more often associated with a system of medical Principlism
which has little relation to Christian ethics. This system, championed by
Beauchamp and Childress,[6] holds that the four principles of "autonomy, be-
neficence, nonmaleficence, and justice are intersubjectively valued in and of
themselves."[7] Each of these principles factors into ethical medical decision-
making, but the subsequent system is unrelated to the system employed by
Maston except by name alone. Concurrent and posthumous presentations
of Maston's ethical thought, from dissertations to his *festschrift*, similarly
lack the concrete specificity needed to classify his work as much of what
has been done primarily concerns discussions of a Mastonian hermeneutic.

This chapter argues that Maston's "Principlism" can be understood as
consistent with Deontological Virtue Ethics as it supplements an elevation
of virtuous being with a biblical deontology. In a presentation and clarification of Maston's ethical system, a proper understanding and evaluation may
be given towards his arguments for integration. To this end, this explanation
includes an application of this system as it specifically relates to Maston's
racial ethics and the extents of integration. The result is a description and
systemizing of Mastonian ethics that are evaluated and applied as theologically and biblically coherent.

The argument first offers previous evaluations of Maston's ethics with
the intent to show the weaknesses of these brief assertions. Secondly, the
chapter defines Deontological Virtue Ethics. Then the case is made that
Maston's ethical thought aligns squarely with Deontological Virtue Ethics

2. Scudder, "Theology and Ethics," in *An Approach to Christian Ethics* edited by
Pinson, 111.

3. This is the extension of the initial discussion in pages 19–21, and thereby
builds on the base facts given there.

4. See Kaiser, "Principlizing Model," 19–50.

5. Hays, "Applying the Old Testament Law Today," 35.

6. See Beauchamp and Childress, *Principles of Biomedical Ethics*.

7. Bulger, "Principlism," 92.

before raising possible critiques. Next, the system is applied to racial ethics and offers its final conclusions in steps towards integration.

Previous Evaluations of Mastonian Ethics

Part of the reason the Mastonian system is unclear is that its formation was never a primary goal of Maston's work. In his 1974 book, *Why Live the Christian Life?*, Maston sets out to give his account of basic Christian ethics. This was part of a larger intention to cover the entire field of Christian ethics in four works. Two of these works had already been written to show perspectives of biblical ethics, in his most popular work *Biblical Ethics*, and social or applied ethics, in *Christianity and World Issues*, as well as later supplemented by *The Christian, the Church, and Contemporary Problems*. Maston's fourth work, which would cover the history of Christian ethics, was never completed. Though he notes in the preface of *Why Live the Christian Life?* that "there is no attempt to conform to or promote any particular theological position for ethical system or theory [or] to force the Christian life for its ethic into one descriptive term,"[8] this work, and the other three mentioned above, are paramount to understanding Maston's framework.

There are of course several systems which are easy to eliminate as Maston addressed and rejected numerous of them. Likely the chief system in which he found the most distaste was that of the situation ethics of Joseph Fletcher.[9] Maston lamented the association of liberal theology with social concern and saw situation ethics as chief contributor in this association. Concerning moral relativism, he concedes that there is indeed a place for a shift within morality. However, he clarifies saying that "while that which is right in itself may become wrong because of the attitude of others and the general environment in which the activity is ordinarily found, an activity that is wrong within itself can never be made right."[10] He continues in his pattern of refusing an either/or in favor of a both/and saying "thus we can conclude that right and wrong are not absolute or relative, but may be *both* relative *and* absolute."[11]

8. Maston, *Why Live the Christian Life?*, xi.

9. Fletcher, *Situation Ethics*.

10. Maston, *Right or Wrong?*, 19.

11. Maston, *Right or Wrong?*, 20. Italics added. Perhaps an alternative non-technical description of Maston's system could be titled "Both/And Ethics," as it would avoid the clunky mouthful of "Deontological Virtue Ethics" and aptly reflect Maston's hallmark expression.

Maston addresses additional systems across many of his works, most often in passing comments. One of the most sweeping judgments which reveal his opinion on several systems comes in his book *Right or Wrong?* Here Maston sets out to offer an approach for moral decision-making for issues faced by teenagers and youth leaders, though he notes the process is the same for all believers. In his chapter, "Determinants of Right," Maston proposes that two questions represent the task of ethics.[12] The first is to ask what is good, and the second is to ask how man can attain the good. He then offers three options for approaching these questions. Beginning with the individual, Maston addresses traditional understandings of hedonism and utilitarianism based upon man's reasoning and rejects each as insufficient due to the state of man's sinful nature. The second approach raises the conflicting ideals of group ethics, clearly drawing a connection to the faults raised by Reinhold Niebuhr.[13] The final option he suggests as the most hopeful and constant, is to determine the will of God. This task is not as simple as divine command theory either, as Maston is critical of the rigid conception of the Bible as a rule book. One of his most prolific students, Foy Valentine, states that the authoritative will of God, for Maston, is "the Christian's absolute *summum bonum* in life."[14] Maston further explains that "the will of God evolves from and is expressive of the nature of God."[15] The task then is to determine the will of God. Few have attempted to offer a category for this process, and those that have seem to do so from partial aspects of Maston's work.

The clearest attempt at qualifying Maston's framework into an existing system is found in a brief statement by Bob E. Adams in his chapter, "Maston, Missionaries, and Missions," within the Maston *festschrift, Perspectives on Applied Christianity*. Here, Adams suggests that Maston would fit under a natural law system.[16] While there is some evidence to accept this framing, this is inconsistent with a full understanding of Maston's ethics. Adams himself notes the weaknesses of this assertion which lie in the disjointed nature of natural law and Maston's elevation of individualism expressed especially

---

12. Maston, *Right or Wrong?*, 22.

13. Niebuhr, *Moral Man and Immoral Society*. These faults include what Niebuhr refers to as the mob mentality and is key to the thesis of the work as reflected in the title of the book. Against internal confusion, it should be noted that Reinhold Niebuhr is the older brother of Maston's supervisor Richard Niebuhr.

14. Valentine, "To Christian Ethics," in *An Approach to Christian Ethics* edited by Pinson, 49.

15. Maston, *Why Live the Christian Life?*, 94.

16. Adams, "Maston, Missionaries, and Missions," in *Perspectives on Applied Christianity* edited by Tillman, 13.

as the priesthood of the believer as well as the voluntarist church.[17] Two further critiques are needed here. The first is there is a clear teleological component of Maston's framework which natural law theory fails to address as fully as Maston does. This component will be discussed in depth below. The second critique is that Maston echoes the classic response to natural law theory, of its failure to heed the gravity of the fall. At large, Maston was hesitant to affirm any predominately rationalistic approach because of the effects of the fall on the mind. He states that with moral questions, "an important step in any wise decision concerning a major problem is a proper sense of our own limitations. We should acknowledge that we cannot think as clearly as we should unless we have the leadership of the Holy Spirit."[18] This is not to say that Maston eliminates the need for reason, as a divine command theorist, for example, might. Maston instead looks at a number of sources towards ethical decision-making, of which reason and specifically what he describes as common sense are included. For these reasons, the Mastonian ethic is incompatible with the propositions of traditional natural law theory.

Charles McCullough, in his dissertation "An Evaluation of the Biblical Hermeneutic of T. B. Maston," argues that Maston offered a unique appeal to a number of systems and did not fit one distinctly. He writes, "his hermeneutic evidenced an eclectic nature which brought together the interests of rules ethicists, contextualists, virtue ethicists, and response ethicists."[19] The Mastonian ethic is simply not well measured by these systems individually and McCullough does not consider a more nuanced approach to understanding Mastonian ethics. Enter Deontological Virtue Ethics.

Clarifying Deontological Virtue Ethics

Before moving to the argument for Maston's ascription to the system, it would be most helpful to first define Deontological Virtue Ethics as it is used here, as well as demonstrate the need for this classification. Beginning with the need, it quickly becomes clear that the most dominant ethical systems historically each have significant faults—no doubt contributing to debate concerning which is the most valid. For example, utilitarianism's emphasis on the majority rule has a tendency of withholding justice from the minority. Divine Command Theory has no clear answer for circumstances

17. Adams, "Maston, Missionaries, and Missions," in *Perspectives on Applied Christianity* edited by Tillman, 16.

18. Maston, *Right or Wrong?*, 45.

19. McCullough, "Evaluation of the Biblical Hermeneutic of T. B. Maston," 238.

outside of that which is commanded. Cultural Relativism is self-refuting, as it assumes itself to be a moral absolute. Natural Law Theory falls victim to justifying the fallacy that *is* determines *ought*.[20] Likewise, the dominant theory examined herein, Virtue Ethics, is not without its weaknesses. Virtue Ethics tends to be ambiguous both in its application and in its codifying of which virtues qualify as a distinct list of the virtuous. The proposed answer then seems to take an existing dominant system and supplement it in such a way to compensate or eliminate its traditional weaknesses.

Previous attempts to supplement a dominant system can be seen in such works as William Frankena's *Ethics*, in which Frankena takes utilitarianism—a traditionally teleological system—and attempts to balance it by supplementing a "principle of justice" saying,

> we should recognize two basic principles of obligation, the principle of utility and some principle of justice. The resulting theory would be a deontological one, but it would be much closer to utilitarianism than most deontological theories; we might call it a *mixed deontological theory*.[21]

Here, Frankena has addressed to some degree the critique of Utilitarianism above by supplementing a component of deontological justice. His "mixed deontological theory," if applied rightly, should compensate the concern of injustice towards the minority in his prominent Utilitarianism, which is no small accomplishment. However, as Timmons notes, the difficulty remains in identifying possible consequences and extents of results, essentially requiring omniscience on the part of the moral participant.[22] To this end, Frankena's nuanced system still falls short. Therefore, any subsequent attempt at a balanced system should not be content with addressing partial critiques but rather stand as a comprehensive response. Deontological Virtue Ethics (DVE) offers this response.

The most cogent discussion of DVE is found in *The Convergent Church* by Mark Liederbach and Alvin Reid.[23] Liederbach and Reid argue that the question of character addressed in Virtue Ethics must be supplemented with a deontology because of Scripture's teaching, the content of virtuous norms, the proper expression of these norms, and the symbiotic relationship they

---

20. For a concise outline of each system and its strengths and weaknesses, see Wilkens, *Beyond Bumper Sticker Ethics*.

21. Frankena, *Ethics*, 43–52. Italics original to the author.

22. Timmons, *Moral Theory*, 130–31.

23. Liederbach and Reid, *Convergent Church*. Later expanded in Liederbach and Lenow, *Ethics as Worship*.

form.[24] The consequential system espouses a full understanding of biblical ethics in a balance of character and action. Their presentation of DVE is consistent with the balanced Principlism expressed by Maston and will be drawn from in depth. Dealing then with each component of the system's terminology, the system is foundationally a virtue system.

Virtue Ethics

It was nearly four hundred years before Christ when Plato first introduced the cardinal virtues of wisdom, courage, justice, and temperance,[25] but it was his student Aristotle who developed a fuller understanding of what virtue is at its core. The goal of these philosophers was a complete life, namely, for Aristotle, this was portrayed in the magnanimous man's life as "the good for man is a complete human life lived at its best and the exercise of the virtues is a necessary and central part of such a life, not a mere preparatory exercise to secure such a life."[26] Aristotle posited that every good virtue man could be or attain lies between two vices as a golden mean.[27] Both the virtue in deficiency and in excess were a detriment to character of the virtuous man.

While Plato and Aristotle each were able to observe objective truth in the world, their minds were still unable to grasp the fullness of revelation and truth that came with Christ. Salvation brings with it a regeneration of the mind and an understanding only given by the Holy Spirit. As Paul wrote in 1 Cor 2:14, "but the worldly man does not receive the things of the Spirit of God for they are foolishness to him; and he is not able to understand them, because they are spiritually discerned." As noted above in his critique of purely rationalistic approaches, Maston would point to this level of insufficiency on the part of Plato or Aristotle.[28] The Spirit's role can never be reduced to convicting, leading, or calling alone, but must see every component of his power manifest. As Bernhard Anderson notes, "the Holy is not just power—the awesome power manifest in the storm, 'earthquake, wind, and fire,' but is power manifest in relationship with people, saving power and ethical concern."[29] This ethical concern is developed into a distinctly Christian virtue through Augustine of Hippo and Thomas Aquinas.[30]

24. Liederbach and Reid, *Convergent Church*, 188–98.

25. Plato, *Republic*, Book IV, line 428a.

26. MacIntyre, *After Virtue*, 149.

27. Aristotle, *Nicomachean Ethics*, 26–29.

28. Maston, *Right or Wrong?*, 45.

29. Anderson, *Contours of Old Testament Theology*, 48.

30. Augustine, *Writings Against the Manicheans and Against the Donatists*, ch. 15, para. 25. Clarified further by Thomas Aquinas, in Aquinas, *Summa Theologica*, 2-1.62.1–3.

Augustine and Aquinas recognized the cardinal virtues but added to them in the theological virtues seen in 1 Cor 13: faith, hope, and love. Peter Kreeft notes this addition as necessary as "without the supernatural virtues, the natural virtues fail."[31]

The addition of the theological virtues, with the Christian understanding of inner transformation, reveals the full meaning of a virtue ethic system. Dallas Willard explains that "the effort to change our behavior without inner transformation is precisely what we see in the current shallowness of Western Christianity that is so widely lamented and in the notorious failures of Christian leaders."[32] In the same way that ignorance or surrender to the difficulties of the task sell the issue short, so do faulty systems and empty rhetoric. Alasdair MacIntyre offers his classic definition stating that "a virtue is an acquired human quality, the possession and exercise of which tends to enable us to achieve those goods which are internal to practices and the lack of which effectively prevents us from achieving any such goods."[33] This definition expresses the concept of ethical being better than most. Virtue ethics is an ethic of character. The weakness of this definition is that it fails to offer the source of virtue. For Plato, virtue finds its fullness in the world of the forms. For the Christian, however, the fullness of virtue is found in the character of God. This ethic could be bound up in the echo of Lev 19:2, as God declares, "be holy, for I am holy." This call to holiness is the content of morality. Man is called to express and reflect the holiness and character of God. Maston explains that

> God's ultimate ideal or will for us is our holiness or sanctification. . . . Sanctification involves separation from the evils of the world to a dedication to God. . . . The ultimate goal of the Christian's life, which is a glorious one, is that he shall awake at the end of life's journey in the likeness of the resurrected Christ.[34]

Concerning the aforementioned virtues then, it is insufficient to be just as man conceives justice. Holiness requires that true justice reflect the justice of God (2 Chr 19:7). This connection to the source of God is the case for all virtue. The virtuous is only such to the degree it reflects the fullness of God's character.

---

31. Kreeft, *Back to Virtue*, 72.

32. Willard, *Renovation of the Heart*, 79.

33. MacIntyre, *After Virtue*, 191.

34. Maston, *God's Will and Your Life*, 48–49.

Two classic faults of this system have already been mentioned in the inability to offer a distinct list of virtues and the ambiguity of its application. The former criticism is answered here, in that the comprehensive list ought to reflect the eternal character of God.[35] Simply put, "a deontological virtue ethic gives specific direction to how we can become like Christ in character and respond to God in every moment with both a proper attitude and God-honoring content."[36] The latter critique is answered in the supplementation of deontology.

Supplementing Virtue with Deontology

There is little room for ambiguity in deontology. Whether phrased in a Kantian deontology or divine commands, duties expressed in actions and imperatives allow for intrinsic judgement and clarity. In one of the earliest presentations of the distinctions of teleology over against deontology, C. D. Broad writes "that *purely* deontological and *purely* teleological theories are rather ideal limits than real existents. Most actual theories are mixed, some being predominantly deontological and others predominantly teleological."[37] Supplementing virtue ethics with deontology seeks to offer a more balanced mixture than a nearly pure one. This is the balance of not only duty and ends, but also of being and doing. Liederbach and Reid explain,

> Commands and principles demonstrate the proper form of action and obedience (John 14:15). Repeated obedience, in turn, leads to habits of practice. Eventually these habits of practice will become habits of the heart, or virtues. These virtues in turn will form the basic building blocks of godly character. And people who have godly character love to obey the commands of Jesus (John 14:21). What emerges, then, can best be described as a "deontological virtue ethic," where deontological is the adjective that describes how to order virtues to the proper ultimate goal (loving God) and how to properly express them in particular circumstances. Rightly understood, the commands

35. Only one virtue escapes this categorization, and even then, only partially. Humility is not a virtue found in the eternal and unchanging nature of God. On the contrary, his glory excuses him as the only being who is free from the need for it. However, as Phil 2 notes, in his incarnation and death, Christ offers the ultimate picture of humility and is man's point of imitation here as well. Humility is not eternal as Christ lacked it prior to the incarnation. It was something he had to put on, which he did in perfection, and put off in his glorification. While humility is absent from the eternal nature, it undoubtedly still sees fullness in the person of Christ.

36. Liederbach and Reid, *Convergent Church*, 201.

37. Broad, *Five Types of Ethical Theory*, 207–8. Italics original to the author.

of Scripture should not be relegated to prima facie principles that are relevant only in light of relevant virtuous motivations and intentions; rather they are given by God to instruct, guard, and guide virtues. They champion the cause of virtue by keeping them from becoming the basis of moral situationalism and circumstantialism. The absolute commands of God are not ends in themselves; they are means to the end of rightly ordered worship expressed ethically in the lives of God's people, who are virtuous in character because they are obediently striving to be like Jesus. It is through a deontological virtue ethic, then, that the Christian life enters the self-feeding loop of obeying God to demonstrate love for him and loving him by obeying him as John 14:15 and 14:21 instruct.[38]

Deontology further allows for a concrete standard of evaluating what is morally right in pursuit of the virtuous. A scale of the virtuous tends to leave enough room for interpretation for critics to associate it with moral relativism.[39] By supplementing deontology there is a standard for both the resulting character and ends, as well as right actions. Being and doing intersect in Deontological Virtue Ethics and can be seen in the ethics of T. B. Maston. However, it is one thing to assert a framework and another to demonstrate ascription to said system.

Evidences for Mastonian Deontological Virtue Ethics

Maston's Principlism and the task of Christian ethics are rarely defined in a formal sense in his writing. The closest full definition comes in Maston's work on basic Christian ethics, *Why Live the Christian Life?* He writes, "Christian ethics may be defined as a critical reflection on the moral decisions and actions of individual Christians and of the Christian community. Christian ethics performs both an analytical and a prescriptive function, with the former preceding the latter."[40] The immediate appearance of fault in this definition towards the present task is it offers little explicit notion of the being or goal which is an obvious component of DVE. This is not to say his ethic lacked this component, just that this expression of it does not make it abundantly clear.[41] Subtly however, each aspect is present. In the dualistic

38. Liederbach and Reid, *Convergent Church*, 199–200.

39. Hursthouse, *On Virtue Ethics*, 33.

40. Maston, *Why Live the Christian Life?*, 11.

41. It might be more beneficial to the present argument to exclude this definition. However, to make the most compelling case for a Mastonian ascription to DVE,

function of analysis and prescription, there are components of deontology and teleology. Analysis speaks to the ability to judge actions themselves as moral or immoral. Prescription is the expression of what is good. The full body of his work illustrates the full weight of this argument. Firstly, this is seen in his emphasis of the will of God as a complete and perfect ideal akin to the virtue foundation. Secondly, this is seen in his implementation of principles as a deontological component. Finally, this is seen in his balanced tension or "both/and" ethic as it is so often described.[42]

Mastonian Virtue

The authoritative virtue lies in the character of God. The Mastonian ethic understands and seeks after this truth. This character is not only seen in rational observation, but in special revelation. Maston writes, "The chief tangible source for a knowledge of the will of God is the Bible. We find in the Bible a record of God's revelation for disclosure of himself to man; a self-disclosure that was climaxed in his son who was the very stamp of his nature."[43] So then, for Maston this level of virtuous character is seen especially in the person of Christ. In his most Christological work, *To Walk as He Walked*, Maston takes to task a description of Christ's character and actions to replicate each in the Christian life. His argument is that the authentic Christian is not the one that follows the commands of Christ most closely, shares their faith regularly, and expresses orthodoxy in their theology—though these all are to be included as vital aspects of the faith. The authentic Christian is the one who takes *inward* root in the character of Christ as the expression of their being.[44] This is the pursuit of the Christological ideal. Scudder affirms that "Maston believes that the perfect ideals are the most relevant part of the Bible."[45]

Maston claims the standard of perfection is to be found in the essential nature of God and that "the ultimate ideal for the Christian is not so much complete obedience to the will of God as it is to complete conformity

evidence cannot be appropriated. Even data which may seem contradictory, such as this definition, are only apparent contradictions and are more indicative of the fact that Maston would rarely formally systematize his thought. The full body of his work illustrates the full weight of the present argument.

42. This phrase can be seen in nearly all of Maston's works and obviously is reflected in the title of the 2011 Maston reader (Maston et al., *Both-And*).

43. Maston, *Right or Wrong?*, 26.

44. Maston, *To Walk as He Walked*, 162–68.

45. Scudder, "Theology and Ethics," in *An Approach to Christian Ethics* edited by Pinson, 117.

to the nature and character of God."[46] This represents the first task of the Christian life as concerned with the teleological being. While DVE at some point becomes symbiotic in its action of ethical norms and virtuous habits, it begins with sanctification. Maston is emphatic that the Christian ethic is dependent upon a renewed heart. So, while an unbeliever may in fact produce actions which may be consistent with virtue, these persons are not in themselves virtuous. Sin has marred the image of God and the sinner must be justified by Christ to restore this image. The elevation of virtuous character in the pattern of God's revealed will and nature then become the goal of the Christian ethic. Maston explains,

> the Christian ethic as in the Christian Life in general, the imperative is preceded by the indicative, oughtness by isness . . . [it] is not something put on from the outside; it is something that naturally and inevitably evolve from an inner relationship. The ultimate ideal for the Christian is a complete harmony between the inner and the outer.[47]

In his review of Maston's use of biblical ethics, James Giles writes that Maston insists "that the holiness mentioned in Leviticus 19:2 and other passages implies moral purity and blamelessness as well as a separation unto God . . . [and] to survey the ethical teachings of the Bible is to hold before one the ideals that lead to perfect (healthy and complete) living."[48] This is to say that the ideal and virtue are synonymous. The goal of the Christian is to reflect the nature and character of Christ. Maston says elsewhere that "the real Christian is one who lets the resurrected Christ live in him and express himself through him. In other words, we are real Christians to the degree that we are Christlike."[49] This is the emphasis of more than Christian ethics, this is the emphasis of the Christian life. The Christian life was the compass for Maston's work. Joe Trull reflects on Maston's approach to personal morality and growth saying that for Maston, "the ultimate ideal in the Christian life . . . is perfection. Not the kind of sinlessness often connected with perfection but the biblical idea captured in the Greek term *teleos*— 'complete, full-grown, mature.' [written inside] his Bible, 'he who stops being better stops being good.'"[50] Remarking on this perfection, Maston states,

---

46. Maston, *Why Live the Christian Life?*, 130.

47. Maston, *Why Live the Christian Life?*, 10–11.

48. Giles, "Biblical Ethics," in *An Approach to Christian Ethics* edited by Pinson, 101–9.

49. Maston, "Who Is the Good Christian?," 19.

50. Trull, "Personal Morality," in *An Approach to Christian Ethics* edited by Pinson, 179.

"perfection involves more than sinlessness unless sin is interpreted in broad terms. An adequate conception of sin would include both sins of omission and commission. Also, sin would have to be interpreted as inner as well as outer."[51] This inner/outer paradigm is not an interchangeable process for Maston, but is clearly concerned with the foundation of being. He writes,

> the movement in the Christian life is from the inside to the outside. This is the reason why the Christian religion and the Christian ethic are primarily concerned with Christian character rather than with Christian conduct. The latter will result from the former. The only sound, dependable basis for Christian conduct is in Christian character, which stems from union with Christ.[52]

This is decidedly teleological. This is decidedly virtuous. But it is not decidedly complete.

Mastonian Deontology

Maston's virtuous ideal is supplemented with deontological components in the use of Scripture. This is supplementary as he is clear that Scripture is not an unyielding set of rules. Maston shows deference to both context and culture in such affirmations as Martyr's threefold distinction of Old Testament law,[53] but he always sees the words of Scripture as relevant and authoritative for the believer. Charles Myers writes that

> it is [Maston's] conviction that the method of change must be just as much in harmony with the spirit and teaching of Jesus as the idea calling for the change. He maintains that good can never be attained by doing evil. There are Christian methods as well as Christian goals and only those methods that can stand at the tests of Christian principles should be used to achieve Christian ends.[54]

This method is revealed in the principles of Scripture and become the foundation for ethical decision making for Maston. In *Right or Wrong?*, Maston elaborates on what this process looks like. He writes that

51. Maston, *Why Live the Christian Life?*, 128.

52. Maston, *Segregation and Desegregation*, 119.

53. Martyr, *Dialogue with Trypho*, 37–46.

54. Myers, "Race Relations," in *An Approach to Christian Ethics* edited by Pinson, 171.

fundamental principles . . . will give you a basis not only for one but for every decision. These principles if closely related or properly unified will make up your philosophy of life. They will not only give you a basis for the decisions of life but they will also give you the poise and strength to face courageously and victoriously life and all that life brings.[55]

Greenfield defines Maston's use of Principle as "a *concept* that reflects an ideal that flows out of the revealed will of God."[56] Though this ideal, as Greenfield sees it, is to be understood as the commanded action more so than the desired virtue. This is where his Principlism demonstrates its namesake. One of Maston's last students at Southwestern, William Goff, notes that "Maston took quite seriously the biblical imperatives . . . he pointed out that if you have a principle, it is as strong as an imperative. If you have a principle, you live by it."[57] These principles are the actions revealed in Scripture, understood to give a component of obligation for the Christian, but may not necessarily be stated as imperatives clearly in the text. A distinct illustration of this can be found in a paper Maston presented to the Christian Life Commission in 1977, where he explains that

among these principles are: (1) Life is a creation of God and should be considered sacred. (2) The individual will be held accountable by God for his decisions (Gal. 6:7–8). (3) One's body belongs to the Lord, is a temple of the Holy Spirit, and should be dedicated to the purposes of God (I Cor. 6:13–20; Rom. 12:1). (4) Right for the child of God is determined not only by what he thinks is right but also by what others think and by the effect of what he does on the lives of others (Rom. 14:1-23; I Cor. 8:1–13) (5) closely akin to the preceding is the fact that the strong should serve the weak (Rom. 15:1–3). (6) Whatever the Christian does should be for the benefit of others, for the good of the church, and for the glory of God (I Cor. 10:24, 31–33). (7) We who have been recipients of the comfort of God should be instruments of that comfort, letting our father reach out through us to those who have sinned and fallen short of the glory of God (II Cor.1:3–7).[58]

Notice each of these is not a code or list of commands quoted verbatim in the way that the Ten Commandments would be, but at the same time they

55. Maston, *Right or Wrong?*, 3.

56. Maston et al., *Perspectives on Applied Christianity*, 41.

57. William Goff, personal phone interview, April 10, 2018.

58. Maston, "Principles of Christian Social Concern and Action," 20.

call the believer to commanding action. These principles, among others, demonstrate Maston's concern for both the being and doing of the Christian life. The character of God is patterned by believers to the extent they obey the commands of God. He writes, "One must know what and who he is if he is to know what to do. One may scrupulously avoid the words 'ought' and 'should,' but there is present an element of obligation whatever may be one's approach to Christian ethics and the Christian life."[59] This obedience in turn produces both virtuous actions and movement towards the ideal. DVE is the balanced ethic.

Mastonian Balanced Tension (Both/And)

The question of balance within DVE is paramount to a full understanding of the description of virtue and ethical decision-making. Maston posits the question of balance is key to the Christian life. Maston would frequently warn his students in his doctoral seminars that "one of the hardest things for us to do as Christians is to maintain balance. We will tend to go towards one extreme or another, but to maintain the balance between the different poles, different polarities that draw us, is very difficult to maintain over a long period of time."[60] He would often describe this task with the picture of a rubber band. The rubber band is created to operate with tension. Too loose and the rubber band would be ineffective. Too tight and the rubber band would snap. Instead it is created to find a "'creative tension' . . . stretched to accomplish its purpose but not stretched to the breaking point."[61]

DVE is a third option between more strictly teleological and deontological options. This task is emblematic of Maston's imitation of Christ as he found the "creative 'third options' set out so often by Jesus when he was offered to unacceptable alternatives."[62] The Christian likewise is called to find the third option between the two extremes. Greenfield suggests that in his own day, Maston would reject fundamentalist legalism as well as extreme liberalism saying that, "both overemphases are wrong. Heresy is always found at the extremes; orthodoxy stresses balance. Again, not either/or but both/and is needed in grasping the Bible's message."[63] This dyadic "both/and" structure is likely the most indicative display of Maston's balance in his ethics. It is not seen in either the being or the doing of the Christian walk, in

59. Maston, *Why Live the Christian Life?*, 12.

60. William Goff, personal phone interview, April 10, 2018.

61. Maston et al., *Perspectives on Applied Christianity*, 26.

62. Maston et al., *Perspectives on Applied Christianity*, 25.

63. Maston et al., *Perspectives on Applied Christianity*, 36.

either the teleology or the deontology. Instead it is in the both/and. Maston clearly and frequently asserts that,

> we should have a deepening desire that our lives will increasingly express the same character traits found in God and that these traits will be the expression of a unified or integrated personality. This will be true as and to the degree that the outer expressions of our lives are the normal, natural expressions of the inner life.[64]

Possible Critiques

There are of course going to be criticisms of the argument made here. The primary concern is that of anachronism. This is to say that applying contemporary terminology across more than five decades could reap errant conclusions. However, the attempt here has been to avoid sweeping errant anachronisms, while still seeking a linguistic prochronism.[65] It is best to anticipate and answer two of these critiques here.

There is first a question of why Maston did not use virtue ethic language if his system supposedly echoes it. Firstly, this is because the specificities of virtue ethics were primarily unknown to Maston, given that the resurgence of the discipline by MacIntyre and others was just picking up speed in the final years of Maston's life.[66] Though, Maston did have a firm grasp on a more classical understanding of the virtues, and discusses them at some length in *Biblical Ethics*. Maston affirms the theological virtues as discussed by Aquinas describing them as "inward dispositions that provide the basis or foundation for the outward expression of the Christian life."[67] His understanding of virtues was solid and affirmative, though he was unfamiliar with the surging discipline.[68] It is interesting that while his basic Christian ethic did not espouse a distinct system, the answer to the title question elsewhere is consistent with DVE. He concludes, "so, why live the

---

64. Maston, *Why Live the Christian Life?*, 21.

65. It would be foolish to assert that Maston fully held to a system of which he was unaware. Instead it is posited here that Maston's ethical framework can be well measured and described by DVE.

66. See Kotva, *Christian Case for Virtue Ethics*; Kreeft, *Back to Virtue*; MacIntyre, *After Virtue*; and Meilaender, *Theory and Practice of Virtue*. Notice particularly the earliest of these works were published in 1984, well after Maston's career, and only five years before his death.

67. Maston, *Biblical Ethics*, 206.

68. William Goff, personal phone interview, April 10, 2018.

Christian life? Because the virtues God offers, over against potential vices, are better for us and reflect the character of God."[69]

There is also a question of the contemporary nature of DVE. A critique of this assertion may be that this work is trying to force a new system upon a man who may or may not have ascribed to it had it been presented to him, and that it merely reflects the development of the field in a way that would have been unfamiliar to Maston. The system is not a new presentation in the development of Christian ethics, but rather new terminology which embodies an attempt to see the balance of obligation and being original to Scripture and the subsequent attention to the maturity expected of followers of Christ.[70] The affirmation of DVE is to affirm a distinct description of the biblical ethic, an ethic which T. B. Maston consistently applies.

While Steve Wilkens has no chapter or bumper sticker to give Deontological Virtue Ethics, perhaps one might be proposed that would fit it well. This bumper sticker has been brandished, embroidered, printed, and scrawled on the heart of all familiar with church youth culture since the 1990s: What Would Jesus Do? The question has become trite through overuse, but it nonetheless expresses the heart of DVE. In DVE there is a balance of action and character, namely the character of Christ. It is not enough to ask Who Was Jesus? (Virtue alone) or What Should I Do? (deontology alone) but to bear the mark of biblical ethics—and the woven bracelet of 1996—W.W.J.D.

69. Maston et al., *Both-And*, 60. While this conclusion is more obviously a pure virtue ethic, the aforementioned reasons for the insufficiency of virtue alone show the need for DVE.

70. Precursors to DVE as an attempt to espouse the biblical ethic might include iterations of Divine Command Theory well as assertions of the pattern of Christ.

Chapter 8

Integration and Virtue

Virtue as a Societal Alleviation

HAVING ESTABLISHED A BASIC understanding of DVE, the question is now raised of the efficacy of a change in individuals towards changes in culture. Many would argue that legislating morality is the most effective approach to quick societal change as in the case of desegregation,[1] but with the issue of underlying prejudices there are no hard and fast solutions. Even as legislation is a key part of ensuring justice, lasting change must begin concentrically from the individual as "culture is what *we* make of the world. Culture is, first of all, the name for our relentless, restless human effort to take the world as it's given to us and make something else."[2] This change and creation is not of words alone, but requires action and growth. Peter Kreeft describes culture as sliding towards a precipice from which it cannot recover, and the only solution is seen in actionable virtue as simply "Crying 'progress' as we die will not raise us from death."[3] Actionable virtue is a deep concern of DVE.

Concentric change, on the other hand, offers a restoration first on an individual level and then builds to social groups at large. This is particularly necessary within the conversation of race, as race is a socially constructed grouping much like culture itself. Maston's teacher, Richard Niebuhr, in his famous work, *Christ and Culture*, defines culture as "the 'artificial, secondary environment' which man superimposes on the natural. It comprises

---

1. See Johnson, "Legislating Racial Fairness in Criminal Justice," 233.
2. Crouch, *Culture Making*, 23. Emphasis added.
3. Kreeft, *Back to Virtue*, 56.

language, habits, ideas, beliefs, customs, social organization, inherited arti-facts, technical processes, and values."[4] Within this definition, the individual holds the power to influence nearly every part of what culture is as a whole by what they choose to sustain and dismiss. Of course, Niebuhr turns to offer five possible types of Christian engagement of culture.[5] Maston clearly adopts the last of these types in Christ the transformer of culture, though as Adams notes, "with Mastonian alterations."[6] These alterations are best understood through the present task of DVE.

The elevation of virtue in the life of the individual becomes increasingly effective as that individual models virtue winsomely and inspires others to do the same. While many would see this as a fault of the approach, it carries a particular strength within the church. The church carries a distinct ability to influence and shape thinking and to confront the vices of sin behind the authority of Christ revealed in Scripture.[7] Sin is to blame for all social woes and is the single enemy of virtue leading each person away from holiness and the complete life. It is easy to tie sins together and attempt to trace lines of influence or gateways, but in the end, it is a comprehensive nature which is to blame. In short, "Sin survives, takes root, and hangs on. This is part of what it means to say that human beings are all sinners. But social sins, in particular, survive, take root, and hang on because people benefit from those sins—often without being willing or able to notice either that they are sinning or that they are benefitting."[8] Racism, partiality, and prejudice persist as some of these beneficial pains, and require specific attention.

Applying Deontological Virtue Ethics to Race

DVE can be demonstrated in its application to race relations. This is seen in Maston's work towards integration as the ultimate goal for the church within race relations. This integration, over against desegregation, demon-strates both an appeal to the being and becoming of virtue as well as the doing of specific biblical commands and principles which pertain to racial ethics. Again, Maston asks, "If Christians do not attempt honestly to apply the Christian spirit and Christian principles to race relations, how can they

4. Niebuhr, *Christ and Culture*, 32.
5. Niebuhr, *Christ and Culture*, xliii.
6. Maston et al., *Perspectives on Applied Christianity*, 13.
7. Holder, "Issue of Race," 45.
8. Stassen and Gushee, *Kingdom Ethics*, 15.

expect others to respect their Christian claims or to hear and accept the message they proclaim?"[9] The spirit and principles then must be explored.

The portrait of virtue here is more than just the characteristics of the person of God, such as his roles as a moral person, creator, ruler, sovereign, and father. Instead, this is the discussion of the ideals in which each of these characteristics find root. If virtue is to be applied to the race discussion, it must be determined which virtues are the most relevant. A case could be made for several as courage is required for many to discuss as Maston warns against "moral cowardice,"[10] and wisdom would be an obvious requirement regarding any subsequent actions to that discussion, but it seems that two virtues rise to the forefront. These virtues are that of justice and love. The implementation of these virtues causes subsequent virtues to be satiated as well. Each of these must be examined at greater depth as Maston especially implements them.

Justice

To move towards integration, one must first illuminate the development and understanding of the virtue of justice as "the concept of reconciliation is empty of content unless it is built upon the sturdy foundation of justice."[11] As each virtue lies between vices of deficiency and excess, justice is no exception.[12] While either vice could be referred to simply as injustice, more detail can be given towards a fuller understanding. Most often, when justice is considered, it is accompanied with some payment of that justice. For Maston, no illustration of this payment exceeds the cross. He writes, "the cross . . . reveals that God loves the sinner while hating his sin, that he condemns man for his sin but that he also saves man from his sin. He is a God of justice and love."[13] Simply calling attention to an injustice does not appease the demands of justice. Justice is the due reward for any action, positive or negative. Should that be right payment for a task preformed or right punishment for a crime committed, justice is concerned with what is

9. Maston, *Bible and Race*, 95.

10. Maston, *Christianity and World Issues*, 99.

11. Stassen and Gushee, *Kingdom Ethics*, 396.

12. As a point of interest, it is unclear "exactly how Aristotle understands this arrangement, or the nature of the vices of excess and defect which this particular justice is to counteract." The vices of deficiency and excess then in this case have been extrapolated accordingly. LeBar and Slote, "Justice as a Virtue," 1.

13. Maston, *Christianity and World Issues*, 284.

rightly due.[14] Justice is considered first as Maston affirms that equal justice is attainable in society.[15]

Vice of Deficiency

The first side of injustice is in a deficiency of justice, which could here be more specifically called disregard. This is the most common reality of injustice and with it comes a recognition of some person or action going unseen or unpunished. The more apparent the slight, the greater the injustice seems. Unjudged disregard is a result of one of three causes; a double standard based on the person accused, an ignorance or apathy towards justice being done, or a delight in injustice and corruption. While the frequency of the third cause is not as common, the first two run rampant and often together. A double standard can be seen financially, in social classes,[16] and notably to this discussion, racially. There is no shortage of statistics for a racial double standard in drug prosecution based on the color of the accused's skin as more Caucasians go unjudged or unprosecuted than any other people group, even when there are the same number of those culpable.[17] Further, when partnered with an apathy towards justice caused by apartness or the difficulty involved in resolution, the unjudged touches the race issue closely. Maston recognizes this level of disregard towards justice in messages of the prophets. As God calls his mouthpieces to speak, "God is revealed as strongly condemning injustice."[18] This condemnation echoes God's answers to the questions of the wicked going unpunished (Jer 12:1; Job 21:7–13): where man may disregard justice, the Lord does not.

Vice of Excess

The second injustice is in an excess of justice. This is not truly an abundance of justice as there cannot be in reality an excess of something that has been satisfied in the sense of a debt paid, but rather the excess here is an abundance of principle distorted by terminology. Excessive injustice inflates the

14. "Justice and Peace," in *New Dictionary of Christian Ethics and Pastoral Theology*, edited by Holmes et al., 15–21.

15. Maston, *Christian, the Church, and Contemporary Problems*, 158. Equal justice is a Niebuhrian perspective and should not be conflated with the similar Rawlsian language of *Justice as Fairness*.

16. For an example of class divisions beyond race see Wray, *Not Quite White*.

17. Bradley, *Black and Tired*, 1.

18. Maston, *Biblical Ethics*, 41.

results or payment of justice in either punishment or reward, which could here be more specifically called tyranny or, more commonly, oppression. The alternative to a deficiency of justice in Caucasians uncharged with drug possession can be transversely seen in an excess of punishment in the sentencing of minorities for the same crimes as their Caucasian counterparts.[19] The elimination of these vices is in part the task of desegregation, but there is also a deeper root to be addressed.

Excess of punishment is often rooted in prejudices spurred on by apartness. This is a tragic distortion of the hatred in the hearts of men, and its awareness is the first step. The sad reality is that many who deem themselves progressives regarding race, harbor prejudices and judgments they rarely think about on a surface level in stereotypes and presuppositions of people they have never met.[20] The move to virtue is an attack of the inclination to be judge and jury, and go beyond what is right to what is vindictive. Maston sees this concern against oppression especially in the prophets. He summarizes them saying, "God looked for justice (*mispat*) among them and found bloodshed (*mispah*), for righteousness (*tsedaqah*) and 'behold a cry (*tseaqah*)!' [(Isa. 5:7)] . . . [God] speaks in defense of . . . the oppressed."[21] When change begins within the individual heart, the community can then be affected for good.

The Golden Mean

Once awareness moves both vices towards the golden mean of justice, much must be done to sustain it. This is as much a task of the state (Rom 13) as it is a task of the church as

> God's work in the world consists of more than churchy accomplishments like baptisms and filled sanctuaries. It consists of more peace, more justice, more reconciliation, more deliverance—through the church whenever the church makes itself available, through others when we are not available, or when we stand opposed.[22]

The golden mean is one that seeks justice wherever it is absent. This is the continuance of acting justly. In private affairs, there is a call for right

---

19. Bradley, *Black and Tired*, 12. See also, Bradley, *Ending Overcriminalization and Mass Incarceration*.

20. This claim will be explored more in the next chapter.

21. Maston, *Biblical Ethics*, 45.

22. Stassen and Gushee, *Kingdom Ethics*, 19.

dealing and practice and publicly there is a call for justice in every school, courtroom, and political office. It is to point out deficiencies of justice and excesses of punishment, to create accountability among the likeminded, and to persuade the obstinate. "Now we pray to God that you do no wrong—not that we may appear approved, but that you may do what is good," (2 Cor 13:7). Justice precedes love as it removes the barriers of integration through desegregation. Maston elevates the question of justice to be consistent with the concerns of objective rights and wrongs of morality. He describes this as part of the "conformity to [the] ideal."[23] Justice for the issue of race is a concern against injustices made because of race. These can be seen in everything from base prejudices and discrimination which leads to apartness, to more overt forms of systemic injustices.[24] The goal then of implementing justice is to be just in character, to call for justice, and to move towards a just society.

Love

Justice alone is insufficient. It is not even a uniquely Christian virtue. In addition to Plato and Aristotle's lists, justice is recognized as a universal duty of governing authorities in Rom 13. Faith in the Triune God is not a requisite for justice to be handed down by those whom God has given the sword. In fact, it is often that those to whom justice is expected, are the ones who find it in great excess or deficiency. But those that abuse the authority given to them by God will stand in judgment before him. Love, on the other hand, is a unique expression of Christian virtue insofar as it is tied to a relational knowledge of God (1 John 4). The virtue of love is one referred to in a number of ways, the most applicable here being compassion. For Aquinas, it was his overarching *Caritas*,[25] for others it is simply a facet of love, but the case remains that compassion is one of the greatest characteristically Christian virtues.[26] For Maston, it is *agape*. The sacrificial expression which is only sourced from God.[27] Compassion is the recognition, empathy, and regard for the lost and other believers as persons made in the image of God. Love is the fullness of life in Christ and the greatest hope for the issue of race.

23. Maston, *Christian, the Church, and Contemporary Problems*, 153.

24. See Bradley, *Black and Tired*.

25. Aquinas, *Summa Theologica*, 2-1.65.4. It should further be noted that Aquinas did not present *Caritas* as necessarily lying between two vices. This is likely for the same reason Aristotle does not give explicit vices for justice, as it is the ultimate virtue in each of their minds. See Hardon, "Meaning of Virtue in Thomas Aquinas," 1.

26. Hauerwas and Pinches, *Christians Among the Virtues*, 69.

27. Maston, *Christian, the Church, and Contemporary Problems*, 157.

Vice of Deficiency

The first vice of love is in a deficiency of compassion which could here be more specifically called apathy. This apathy is a result of apartness, and awareness here must be in a cultural absorption rather than ignorance. Immersive behavior is greater than any classroom, and this modern life is rich with the opportunity to hear from wide perspectives. Empathy is both the awareness and the action. Scripture shows the multiplicity and beauty of all that are in Christ, as Ephesians harps on the unity of the body: "the point is not merely that all Christians are equal [or the same for that matter]; rather, the point is that all Christians have been joined."[28] This is where compassion steps in, a regard for the full body, not just hands for other hands or feet for other feet, fullness and diversity joined. Awareness of apathy calls for the individual to step out of their circle of comfort and into the shoes of others. This is in conversation, relationship, repentance when necessary, and intentional engagement with people of different backgrounds. Maston writes, "Even if love is not immediately attainable in society, the Christian has a personal responsibility to live by the law of love in every area of his life."[29]

Vice of Excess

The second vice is in an excess of the principle which could here be more specifically called paternalism. Paternalism is an overstepping of compassion which goes to shelter and infantilize the receiving party to a detriment of their independence and responsibility. It is an excess of compassion which actually undercuts compassion's desired result of the recipient's wellbeing. For Maston, this comes by many in place of the proper fraternal regard.[30] Paternalism is the great fear of many seeking an excuse not to show compassion, as the recipient might be enabled by this new kindness or just take advantage of nice men and women who do not know any better. An overstep of this fear is used to justify a continuance of prejudices and cripples progress. That being said, this vice remains a reality for the tenderhearted. Maston writes, "we are beyond the time, if there ever was such a time, when the paternalistic approach will be effective. Fraternalism must be substituted. Paternalism stems from a sense of superiority. Fraternalism is a product of a deep sense of oneness in Christ."[31]

28. Snodgrass, *Ephesians*, 151.
29. Maston, *Christianity and World Issues*, 284.
30. Maston, *Bible and Race*, 26–27.
31. Maston, *Conscience of a Christian*, 118.

Awareness here is to see the bounds of compassion fraternalism, namely that the recipient never be stripped of their personhood. Compassion is not a charity to pity the inferior. It is to recognize the deficiencies in the self and the egoism surrounding it and reach out to value another person. Pity and paternalism in the issue of race do no good to the marginalized, but showing concern and walking alongside the marginalized is a different thing entirely, one that moves ever closer to that golden mean.

The Golden Mean

Where justice can have a propensity of being cold, compassion's expression is one of warmth. The virtue of love in compassion is not an academic exercise or charity in the sense of building self-worth through service, rather, it is concerned with walking alongside one another and loving as Christ. This is the command to bear one another's burdens after all, "Christians must be those who are capable of sharing their suffering with others."[32] The chief example of this virtue is of course the person of Christ, who time and time again had compassion on those he encountered. Jesus's great illustration on compassion was within the bounds of prejudices and race in Luke 10, in describing the Jewish traveler beaten and robbed, "But a Samaritan on his journey came down to him, and when he saw the man, he had compassion" (Luke 10:33). This story shows the deficiency of compassion in those who passed the man by and it avoided an excess as the man's compassion was selfless, and it did so for his neighbor rather than looking at a cultural or racial division between them.

Maston believes that even justice, while it may pave a way towards integration, is incapable of achieving it without love. He makes an intentional break to describe the ultimate idealistic virtue of love specifically as *agape*. The ideal of love is the transformation of the heart and spirit to be in line with the person of Christ and the Christian spirit. He writes, "the area of attitudes is the province of the Christian religion. It is becoming increasingly clear that there can be no real integration without the application of the Christian spirit to the relation of races."[33] Love, then, is no empty sentimentality, but a true identification with the love of God. He concludes that "God is a God both of love and justice. Both qualities should be maintained in proper balance in our lives. Justice can check and punish evil; love alone can overcome and redeem evil."[34]

32. Hauerwas and Pinches, *Christians Among the Virtues*, 50.

33. Maston, *Segregation and Desegregation*, 63.

34. Maston, *Bible and Race*, 81.

However, these virtues are not left in ambiguity for Maston. The ideals of love and justice find expression for action in both direct commands and overarching principles. There are obvious explicit commands which speak to the race issue which Maston raises in his arguments. In the command of Luke 6:31, Maston notes that "the so-called Golden Rule, which is a practical expression of love, is very definitely and disturbingly relevant to the racial situation."[35] Matthew 22:39 reads of the greatest commandments that "the second is like it, 'love your neighbor as yourself.'" This comprises the command of the virtue of love, and was for Maston a key component of the expectation for ethical action. Another command he notes is in the Great Commission of Matt 28:19–20, where Maston focuses on the gospel going to all nations. He states the command "cannot be true to its genius and set any boundaries for the application of its spirit and principles. To do the latter would tend to rob it of its vitality."[36] These direct commandments are, for Maston, a great clarity of the above virtues, but are in some ways not as clear as the supplementing principles.

Maston includes a number of principles stemming from the significance of a biblical anthropology in the image of God in Gen 1:26 to the common source "of one" in Acts 17:26. But the greatest principle in the discussion of the race issue for Maston is in what he describes as the "no-respecter-of-persons principle . . . or [the] no-partiality principle."[37] Rooting this principle in Peter's vision on Cornelius's roof in Acts 10, as well as echoed by Paul in Rom 2, Maston argues against the limitations of this principle to the spiritual realm alone saying instead that "if God is no respecter of persons, if he shows no partiality, our ultimate goal should be the elimination of all partiality, prejudice, and discrimination from our lives."[38] This principle has clear implications for the believer's actions and character towards the race issue. Man is to move towards the ideal of Christ's revelation of the character of God through his ethical actions which are clarified in commands and principles.

Deontological Virtue offers an answer to apartness and strain through justice and compassion. These virtues must be found between their respective vices of disregard and oppression, apathy and paternalism. Christ is the example of perfect justice and perfect compassion, and is the picture for virtue in the individual as he seeks to change the culture concentrically. The key lies in an awareness of apartness and vices and acting out the virtues

---

35. Maston, *Segregation and Desegregation*, 110.

36. Maston, *Bible and Race*, 87.

37. Maston, *Bible and Race*, 43–44.

38. Maston, *Bible and Race*, 48.

that ought to be attained. Only then can there be a lasting answer to the issue of race.

A rational demonstration of DVE aims at justice, and a religious ethic makes love the ideal. As Reinhold Niebuhr writes,

> A rational ethic seeks to bring the needs of others into equal consideration with those of the self. The religious ethic, (the Christian ethic more particularly, though not solely) insists that the needs of the neighbor shall be met, without a careful computation of relative needs. This emphasis upon love is another fruit of the religious sense of the absolute. On the one hand religion absolutises [sic] the sentiment of benevolence and makes it the norm and ideal of the moral life. On the other hand it gives transcendent and absolute worth to the life of the neighbor and thus encourages sympathy toward him. Love meets the needs of the neighbor, without carefully weighing and comparing his needs with those of the self. It is therefore ethically purer than the justice which is prompted by reason.[39]

Maston's application of DVE in race relations can be traced through the expressions of justice and love. They each factor in the movement from segregation to desegregation and finally into integration. This movement utilizes each in turn. Maston writes, "Justice may be able to check and punish evil; love alone can overcome and redeem evil."[40]

Conclusion

The ethical system of T. B. Maston, while not historically systematized, can be reasonably evaluated as a Deontological Virtue Ethic. This is seen in his elevation of virtuous being, its supplementation of a biblical deontology, and the overall push towards a balanced tension expressed in the Both/And. This ethic can be applied to racial ethics through an elevation of the virtues of love and justice as well as obedience to the commands and principles of Scripture. This obedience in the life of Maston proved costly. Maston writes that obeying the will of God often causes Christians to create a balanced tension in a way that often causes them to become "the martyrs of one generation and the heroes of the next."[41] Maston became such a martyr, socially estranged and removed from his post for his disruption to the status quo. Nevertheless, he was faithful to his conscience and to the will of God

39. Niebuhr, *Moral Man and Immoral Society*, 57.

40. Maston, *Christianity and World Issues*, 282.

41. Maston, *Christian, the Church, and Contemporary Problems*, 154.

as he understood it through his ethic. This faithfulness demonstrated the theological and biblical ethics required to move into the ideal of integration. Having established the nuances of Maston's ethic, this work will now move to examine its applications through integration.

Chapter 9

Maston's Levels of Integration

Introduction

MASTON'S RACIAL ETHICS AND his larger framework of DVE were never intended to be ethereal concepts or academic exercises alone. He made patient yet effective strides towards the biblical ideal as he best understood it. These ideas drove him to action as he sought to move from desegregation towards integration wherever possible. To this end, Maston wrote and engaged racial reconciliation on several fronts. The application of his ethics through proposed actions engaged his commitments to a traditional Baptistic understanding of the priesthood of the believers and individualism as well as his concern for the SBC, Southwestern, and the church at large. These levels of integration could be viewed as concentric elevations of a consistent concern for integration. Beginning with the individual and moving to the academy, the local church, and finally to the Convention, this chapter will continue to apply the Mastonian ethic in integration.

Maston's three methods towards integration are those of regeneration, education, and demonstration.[1] Regeneration is the concern of the individual. Education has an obvious, though not exclusive connection to the academy. Demonstration concerns the corporate witness and life of the local church. The added level of the convention reflects the additional engagement Maston placed on wider denominational engagement as an extension of the church, which is a necessary division for the purposes of this work. Each level carries with it distinct challenges and solutions which taken

---

1. Maston, *Of One*, 104–7.

together offer a comprehensive assessment of the race problem as it stands and Maston's ultimate solution in the pursuit of the integrated church.

Concerning methods for integration, here only Christ will be sufficient. Maston argues that "there is no real integration, which should be the ultimate goal in human relations, without a removal of separating barriers in the minds and the souls of men. The only hope for the elimination of these barriers or walls is in Christ."[2] The present society stands in the mire of desegregation. Admittedly, it was this same society that has been at times a step ahead of the church, or at least the Southern Baptist Convention. As Maston notes, in times past the forces of change in regard to race were generally spearheaded by secular means and people, and the church has been slow to catch up and, in some places, remains steps behind.[3] However, secular society has hit a wall and is only sufficient towards desegregation. Society has the ability to reshape laws, but only Christ has the ability to reshape hearts.

Integrating the Individual

Beginning with the individual, Maston holds the priesthood of the believer with great regard. His commitment to this concept was likely that theological distinctive which kept him most established in the Baptistic tradition he was raised. His ethic stresses individual and corporate culpability and he gives great value to the individual's conscience as a substantial determinant in the application of ethics. Maston would correspond often to former students seeking his counsel. He would offer his thoughts and the nuances to consider in each situation but would often open or close with the reminder that "in the final analysis the decision must be entirely yours."[4]

Maston's efforts were to shape and instruct the individual to affect greater change in the capacities in which the individual served. For the issue of racial reconciliation, integration of the individual has several facets. These include a recognition of existing prejudices, addressing apartness through exposure and social relationships, and finally through a diverse program of personal development. To be sure, this is not some trend of self-help or a strategy to cultural winsomeness but is a discipline of the individual heart and conscience to root out sin and take on the character of Christ. Anything short of the integrated heart is a white-washed tomb (Matt 23:27).

2. Maston, *Christian, the Church, and Contemporary Problems*, 158.
3. Maston, *Bible and Race*, 41.
4. Martin, *Passport to Servanthood*, 58.

Turning to the *Telos* of the matter, there are a great number of motivations considered in this discussion for integration to take place. First and foremost is obviously the continued repudiation of racism from the body of Christ at all levels. The God of Scripture is holy and will not stand to be in the presence of sin. To this end, the church, and each individual member of it, must publicly and privately oppose any and all forms of racism as staunchly as it would oppose sin of any kind, especially as it attacks and holds disdain for persons made in the image of that holy God. The heart of this task is done first on the level of the individual.

For Maston, the first step towards integration lies in an assessment of the problem. This is more than the assessment of any cultural divide or church division. This is an examination of the individual's heart. Maston writes that "all racial groups are prejudiced, at least to some degree. The reasons for their prejudices and the expression of them may differ, but none is entirely free from prejudice."[5] Maston calls for a "probing [of] our prejudices" in determining both their source and solution.[6] These prejudices are an extension of the fall of mankind. As sin is rooted in the heart of every person, so is racial prejudice or partiality. The concern here is to not blame social woes on society alone, but to recognize the extents of depravity in every individual. There is a sense in which even believers may excuse or ignore racism in their own hearts. This is the both narrow and broad concept of synecdoche with which Christ teaches that to hate is to murder, and to lust is to commit adultery (Matt 5:21–30). The modern believer may have never owned a slave or participated in a lynching, but even the slightest prejudice or partiality can begin to form a racist heart. Yet there is hope in Christ to recognize, repent, and root out prejudice. This prejudice expresses itself most clearly in the expression of pronouns in what Maston calls "'we-you' psychology."[7] This "we-you" divide is the compartmentalizing of groups as primarily racial. To say it another way, the racial division of the majority or minority becomes the first demarcation of identity. This, Maston asserts, is at odds with a biblical understanding of humanity, race, and the church.

Maston is not appealing for colorblindness as a dismissal of the created nation and tongue which will exist even in glory. He is lamenting that those in Christ would find more in common with an unbeliever who shares their skin color (or any other marker, for that matter) than a brother or sister in Christ who does not. This is an affront to the unity which is found in Christ for the church. Maston's concern instead is for Christlike treatment across

5. Maston, *Bible and Race*, 64.
6. Maston, *Bible and Race*, 62.
7. Maston, *Bible and Race*, 62.

economic, social, and racial lines. A fraternal concern for those that are in Christ and regard for those made in the image of God who are potential brothers and sisters.

In his 1952 work, *The Christian in the Modern World*, Maston notes, "whatever may be the social or psychological source of racial prejudices, it is not Christian . . . race prejudice is largely a part of our social heritage and that we catch it very much like we catch the measles. We are exposed and it takes."[8] If exposure then is a primary cause of racial prejudice, then its alternative can serve as its undoing. Exposure to expressions of the integrated heart, the example of Christ, and an intentionally developed care for neighbor, which goes beyond the color line, will substantially address the apartness of the individual's heart. Maston often points to shifts in attitudes as the result of exposure to someone of a different race in the military or workforce. The military specifically, as one of the first bulwarks of society to desegregate, formed integrated bonds through community and shared goals and vision. A common enemy, a common task, and common spaces, over time, chip away at the prejudices which would otherwise separate. However, common space by itself is insufficient towards the completion of the task. As noted earlier, Maston views only the spirit of Christ capable of bringing real integration. He writes that God's "authority becomes supreme in the lives of individuals only as they become new creatures in Christ Jesus (2 Cor 5:17). One who seeks to build a Christian society on any other foundation than redeemed personalities is building on sinking sand."[9] As prejudice is a concern of sin, so its solution must include its atonement and subsequent ethical applications. One such application is through a recognition of the biblical neighbor.

For Maston, the call to integrate social relationships is the logical extension of loving one's neighbor. He notes Christ's answer towards the limitation of neighbor in Luke 10:25–28 through the good Samaritan, a significant racial divide to his Jewish audience. Maston writes, "even if we legitimately could limit 'neighbor' to fellow Christians and hence limit our obligation to love, would this by any stretch of the imagination any class or racial limitations? All who know Christ as Saviour are our brothers in Christ."[10] So then a practical step towards integrating the individual for Maston is to intentionally expand social concern and engagement to every neighbor. This was demonstrated in Maston's own life at an early age. As a teenager, Maston's mother became ill and was cared for by "a Negro woman

---

8. Maston, *Christian in the Modern World*, 60.

9. Maston, *Of One*, 105.

10. Maston, *Bible and Race*, 71.

who came to help."[11] This woman would eat meals with the Mastons and clearly made an impression on young Tom. In the same way, engagement of every neighbor at the figurative and literal table would go a long way towards integration of the heart.

Against Tokenism

One caveat should be given towards a problem that may arise in the pursuit of the ideal of integration. There can be a tendency in the interest of integration for an individual to resort to tokenism. Tokenism "gives the illusion . . . [of] addressing the issue of discrimination without really challenging the existing balance of power."[12] Tokenism for the individual is the idea of filling some quota of appearance through targeting relationships racially without fostering genuine community. Tokenism is, simply put, false integration. It trades an appearance of diversity for the greater struggles of integration and draws elbows together for a postcard more than hearts together for genuine life together. Tokenism might further give an excuse to stagnancy. If the individual already has a relationship with someone of another race, they may think the task of integration to be achieved or to apply to someone else. Integration is concerned with the full acceptance of a community, and a specific elevation of only some individuals while neglecting the greater demands falls short of the ideal. So then, integration must pronounce the goals of simple tokenism as an insufficient perpetuation of desegregation.

A Question of Achievability

An obvious question concerning integration at any level is its achievability. Undoubtedly, individualistic integration is the heart of this question. If the individual is unable to move from desegregation to integration on this side of heaven, the present conversation is moot. As integration has been described as a full acceptance into community and further as the repudiation of partiality and prejudice this is at its core a question of sanctification. That is to say, integration is only achievable to the extent that the heart is transformed. Maston views salvation in a triadic fashion of justification, sanctification, and glorification corresponding to Christ's saving work in man through time past, present, and future, respectively.[13]

Therefore Maston would not view integration here as an attainment of the perfect ideal which will be found in glorification as pictured in Rev 7:9.

---

11. "Oral History Collection: T. B. Maston," 78.

12. LaPointe, "Tokenism."

13. Maston, *Why Live the Christian Life?*, 66.

Instead, it is the conclusion of justification and the process of sanctification. Individualism, as Maston conceives it, is not an elevation of the self, but a proper ordering of God's creation. He writes, "the right kind of Christian individualism stresses both the rights of the individual, particularly the rights of other individuals, and the responsibilities of the individual to others, to the Christian community, into the world in general."[14] So then, integration in the heart of the individual is achievable to the extent they deny themselves and follow Christ (Luke 9:23). This denial will reorder the priorities of the heart to consider the will and love of God as utmost, and then the consideration of neighbor as the reciprocal and indispensable implication of that love.

Maston's concern for the integration of the individual is one that necessarily carries over into integrating the academy, the church, and the convention, as most obviously, these entities are made up of individuals. So, in this simple regard, many of the principles which apply towards one area inevitably overlap onto the next. This work seeks to avoid redundancies wherever possible but will continue to evaluate the nature of Maston's argumentation, as well as examine his larger blueprint of integration. Integrating the individual is the first step. The second is of obvious concern to Maston in integrating the academy.

Integrating the Academy

Moving to the question of religious education, this section examines positions concerning racial diversity and religious education in order to offer a biblically sound case for integration. While this topic could be overwhelmingly broad, it is helpful to first set a few limitations and assumptions. First, this discussion limits itself to evaluating religious education within the SBC as the primary engagement in Maston's life. Maston taught most obviously at Southwestern but also served as a guest professor at every other SBC seminary except New Orleans Baptist Theological Seminary. Religious education was the calling of Maston's life, and this chapter reflects this focus with appropriate emphasis. This examination must include at its heart the theological and biblical motivations of the conversation in order to offer a few guiding principles. Next, as cannot be avoided in such a discussion, the examination turns to an assessment of affirmative action as it has been formulated in recent academic theory. This requires evaluation from the previously mentioned principles in order to determine the cohesion of affirmative action and religious education. Finally, limited practical applications

14. Maston, *Christianity and World Issues*, 45.

of these principles as they relate to administrations, curricula, and student bodies at large are discussed.

Beyond its initial formation, the SBC continued to wrestle along "the color-line,"[15] in its seminaries. However, even from its foundation, the SBC evinced concern shown towards those of other races, though obviously short of the ideal integration discussed here. From 1845–2018, the SBC has made no less than thirty-five formal resolutions on race, several which pertain specifically to education.[16] In the year of its founding, the Convention "RESOLVED, That the Board of Domestic Missions be instructed to take all prudent measures, for the religious instruction of our colored population."[17] As the denomination grew and slavery was brought to an end, subtle changes began to occur but seemingly always with reluctance by the White majority. In 1944, there was a greater clarity brought to previous statements of education with another resolution focused specifically on the education of Black Baptists. It reads,

> In view of the appalling spiritual need for an adequately developed ministry for the vast and perilously neglected Negro host within the bounds of our Southern Baptist Convention and due to the clear indication of Providence that this is the opportune time to move forward more aggressively and on a wider scale in the help to this worthy and highly strategic cause of ministerial education for Negro Baptists, therefore be it resolved:
>
> First, that the Convention go on record as reaffirming our loyalty and increased cooperation with the American Baptist Theological Seminary in Nashville, and
>
> Second, that it give its vote of approval of the work of a large group of brethren of both the white and Negro races in and around New Orleans, who have in view the imperative local and regional needs projected on the basis of local self-support and with an interracial faculty and trustee organization such a school as under Divine Providence has greatly helped already in

15. Du Bois, *Souls of Black Folk*, 20.

16. See Williams and Jones, *Removing the Stain of Racism*, xxxv, where the authors reference 31 distinct resolutions prior to *2017*. Since that book's release, additional resolutions have been made "On The Anti-gospel Of Alt-right White Supremacy," in *2017*, "On Renouncing The Doctrine Of The 'curse Of Ham' As A Justification For Racism" in *2018*, "On Critical Race Theory and Intersectionality" in 2019, and "On the Sufficiency of Scripture for Race and Racial Reconciliation" in 2021, bringing the total to at least 35 distinct resolutions. This number only grows when considerations are made for the connected issues and language seen in other resolutions such as those made "On Immigration" in 2018, or "On The Uyghur Genocide" in 2021. See https://www.sbc.net/resource-library/resolutions/ for a full catalog of SBC resolutions.

17. Williams and Jones, *Removing the Stain of Racism*, xxxv.

the better equipment of a considerable number of local pastors during the seven years of its existence.

Third, that the Convention thus express its approval on this local effort as a worthy missionary project as is evidenced by its rapid growth, reaching a matriculation of over two hundred students last year; also, by the fact that it has unified the seven Negro Baptist Associations numbering a constituency of over a hundred thousand Negro Baptists; and further, by its ability to attract and hold the sympathies and cooperation of the white Baptists of New Orleans who have contributed through their churches liberally for several years to its support; and further, by the approval it has received by the Baptists of the state of both races, substantially expressed through their state organization and by many prominent leaders of the National Baptist Convention and of the Southern Baptist Convention.

Finally, that we commend the Baptist Bible Institute for the large part it has taken in Negro Education through this missionary project which grew directly out of its own missionary activities and has been largely supported by a large number of its graduate student instructors who serve every year on the faculty, along with a number of Negro teachers who give their services sacrificially for a salary scarcely more than nominal.[18]

This resolution affirms the work seen at many Baptist colleges and seminaries to show special concern towards Black ministers, but did not yet regard them as equals. At Southwestern, this was seen when Maston and a handful of other faculty took it upon themselves to train Black pastors.[19] For Maston, concern for the souls of Black congregations necessitated concern for the education of Black ministers. He writes, "I do not know anything that needs to be done more and will contribute more to the program of Christ and to the strengthening of the Baptist cause among Negroes than such an aggressive program of theological extension work."[20]

In the book, *Removing the Stain of Racism from the Southern Baptist Convention: Diverse African American and White Perspectives*, Kevin M. Jones, Assistant Professor of Teacher Education at Boyce College at Southern Seminary, suggests that "if Southern Baptists want to see the stain of racism removed from seminary to the pew, then the entire denomination must critically and seriously consider a widespread curriculum change that includes

18. Williams and Jones, *Removing the Stain of Racism*, xl–xli.

19. This is not to say that Maston "did not yet regard them as equals," but rather, their status as students on that campus was not yet as equal to their white counterparts.

20. Maston, "Southern Baptists and the Education of Negro Ministers."

more vetted writers/authors, professors, pastors, and leaders from ethnic groups that have been traditionally marginalized."[21] In 2015, the Southern Baptist Convention affirmed this sentiment with a resolution stating,

> RESOLVED, That the messengers to the Southern Baptist Convention meeting in Columbus, Ohio, June 16–17, 2015, rededicate ourselves to the holy responsibility and privilege of loving and discipling people of all races and ethnicities in our communities; and be it further
>
> RESOLVED, That we urge churches to demonstrate their heart for racial reconciliation by seeking to increase racial and ethnic diversity in church staff roles, leadership positions, and church membership; and be it further
>
> RESOLVED, That we urge Southern Baptist entities and Convention committees to make leadership appointments that reflect the racial and ethnic diversity of the body of Christ and of the Southern Baptist Convention.[22]

In 1991 there was not a single African American serving full-time at any of the six SBC seminaries.[23] Today there are nine. Progress is applauded, but the question of continuance remains.

An additional concern is that of a need for a diversity of perspectives. This is to say that not only is it right and just to have equal standing in community, but that it is beneficial. Proper and orthodox doctrine aside, total uniformity in academic thought is generally a sign of a lack in critical thinking. By expanding scholastic voices beyond those of a single demographic, there grows a better equipment on the part of the institution towards its students. Specifically, in regard to religious education, the Baptist Faith and Message describes the goal as stating, "the cause of education in the Kingdom of Christ is co-ordinate with the causes of missions and general benevolence, and should receive along with these the liberal support of the churches. An adequate system of Christian education is necessary to a complete spiritual program for Christ's people."[24] As religious education then is preparation for ministry at every level, to peoples in every position, monolithic education will not suffice. While experiential knowledge itself is not communicable, a knowledge of various experiences, perspectives, and traditions is. To be prepared to minister to the nations, it is most helpful to

21. Williams and Jones, *Removing the Stain of Racism*, 93.

22. See "Resolutions on Racial Reconciliation," at https://www.sbc.net/resource-library/resolutions/on-racial-reconciliation/.

23. Swift, *Religion and the American Experience*, 245.

24. See "Baptist Faith & Message 2000," https://bfm.sbc.net/bfm2000/.

understand the nations. David Dockery states that, "We now live in a multiracial, multicolored, multiethnic context. We have the pleasure of seeing God's creation in all of its variety, which is a great gift from God."[25] Variety of training is beneficial to reach the variety of the kingdom. This then is the desired end: to repudiate sin and be well-equipped for ministry.

Guiding Principles

In higher education, affirmative action and subsequent strategies alone merely address proximity and quota. While these ends may be satisfactory for some, anything less than the ideal of Christ should find itself wanting in the eyes of the church. Practical action in religious education must be considered and offered that reach these ideals. This will be shown through a reversal of the previously mentioned desired ends: principles of action concerning the benefit of diversity followed by principles of action concerning the repudiation of racism through education.[26] For these ideals, it will be helpful to consider the biblical picture of integration as it relates to education. This can be seen both by demonstration as evaluated through such biblical narratives as Acts, as well as direct instruction and command as it seen in a number of epistles, especially the Pauline letters. Considering the structure for the church-planting efforts of the New Testament, it is clear the command of Christ is one of reproduction and education. Namely, in order to make disciples of all nations, all nations must be reached. Faithful men, called by the Spirit and affirmed by the church (see Acts 13), were sent to the nations. Maston writes, "Just as [the Christian religion] cannot be true to its genius and establish any boundaries for its missionary endeavor, likewise, it cannot be true to its genius and set any boundaries for the application of its spirit and principles. To do the latter would tend to rob it of its vitality."[27] First John 2:2 echoes this heart saying that Christ, "Himself is the propitiation for our sins; and not for ours alone, but also for the whole world."

To take this to the whole world then, the church was commissioned by Christ and a strategy was quickly seen in his instruction in Acts 1:8, "'you will receive power when the Holy Spirit has come upon you; and you will be my witnesses in Jerusalem, and in all Judea and Samaria, and even to the ends of the earth.'" These widening circles begin with the church in Jerusalem, and by the eighth chapter of Acts, continue with Paul to those

25. Dockery, *Renewing Minds*, 143.

26. It should be noted at this point that these principles speak to concerns Maston held throughout his career, yet implements modern terminology, such as affirmative action. These principles are consistent with Maston's picture of integration.

27. Maston, *Bible and Race*, 87.

ends of the earth. As Paul and his cohorts travel from place to place planting churches and encouraging brothers, there is a clear pattern of development. Take Timothy for example. Acts 16:1–5 records that Paul,

> came also to Derbe and to Lystra. And look, a disciple was there, named Timothy, the son of a believing Jewish woman, but his father was a Greek, and he was well spoken of by the brethren who were in Lystra and Iconium. Paul wanted this man to go with him; and he took him and circumcised him because of the Jews who were in those parts, for they all knew that his father was a Greek. As they were passing through the cities, they were delivering the doctrines decided upon by the apostles and elders who were in Jerusalem, for them to observe. So the churches were being strengthened in the faith, and were increasing in number daily.

It is clear that the plan was established to reach the nations by raising up the nations, here demonstrated by Paul raising up a local man named Timothy. Timothy of course would go on to be one of Paul's most effective partners and faithful protégés. In fact, the incredible nature of this plan is that the concrete churches established by Paul exist today only in his letters. Timothy, however, is alive in Christ. The building of the church universal does not find its construction in groupings of the church local, but in the individual believers that comprise the local church. As is disclosed in Revelation, these believers come from every nation, people, and tongue. The first principle is to equip all peoples. The efficacy of missions would be severely limited if it were to rest solely upon those who were sent. Indeed, the church likely would not exist today if it had been forced to work in this fashion. If the biblical church is not limited in this regard, neither should this limitation be placed on higher education which serves the church. Maston understood and posited this fact in his works.[28] The equipping of ministry should be an equipping of the nations.

This is generally done well on the international scale with extension campuses of the major SBC seminaries in numerous countries in Europe, Asia, and South America and is being pursued more as a facet of missions in these places. The question then becomes how well it is being done here in the States. Here, the annual reports of the Convention's six seminaries and various entities are helpful. As referenced earlier, in 2015 the Convention, "RESOLVED, That we urge Southern Baptist entities and Convention committees to make leadership appointments that reflect the racial and ethnic

---

28. Maston, *Segregation and Desegregation*, 143–62.

diversity of the body of Christ and of the Southern Baptist Convention."[29]
To this end, each seminary offers in its annual report a section titled, "Ethnic Participation," where it details the efforts made in that calendar year at its respective institution.[30] This should be celebrated as consistent with the ideal of diversity, but should not offer the satisfaction of a completed task. There is a sense in which this task is never complete. Full integration cannot be measured in a report as the ultimate integration is one of the heart and character of the individuals that make up the larger institution. This is not to say the task is purely individualistic, but that there is a balance to be struck in the pursuit of diversity.

Not only is this diversity pursued, but its antithesis is also renounced. This is of course the heart of much controversy in the early church between Jews and gentiles, culminating in the Jerusalem Council and in the life of Peter on the rooftop of Simon's house (Acts 15:1–35; 10:9–16). The resolution of these issues is an examination of the person of God, namely that God is no respecter of persons. Maston explains, "if God is no respecter of persons, if he shows no partiality, our ultimate goal should be the elimination of all partiality, prejudice, and discrimination from our lives."[31] Practical action of this elimination of this vice in the Convention is best demonstrated by the 1995 Resolution on Racial Reconciliation on the 150th Anniversary of the Southern Baptist Convention which states,

> Be it further RESOLVED, That we apologize to all African-Americans for condoning and/or perpetuating individual and systemic racism in our lifetime; and we genuinely repent of racism of which we have been guilty, whether consciously (Psalm 19:13) or unconsciously (Leviticus 4:27); and
>
> Be it further RESOLVED, That we ask forgiveness from our African-American brothers and sisters, acknowledging that our own healing is at stake; and
>
> Be it further RESOLVED, That we hereby commit ourselves to eradicate racism in all its forms from Southern Baptist life and ministry; and
>
> Be it further RESOLVED, That we commit ourselves to be doers of the Word (James 1:22) by pursuing racial reconciliation in all our relationships, especially with our brothers and sisters in Christ (1 John 2:6), to the end that our light would so shine

29. See "Resolutions on Racial Reconciliation," https://www.sbc.net/resource-library/resolutions/on-racial-reconciliation/.

30. See https://www.sbc.net/resource-library/ministry-reports/.

31. Maston, *Bible and Race*, 48.

before others, that they may see (our) good works and glorify (our) Father in heaven (Matthew 5:16); and

Be it finally RESOLVED, That we pledge our commitment to the Great Commission task of making disciples of all people (Matt 28:19), confessing that in the church God is calling together one people from every tribe and nation (Rev 5:9), and proclaiming that the Gospel of our Lord Jesus Christ is the only certain and sufficient ground upon which redeemed persons will stand together in restored family union as joint-heirs with Christ (Rom 8:17).[32]

This demonstrates both remorse and a heart for reconciliation on a Conventional level. It must also be noted that the SBC has traditionally elevated the biblical principle of the autonomy of local churches.[33] This means that while on a large scale, there has been a step of corporate repentance, no individual church is obligated to act beyond this statement.[34] John E. Rouse reflects, "The priesthood of the individual believer and the zealous regard for the autonomy of the local church often lead to a nonconformity on both theological perspectives and governance procedures among leaders and laymen."[35]

It is helpful then for individual congregations to make similar declarations when necessary, lest there be a question of disjointed theology and action. Race is an issue that will not likely go away in the foreseeable future. Building upon the integration of the individual, the problem stems from the fallen heart of every man and is redeemed only in Christ. Al Mohler writes, "our commitment to Christ requires that we confess in every generation the sin in which this convention was conceived and the sin that remains, while working relentlessly to see racists within our convention redeemed from the powerful effects of this sin."[36] This is where the question of religious education is paramount. The equipment of ministers of the gospel must be as comprehensive as possible for the task that is ahead of them. This necessarily includes instruction of proper hermeneutics, preaching, counseling, and ethics. It is further shaped by the classroom itself, which raises the question of how this classroom is built.

32. Williams and Jones, *Removing the Stain of Racism*, lvi.

33. See a comparison of the 1925, 1963, and 2000 Baptist Faith and Message at https://bfm.sbc.net/comparison-chart/.

34. The autonomy of the SBC further means that no church is ever obligated to act at all.

35. Rouse, "Role of Segregation in Southern Baptist Polity," 21.

36. Williams and Jones, *Removing the Stain of Racism*, 5.

Assessing Affirmative Action

Here, it is necessary to give a preliminary definition to affirmative action. Philip Rubio writes in his book, *A History of Affirmative Action, 1619–2000*, that affirmative action can be understood as "an antidiscrimination tactic to enforce equal opportunity measures and a state device for regulating discrimination."[37] However, its perception today can be one of distorted equality, even among many that it is said to benefit. When considering affirmative action, it is helpful to delineate from the intent as posited in academia at-large over against the goal of integration as discussed in this chapter towards religious education. The general understanding of "the goals are laudable, but the implementation of plans to accomplish those goals has caused frustration for advocates as well as foes."[38] Namely, there is a general fear that the application of affirmative action is a response to a broken system which constructs a faulty one. This is most often expressed in a concern that qualified candidates may be passed over in preference of arguably less qualified candidates who are of a predetermined ethnicity or meet a preferential quota of diversity. This of course could be an overcorrection of equality, which is itself, inequality. For this reason, legal affirmative action has been dismantled in several states, even with the support of many of the minorities it was meant to benefit.[39] The question of equal opportunity is the heart of affirmative action. The difficulty becomes determining whether equal opportunity regardless of ethnicity has been achieved within higher education, or any field for that matter. If there is a genuine equality of opportunity, affirmative action would no longer be needed. This is one facet of the consideration of systemic racism and prejudice today.

Systemic racism is most usually considered in three ways; it asserts primarily that "(1) certain laws and policies continue to imply White superiority over racial minorities, (2) privileges are afforded to people belonging to the White race that inherently place racial minorities at certain disadvantages, and (3) general race-based discrimination continues to pervade the daily lives of racial minorities."[40] The degree of acceptance of these assertions varies greatly. Emerson and Smith describe these levels of acceptance as primarily divided between Blacks and Whites and increasingly so between

---

37. Rubio, *History of Affirmative Action*, 114.

38. Marlow and Rowland, "Affirmative Action," 541.

39. Rubio, *History of Affirmative Action*, 10.

40. Diggles, "Addressing Racial Awareness," 32–33. While the treatment here concerns benefit to "the White race," systemic racism can be found anywhere that promotes or holds any level of racism described herein.

evangelicals.[41] This is generally a question of experience and first-hand knowledge of oppression, perceived or real. However, it is not a question of experience alone. No small number of studies have shown the realities of racial and systemic injustices as ever present in the United States.[42] Wherever realized, these injustices must be decried. Only in awareness is there an ability for injustice to be acted upon and integration to be realized. If inequality and injustice exist as a result of sin, there is a responsibility on the believer to pursue reconciliation. Maston reflects that proper worship cannot occur before this reconciliation occurs, per Matt 5:24, "leave your gift there before the altar and go. First be reconciled to your brother, and then come and offer your gift."[43] Reconciliation precedes unhindered worship which motivates action towards integration.

However, a greater question is if affirmative action is the proper implementation of integration. To this question, clarity is required. Explicitly, it is the degree to which affirmative action is implemented that dictates its cohesion with integration. The present definition poses affirmative action as an enforced policy. As integration is a concern of the heart, affirmative action as forcefully or unyieldingly applied would better be understood as a further implementation of desegregation. However, if the concern of affirmative action is instead couched as the implementation of ideal within limits, integration may in fact still be achieved through it. This must be explored in greater detail.

Here it would be helpful to consider a broader definition for affirmative action. *The Stanford Encyclopedia of Philosophy* defines affirmative action as, "positive steps taken to increase the representation of women and minorities in areas of employment, education, and culture from which they have been historically excluded."[44] This widening of the position allows for integration rather than desegregation to offer lasting and genuine change. In this framing of the position along positive influence, valuing diverse voices as benefits would change the question of opportunity. If viewed in this way, the ethnicity of a candidate has the ability to become an additional qualification in itself. For example, by adding a member of faculty of a different ethnicity who possesses otherwise a virtually identical résumé to another candidate in regards to level of education, experience, and expertise, the former candidate would arguably be a greater addition simply because of

41. Emerson and Smith, *Divided by Faith*, 112.

42. See Bertrand and Mullainathan, "Are Emily and Greg More Employable," 991–1013; and Feagin, *Systemic Racism*; for two such examples.

43. Maston, *Segregation and Desegregation*, 98.

44. Fullinwider, "Affirmative Action."

the diversity of perspective that is brought with them. This is consistent with the Supreme Court ruling in *Grutter v. Bollinger,* where race was held to be a considerable factor in regard to college admission, but not as justification for an imposed quota.[45] Notice here, because the enforced nature of change to meet a certain quota is removed, the policy would not consider race to pass over a more qualified candidate, yet could still be considered as a factor or qualification in itself.[46]

This is where a principled approach would vary from a mandated policy. Integration would seek to elevate and celebrate diversity. This is to say that no candidate should be considered if they are unqualified for the position in order to meet a quota. This would only be a step backwards.[47] In the case of equally qualified candidates, the addition of an ethnic minority will likely have a ranging impact on the institution in a number of ways. First, by valuing a diversity of voice in a leadership position there is given a picture of racial acceptance to students, potential students, and the lost. Maston offers that "the effectiveness with which we reach [others] for Christ will be determined, to a considerable degree, by whether or not we treat them like brothers."[48] The level of acceptance into a community can be directly correlated to the level of influence that group may see in leadership, formal or otherwise. Subservience may be publicly denounced, but this denunciation has not been fully realized if it is not represented at the level of leadership. This seems to demarcate affirmative action as a question of the principles of the repudiation of racism and the valuing of diverse voices.

Here, a natural progression should be seen in the growth of diversity. At times preference will and should be given to those of lesser opportunity due to disparages of wealth, class, or ethnicity. These disparages should be considered as one such application of integration and reconciliation. These

---

45. *Grutter v. Bollinger,* 539 U.S. 306 (2003).

46. This question is still being asked, as made evident by the recent case between Harvard University and Students for Fair Admissions, a group which claims the University systemically discriminates against Asian Americans in its admission decisions because of its affirmative action policy. See Hartocollis, "Does Harvard Admissions Discriminate?"

47. It should be noted that there are more qualified racial minorities in academia than ever before. *The Journal of Blacks in Higher Education* notes that, "Faculty departments traditionally explain their poor performance on the grounds that there are no qualified African Americans in the Ph.D. pipeline. But the fact that many of our great universities have been highly successful in recruiting African-American faculty tends to show that the 'no blacks in the Ph.D. pipeline' thesis is at worst a red herring and at best a weak explanation for poor results." See JBHE Research Department, "Black Faculty in Higher Education," 69.

48. Maston, "Biblical Basis for Social Concern," 1.

principles lend themselves to a discussion of right action in administrations, curriculum, and student engagement. This will include protocol for hiring and developing faculty, the construction of curricula to include a diversity of voices, and student development as the most immediate and possible implementation of these ideals.

Concerning Administrations

Affirmative action to this point has only considered new hires, yet integration speaks just as much to the development of faculty. This concern begins at the top. Leadership in the institution, as in the pastorate, is the foremost model of the institution's values. Maston writes that an extension of integration in education "should have integrated schools with integrated faculty."[49] While race has at times been reduced to a component of sensitivity training obligated by human resources, it will be beneficial in the place of leadership to discuss issues of race from the faculty meetings to the classroom and from curricula to student interaction. The immediate need would be to determine if there are any signs of systemic injustice in the institution. Marilyn Naidoo offers that, "Theological education can facilitate positive social change if faculty make a deliberate attempt and take greater effort to teach in ways that question and dismantle oppressive systems."[50]

At large, a tendency may arise to move from one extreme or the other, here it is necessary to remark again on the nature of virtue as lying between two vices. There is no absolute percentage or measurement at which point integration has been achieved in higher education. Rather, it is the constant reminder of the person of Christ, the image of God, and the nature of the church. This constant reflection is simply to direct people towards the issue of race. Maston reflects that the ideal "may be equated with God's ultimate will and purpose for those institutions."[51]

At schools where a chapel is a part of campus life, whether required for credit or optional, there is another opportunity for a diversity of voices both as a commitment to integration as well as an opportunity for growth. Maston implemented this level of diversity on the campus of Southwestern as early as the 1950s. He would have Black students lead music and give testimonies as well as have Black pastors preach.[52] Intentional exposure such as this is a beneficial first step towards lasting change. This is a simple solution

49. Maston, *Conscience of a Christian*, 119. Though Maston was in this context speaking towards public education, the principle also applies to higher education.

50. Naidoo, "Liberative Black Theology," 173.

51. Maston, *Christian, the Church, and Contemporary Problems*, 188.

52. William Goff, personal phone interview, April 10, 2018.

that can be implemented immediately. Not only can there be a diversity in the speakers invited, but at times a discussion panel for candid conversations concerning race and ministry would also be helpful. The goal would of course be that what may begin as an engagement on diversity concerning race would be extended to having that same diversity address other issues as well.[53] This could foster a framework for cooperation in students that could directly be implemented in their ministry as a tool to cooperate and portray the nature of the body of Christ.

Concerning Curricula

Further development can be made by the existing faculty in course curricula and syllabi. Here, an implementation of racially diverse voices can be introduced into reading lists. It should be noted that in the same way a faculty member must show qualifications, curricula should only consider the most beneficial sources and respective preference should not be given exclusively because of the racial identity of the author. Rather, preference should be shown, as is able, for reflecting various positions and thoughts.[54] For example, when considering proper theology, it can be helpful to assign comparative analysis between classic Western systematics with the development of Eastern or African theology. These additional perspectives again would, under this definition of affirmative action, be positive goals rather than dogmatic requirements as forced integration is no integration at all. At the same time, there should be a level of expectancy and conveyance of the goal of integration placed upon a faculty. This is one such place where the lines between faculty and curricula become blurred.

It is also necessary to consider here the way curricula is formatted at institutions. For example, some schools may have an existing bibliography for a course irrespective of the professor teaching it, or there may be concerns of accreditation. Here, it would beneficial to add diverse writings as recommended further reading in the case that the required list cannot be changed. Even in a day where minority academics were rarer, Maston engaged and reflected on minority author's writings and thought. In his book, *The Christian, the Church, and Contemporary Problems*, Maston fondly reflects, "A keen young Negro Ph.D., in a discussion following an address, asked the searching and pointed question: 'Is there not a danger that

53. For example, panels more exclusive to race would shift to panels on wider issues of theology and expertise such as ecclesiology, missions, et al., elevating diverse perspectives as a sought benefit.

54. See, for example, the "Suggested Reading List on Race and Race Relations" in the appendix of Williams and Jones, *Removing the Stain of Racism*, 166.

Christians will tend to substitute love for justice and make love an empty sentimentality?"[55] The value of diverse voices does not come automatically. Kevin Jones laments in a call to action, "If I do not expose my students to non-Anglo authors, chances are they won't be exposed to them in my field."[56] Additional programs and classes may also be a benefit here. For example, if a seminary were to advertise a class on the Bible and race, a church history elective surveying People of Color, or similar courses, it would both speak to the willingness and effort towards integration as well as practically achieve it within the existing student body. Hearts and minds are shaped while perception of the school is changed internally as well as externally.

Concerning Student Bodies

Finally, concerning racial diversity among students, there should be a desire, wherever possible, to expand the influence and education of the institution to as many students of as many ethnicities as possible. This must include a recognition of where the present makeup is limited or shaped by the monolithic ethnicity of students. It is a general understanding that students are drawn towards schools where they feel they will be accepted.[57] For this reason, it has become the norm, almost to a joking degree, for brochures and advertisements of institutions to feature racial diversity in their photos in order to appeal to anyone who may see it. What may have begun as an honest attempt at integration, or at the very least desegregation, has become glaringly apparent when a student moves from the brochure to the campus, and no such diversity can be found. The portrayed ideal of diversity becomes an empty promise. To this end, it is helpful to consider ways of expanding the genuine diversity of a student body. Putting previous recommendations aside, additional strategies may be helpful. This might include scholarship opportunities, intentional recruiting at racially diverse schools, churches, and programs that have influence in minority communities.[58]

Progress in race relations in higher education must be led by the church. This must be done in a calling and equipping of the church for the work of ministry which must include the repudiation of racism as sin and the reconciliation and valuation across racial lines. This can be done through affirmative action, properly understood as implementing the ideals

55. Williams and Jones, *Removing the Stain of Racism*, 157.

56. Williams and Jones, *Removing the Stain of Racism*, 97.

57. Smith, "Place of Their Own," 128.

58. See The Witness: A Black Christian Collective and The National African American Fellowship, SBC at https://thewitnessbcc.com and http://naafsbc.org, respectively, for examples.

of Christ patiently and diligently in the development and hiring of faculty, the construction of curricula, and the molding of students. These suggestions of implementing these principles are by no means exhaustive or final. None of these applications in themselves offer a sweeping solution to the present issue, but they seek to reflect a Mastonian application of the principles of the integration and reconciliation of Christ onto the issue of race in higher education. The goal, of course, is that the training of ministers and work in higher education would have a direct and consistent result towards integration in the church.

Integrating Ecclesiology

Maston's love for the church is evident in his writings. Even as he elevates the individual and the academy as tools and ends, his ultimate vision for racial reconciliation and integration rests squarely on the shoulders of the corporate body of Christ. Maston describes the church as the solution to shifting values in culture. He explains that "every civilization has an integrating center around which that civilization is built. That center contains the supreme value or values of the civilization. It represents the ends for which men live and die."[59] Even when cultures shift their integrating center to insufficient alternatives, Maston holds that the church remains God's intended center for action and value in the world. The race issue for Maston is a moral problem above all else, and the church is that moral representative of Christ in the world. Maston plainly states that, "If the race problem is primarily a moral issue, then the moral forces should take the lead in its solution. It is the church's business to be the vanguard of the moral forces of society. It will be a tragedy of tragedies for the churches of Christ to surrender their moral leadership."[60] The church then becomes the locus of integration efforts. The individual and the academy engage to serve and equip this larger goal of the church.

The immediate concern here is that the church acts as a model of Christ's program for race relations to the world. This is the demonstration of the Great Commission and acting as salt and light in the world (Matt 5:13–16). The church establishes the pattern of integration not in theory alone, but through demonstration. Maston notes that "one demonstration is worth more than a thousand theoretical lessons."[61] Maston draws this pattern of demonstration explicitly from Scripture. As Christ reveals

59. Maston, *World in Travail*, 90.
60. Maston, *Of One*, 9.
61. Maston, *Of One*, 106.

the biblical pattern for the life of the church, Maston is committed to discerning, applying, and following that pattern. Maston writes, "the basis for Christian concern for the world and for the peoples of the world is not only grounded in the biblical revelation; it also naturally evolves from the nature of the church and the resultant relation of the church to the world."[62] This pattern can be seen in an integration of leadership as well as tradition, but must also address concerns of appropriation and assimilation.

Integrated Leadership

As integration is sought by individual churches, shifts in leadership must be considered. Maston explains that integration "will not occur until Negroes and those of other minority groups are accepted into the life of the church on the same basis as White members. They must be utilized in places of leadership on the basis of their ability, training, and spiritual maturity."[63] There are obvious variations that will occur from church to church in the SBC, as there is no one set polity for the Convention's churches. However, the principles behind integrated leadership will be consistent in churches led by deacons, elders, boards, or individual pastors and do not necessarily speak to vocational positions. The principles of integrated leadership will also have obvious connections to those considered in integrating the academy. Though similar in some areas, the seminary and the church are not equivalent. Integration in leadership will share a similar approach in viewing a candidate's race as another facet of qualifications in representing and reaching the nations, and affirmative action, or tokenism are in their strictest senses incompatible with the goal. Nonetheless, there are distinctions in the leadership of the church which do not translate into the academy ineludibly.

The primary distinction is that while the seminary may draw students from great distances, the local church's primary ministry is done in its immediate community. If said community is not represented in the membership of that church, it may tend towards anemia. But, as the church opens its doors and intentionally engages those around it, especially across racial lines, it better fulfills its mission. One hurdle in this task is if guests feel welcomed. Though signs have been removed which state standards of admittance, the bitterness of desegregation can still make church doorways seem small. Maston's utilization of those of all races, and especially of those in the immediate community, widen the door frames once again. Integrated leadership demonstrates to the surrounding community that a church values

62. Maston, *Christian, the Church, and Contemporary Problems*, 55.

63. Maston, *Conscience of a Christian*, 116–17.

and cares for all races. Even in churches which can only afford to pay a single staff member, integration can be demonstrated in non-vocational positions of leadership, be it in lay-elders, deacons, ushers, or visible acts of leadership such as corporate prayer or announcements. Integrated leadership also brings with it a wider perspective of ministry that a homogenous staff may lack. As noted in the second chapter, the first deacons were selected in Acts 6 in part because of their racial representation of the group they would be serving together.

Maston offers little advice in his primary corpus for the workings of the pastorate or church governance. Though he served as a deacon at Gambrell Street Baptist Church for much of his time at Southwestern and until his death, he wrote little on church leadership directly. His *Biblical Ethics* moves straight through the Pauline epistles without mentioning the word "pastor" or referencing a single pastoral epistle. The primary reason for this exclusion is that pastors were usually not his primary audience. Maston's work was not a top down approach of convincing the influential. He endeavored to speak to the layman, the youth, and women. When he does speak to the distinctions of leadership in the church he writes, "[the pastor] should know the direction in which he believes the Lord wants the church to move. He also should know and suggest ways to attain the goals he has for the church, but he should never seek to force his ideas on the church. He should involve others in refining and defining goals and strategies."[64] The church's leadership is to consider the individual in its efforts.

Maston's instruction to this leadership outside of his monographs was great. Maston regularly kept in contact with his students that left to serve in various ministries and often spoke to ministers at pastor's conferences and leadership meetings. On one such occasion in 1961, Maston encouraged pastors to support the desegregation of schools by decrying racial discrimination in their churches. Though opposition was fierce and obvious, Maston encouraged them, saying, "it's unbecoming in a prophet of God to keep still because he is afraid."[65] Mastonian ethics hold a distinct tension in their execution. The church leader should neither force his congregation, nor stand passively by. Integration requires both prophetic leadership and pastoral care. Anything less will not suffice. By raising up qualified men and women of color to positions of leadership in the local church integration is demonstrated to its members and the surrounding community.

---

64. Maston, *Conscience of a Christian*, 109.
65. "Pastor Should Play Key Integration Role, Dr. T. B. Maston Contends," 9.

Integrated Tradition

A second hurdle which may arise in moving towards an integrated church is the question of tradition. When the American church split along racial lines, each path led to, at times, widely different traditions, histories, and social norms of how a church service looks. Whether this is expressed in service times and lengths or music and preaching styles, there can be cultural expectations that accompany the concept of church. In these cases, the doors may be open, and the staff may even be diverse, but admittance is still on the terms of the dominant culture. In these cases, a spirit of integration will consider what steps can be taken to bridging gaps of tradition. This can be seen in music choices that borrow from varying styles and artists such as hymns, spirituals, and even styles which traverse cultural expectations.[66] This will differ from community to community, but is less of a program than it is a spirit. As Maston writes, "no church is fulfilling its function that does not have a worldwide division and a program commensurate with that vision. The church's ultimate goal should be to make one big neighborhood of the entire world, to make the world into the 'beloved community.'"[67] Genuine integration is making room at the table rather than building a separate one. This is to see the unity of Christ displayed. This is by no means a simple task, and will require, in many cases, great sacrifice. But it demonstrates the wholeness that is offered in Christ: a wholeness that heals. In moving towards these goals, there are still pictures of false integration which would threaten true unity.

Against Appropriation

The first false integration facing the integrating church is appropriation. Like tokenism, appropriation seeks to give the appearance of diversity without the deeper costs of its implementation. Appropriation has been defined as the "*misrepresentation, misuse,* and *theft* of the stories, styles, and material heritage of people who have been historically dominated and remain socially marginalized."[68] This is especially using traditional imagery and style for a benefit without recognizing the significance, meaning, or intention of the other culture's acceptance of it. Appropriation is most often seen in art, music, and fashion. Appropriation is not necessarily malicious or mocking, but is the careless taking of a piece of another culture for the sake of the

66. Lewis-Giggetts, *Integrated Church*, 168–72.

67. Maston, *Christian in the Modern World*, 66.

68. Matthes, "Cultural Appropriation Without Cultural Essentialism?," 343. Italics original to the author.

product, not the people. The most obvious remedy to appropriation comes through integrated leadership. Wisdom and concern are required to show the difference between celebrating the incredible cultures of the nations and a careless show without the affirmation or edification of that culture's representatives in mind. Genuine integration will naturally avoid appropriation through its concern to honor others above one's self (Phil 2:3).

Against Assimilation

The second false integration that facing the integrating church is assimilation. This is the admittance of other cultures on the understanding that they will assimilate to the dominant culture. In some senses, this is the reverse swing of the pendulum which meets appropriation as its opposite. Where appropriation bastardizes a product from its people for the sake of a show, assimilation strips people of their culture in order to be accepted into the community. Minorities are welcome in the assimilated church as long as they think like, look like, and act like the existing culture. Assimilation deprives the minority of its cultural distinctives and history. It is ultimately erasure of a people and their culture. This is a concern to avoid in the integration of tradition. The key to its avoidance is in the celebration of each culture instead of colorblindness.

The uniqueness of every individual is not limited to spiritual giftings alone. There is an explicit uniqueness to be found in the capacities, cultures, and backgrounds of each believer. This is an appeal for the heavenly vision of every tribe and tongue in the kingdom. If these distinctions are reflected in the grandeur of the new creation, they ought to be celebrated in the present creation as well.[69] Maston's elevation of the individual marks his dissent from assimilation. His concern for ministry across racial lines was not a presentation of services offered by the majority culture, but rather a genuine unity of effort. Maston spoke at the 1956 Southern Baptist Convention saying, "if our work is to be effective, it must not be primarily for the Negroes, but rather with them . . . [let us] mature socially, morally, and spiritually, until [we] can work together as full partners, laboring together with God in the promotion of his cause and kingdom."[70] This connection demonstrates the deeper move from the church local into the denomination.

69. Practical steps towards this end might include the merging of previously homogenous churches, including spaces and staffs. While difficulties obviously arise in language barriers, such as an English-speaking church and a Spanish-speaking church deciding to combine services or simply share spaces, there is much that can be done in overcoming the perception of continued segregation.

70. "Southern Baptist Convention," 8.

Integrating the Convention

The integration of the Convention is by necessity an extension of the integration of the church. Maston writes, "for this demonstration of Christian truth to be adequate it must ultimately be broader than the local congregation . . . [The SBC] works from the bottom up—really the leadership of a true democracy is more of an instrument than a cause. It would lose its opportunity to lead if it advanced too far beyond the people it seeks to lead."[71] For Maston, the Convention serves as a middle ground between the church local and church universal. Cooperation between autonomous churches like the SBC allows for a greater kingdom mindset and greater kingdom results. David Roach notes that Maston "worked within the Southern Baptist Convention's denominational structure to create opportunities to speak in favor of social progressivism."[72]

Maston's involvement in the convention is seen most clearly in his work with the Christian Life Commission. Maston was a chief organizer in the Texas CLC and active in the national Commission as a trustee and advisor at various times in his life. Throughout this time, he consistently advocated for racial reconciliation to and through the CLC. In 1965, Maston was awarded the CLC's Distinguished Service Award for his work in race relations. Foy Valentine, CLC president at the time, presented Maston the award and specifically noted that "*The Bible and Race*, is the most thorough and comprehensive single work on race relations ever published by a Southern Baptist."[73] The uniqueness of this work was that its thoroughness did not mitigate its accessibility.

Maston consistently wrote with a question of accessibility in his mind that would not sacrifice its precision. He phrased the question simply as, "is this written so that my mother could read and understand it?"[74] Maston recalled his mother as having only been schooled through the third grade. Though he was highly trained with a bachelor's degree, two masters, and two doctorates, Maston sought to write for the Convention and every man and woman that comprised it. He wrote for every sharecropper and professor to each have the information they needed to arrive at their own conclusion. To this end, he consistently spoke and published on a national level to offer the full picture of integration to the SBC. Beyond a call to Christlikeness in the endeavor, Maston specifically advocated for an integrated Convention.

71. Maston, *Of One*, 107.
72. Roach, "Southern Baptist Convention and Civil Rights, 1954–1995," 69.
73. "Maston Presented Award for Distinguished Service," 30.
74. Maston et al., *Both-And*, 251–52.

Maston writes, "Negro Baptists and those of other minority groups should not just be invited to our meetings. They should help to plan such meetings . . . if we expect their cooperation, let us invite them to share in the planning."[75] Once again, noting the difference between a Convention *for* others and a Convention *with* others, Maston advocates for the latter. This planning and leadership has taken many forms over the years. From Maston's initial Advisory Council of Southern Baptists for Work with Negroes to the present African American Taskforce, the SBC has maintained a consistent concern for racial integration.[76] A great sign of progress was the 2012 unanimous election of the SBC's first Black president, Fred Luter.[77] Victories like this should be celebrated but not viewed as a sign that integration has yet been accomplished.[78] The SBC, or any other association or denomination, must continue in the pattern of Mastonian integration. There will be less of a tendency towards tokenism, assimilation, and appropriation on this level, but the tendencies may still surface. An application of a Mastonian Deontological Virtue Ethic will aid in this fight as it seeks to align with the biblical ethic of both character and action.

Conclusion

The race issue is not one that will go away in the near future, it is rooted in prejudice and sin and will persist in this world, but it does not have to persist in the individual or in the church. The individual, the academy, the local church, and the denomination are each able to move towards integration through bridging apartness in exposure, relationship, leadership, and humility. Only then can there be a lasting answer to the issue of race in a combined effort of integration. While these applications are consistent with

75. Maston, "Problems of the Christian Life," 19.

76. "A group of African American leaders were invited to express the needs, concerns and hopes of the African American Southern Baptist Churches and to advise the Southern Baptist Convention Executive Committee leadership." Southern Baptist Convention, "African American Taskforce Report."

77. Willoughby, "Historic: Fred Luter Elected SBC President," 1.

78. Even as appointments such as Luter's are applauded,—or more recently, the appointment of Dhati Lewis as Vice President of Send Network, the church planting auspice of the North American Mission Board—the long-term nature of entity leadership would mark a greater commitment to integration. Between the work of this research towards an initial dissertation and the present book, five Convention entity heads opened and were filled. The dissertation noted these openings with a hopeful anticipation saying, "It is possible that the SBC could see its first minority head appointed, which would be a great sign of growth for the convention." All five entities appointed white men to the positions.

Maston's integration, there are no hard and fast solutions. The greatest integration will and must come through an application of Christ's spirit and ideals to every aspect of the heart and of life.

Chapter 10

Conclusion

Summary

THOMAS BUFORD MASTON FOUGHT for the biblical ideal of integration in his life, work, and ministry. His works made a distinction between desegregation and integration and affected the very nature of race relations in the Southern Baptist Convention. Maston's theology offered a proper evaluation of segregation in the SBC. Maston's five combatants to segregation in the character of God as Moral Person, Creator, Ruler, Sovereign, and Father demonstrate Maston's adherence and application of biblical revelation as the primary argument against segregationists and their improper theology of God as Segregator. Maston's framework is a commentary on the full circle of integration seen in the New Testament church through the United States, and his subsequent goal is a return to integration.

Maston's anthropology offered the justifications for desegregation as the removal of barriers based upon the image of God revealed in Gen 1:26–28, the common origin of mankind in Acts 17:24–31, and the misinterpretation of the curse of Ham in Gen 9:20–27. Each of these passages factored in Maston's biblical response to the improper anthropology of segregationists and his advocacy for a biblically and theologically robust anthropology. Maston's fight for desegregation in his own lifetime came at great cost to himself and his career. Though great progress was made in Maston's lifetime, he never saw the full realization, depicted here as Deontological Virtue Ethics, applied. Maston's framework has yet to be fully given to the task of racial unity in the American church through integration. Maston's ethic balances the duty and end of the call of Christ expressed in the principled ideal. The virtues of justice and love each carry great weight on the task of integration, align with Maston's ethic, and are biblically and theologically coherent.

Integration, as a consequence of this system, offers a number of proposed actions from integrating the individual, the academy, the local church, and the convention at large as the realization of Maston's work. These actions must wrestle with concerns of integration's achievability, diversity as tokenism, cultural appropriation, and forced dominant-cultural assimilation. This application is the lasting blueprint of Maston's legacy on race relations. There are of course still potential issues and critiques of Maston himself and of the system implemented here.

Issues and Critiques

Potential issues and critiques of this work are likely twofold. In the first, there may be critiques of Maston himself as either inconsistent in his own application of racial ethics, or of suspected liberalities in his hermeneutic and legacy which would question his biblical and theological coherence. Each of these are considered in turn. The second type of issue which may be raised is in the consideration of the Mastonian blueprint presented in this book. This type of critique may raise arguments of alternative approaches towards race relations besides the integration posited here. These critiques will also be addressed as well as they can be foreseen. There is no claim here that Maston or his system are without fault. Maston, like any man, faced his own share of difficulties and sin. The most notable shortcoming in Maston's racial ethics are in his writings on interracial marriage.

Interracial Marriage

As discussed previously, one of the most outspoken fears in desegregation and integration for the SBC was the approval of interracial marriage and the amalgamation of the races. This fear was not lost on Maston. Maston was not unreservedly for integration, as he wrestled with the concept of interracial marriage. This was not to say that he saw it as immoral or wrong biblically, but only that its perception could be harmful in the culture as it stood. He explained, "if by entering into a particular marriage one would lose his opportunity to witness or to minister for Christ, or if his marriage would handicap and hurt the work of Christ, then the marriage would be not only unwise but positively wrong."[1]

1. Maston, *Bible and Race*, 29.

Maston consistently affirmed that there is no biblical argument against interracial marriage.[2] His argument would point to Moses and his Cushite wife as a clear example that the biblical concern was religious rather than racial (Num 12:1). It seems that in the main, Maston's hesitance was one of slowness rather than adverseness. Maston was afraid of the picture an interracial marriage would paint and of the difficulties such a marriage would place on the couple as well as any children that may be born. The problem is of course that these concerns delay integration. There is no doubt great social difficulty was placed on Hosea by his marriage to Gomer (Hos 1:2–3), but it does not change the fact that their marriage would have been incredibly instructive, painting for Israel the nature and character of God. In the same way, the affirmation of interracial marriage would have been deeply instructive to the surrounding religious and secular culture of Maston's day. To say Maston opposed interracial marriage would be a swift inaccuracy. The nuance of his objection as unwise instead shows his own place in the cycle of desegregation.

Hermeneutics and Inerrancy

A second critique of Maston concerns his hermeneutics and statements on inerrancy.[3] Maston was often classified as a liberal scholar because of his social work.[4] In many ways, Maston knew the ways he would be labeled and pressed on despite this. In an interview with the *Baptist Courier* he says that "we can be orthodox in theology and real heretics in the way we live. . . . [We need] men and women who are basically conservative in their theology and are willing to be labeled liberal in their application of theology to life."[5] Maston made stands which, though branded as liberal in his own time, are actually in keeping with theologically sound arguments. The greatest complaint against Maston is he refused to call Scripture inerrant and discouraged the implementation of a statement of faith which would require such an adherence.

The chief question surrounding Maston's hesitance to use the language of inerrancy seems to surround the questions of terminology and comprehensivity. A motion made at the 1969 SBC annual meeting in New Orleans concerning written affirmation of inerrancy specifically by SBC writers and teachers in the seminaries caused Maston to respond that "men who might

2. Maston, *Interracial Marriage*, 9.

3. It should be noted here that Maston's statements in the main use the term infallibility rather than inerrancy. The terms are seen as interchangeable here.

4. Spain, "Oral Memoirs of T. B. Maston," 128.

5. "T. B. Maston: Retired Professor's Emphasis," 9.

have signed such a statement would differ widely in their interpretation of . . . what is meant by 'authority' and particularly by 'doctrinal integrity' and 'infallibility.'"[6] Maston further took issue with such a partial application of the clause. The selectiveness of the statement to only writers and professors, seemed out of step with the purpose of a statement of common beliefs. Maston's love of Scripture should not be in question here. Maston calls the Bible, "the most important possession of the Christian churches, far more important than all their buildings, institutions, and endowments."[7] He describes Scripture as the ultimate authority for the believer. In a fuller description, Maston describes the Bible as

> a divine-human book. It is divine in its origin for initiation, human in its mediation. It was written by men but by men inspired and led by the Spirit of God. . . . The Bible is not only a divine-human book in its writing but also in its contents. It is a record of the revelation of God's nature and character and of his attitude toward and will for humanity but the scriptures also portray the life struggles, the faults and failures, as well as the successes of real men and women.[8]

Maston's affirmation of the authority of Scripture is found in most, if not all, his writings. His discord with inerrancy comes with what level of human interaction there is in the process of revelation. Maston views the fall of man as so weighty upon every aspect of life that he separates God and the word. Namely, he writes that Scripture's "authority stems from the fact that it is a product of and *contains* God's word to man."[9] This separation for Maston does not weaken the Bible's authority, but instead "clarifies and deepens it,"[10] as it reveals that the written word is a reflection of the character of God in Christ as the Word made flesh (John 1:14). It is possible that had inerrancy been more closely defined, Maston may have affirmed the concept. He never formally makes any statement on contradictions in Scripture beyond a question of the importance of the New Testament over the Old Testament.[11] Though, McCullough contends that Maston "allowed for the possibility of inaccuracies in such areas as science and history."[12] But

6. Maston, "Problems of the Christian Life," 19.

7. Maston, *Biblical Ethics*, xi.

8. Maston and Tillman, *Bible and Family Relations*, 17–19.

9. Maston, *Biblical Ethics*, 287–88. Italics added. This statement demonstrates a Barthian influence, which is helpful to understanding Maston's view of Scripture.

10. Maston, *Biblical Ethics*, 288.

11. Maston, "Problems of the Christian Life," 19.

12. McCullough, "Evaluation of the Biblical Hermeneutic of T. B. Maston," 67.

even in his hesitance to affirm Scripture's infallibility, it is clear that Maston had a great regard for the biblical record as authoritative. It seems there is simply not enough written by Maston to suggest which details of inerrancy he took issue with beyond what McCullough posits. Whether Maston would affirm the Baptist Faith and Message 2000 in place of the 1963, or if he would by extension be able to teach at an SBC seminary today is unclear.[13] What is clear is his deep love and reliance on Scripture to lead and reveal the Christian life. There is seemingly no contradiction between the arguments he puts forth in his theology, anthropology, and ethics and his statements on infallibility. Each facet of his overall racial ethics is theologically and biblically sound.

Arguments Against Mastonian Integration

The second wave of critiques comes in the form of critiques against the program of integration. These critiques may be raised by one in favor of a more natural approach instead of what may be perceived as a forced integration. Whether this is founded in a desire for colorblindness or a conviction that conversations about race are part of the problem, this is not an unheard-of concern. The primary issue with this critique is that it is not new. Martin Luther King Jr. famously wrote in his "Letter from Birmingham City Jail" that "for years now I have heard the word 'wait.' It rings in the ear of every Negro with a piercing familiarity. This 'wait' has almost always meant 'never' . . . [but] 'justice too long delayed is justice denied.'"[14] Maston recognized that steps must be taken to address the injustices of segregation and desegregation. This is what the justice of God requires. Waiting on results without action fails to recognize the weight of sin and God's program against it in the body of Christ. Maston sharply contends the tension created by deliberate action is necessary for true growth and efficacy in the Christian life.[15] Returning to Maston's favorite illustration of the rubber band, the tension between the real and ideal require movement towards integration. To be sure, integration is ultimately a concern of the heart, and actions done by man alone will only snap the band. But as man joins in the work of the Spirit as a vehicle of God's work, genuine progress can be made through the deliberate steps of Mastonian integration suggested herein.

    13. See a comparison of the 1925, 1963, and 2000 Baptist Faith and Message at https://bfm.sbc.net/comparison-chart/.

    14. King, *Testament of Hope*, 290.

    15. Maston, *Next Steps in the South*, 3.

Moving the Goalposts

One last critique is that the recent movement in calls for diversity and inclusion are signs of the church bending to the cries of culture. This fear is similar to the pushback against critical race theory and resolution 9 at the 2019 SBC annual meeting, which supposedly mark the edge of a slope which descends into denying inerrancy, biological gender, or other social movements. To bend here would be to move the goalposts. The problem is that these goalposts have been set for millennia. Integration is not a social pursuit of the twenty-first century. Integration is the biblical ideal for the spirit of Christ in a diverse community of believers.

So what is critical race theory? Or, better stated, what is the range of critical race theory? There are some that hold CRT to be an all-encompassing worldview while others regard it only as a tool to measure and combat racism. Some who believe that racism is a permanent state while others view it as a problem to solve. Introductions, summaries, and focal studies of the discipline can begin to inform a general understanding of the field.[16] But a cogent understanding of the internal use and conversations is only begun by those that have immersed themselves in the field. The problem is that many who utilize these terms and critiques have little grasp on the field but speak as authorities on the matter. This is not to say that these conversations should never consult these terms or ideas, but that nuance is necessary to recognize the range of this loaded terminology.

Language is employed to convey a particular meaning within a particular context. If you remove that context, or implement it in a different context, there is a great chance that the intended meaning has shifted or possibly been lost entirely. The jargon of any field—academic, medical, industrial, etc.—is not a group of lofty insider codes. It is language within context. This language can be a helpful shorthand within that context but can also be unnecessarily confusing or dismissive outside of it. The greatest danger is when jargon is used to convey only the extremes of a concept or conversation.

It is the extremes of the spectrum (actual or conceived) which build the best straw men. It would be ignorant and abusive to suggest that every democrat is an ardent supporter of late-term abortions, or that every republican is xenophobic. Might that be true of some democrats or republicans? Of course. But the sweeping partisanship and vitriolic landscape that is the present political climate need not also describe our conversations within the church. To label and dismiss anyone with whom there is

16. Delgado and Stefancic, *Critical Race Theory*.

an apparent disagreement is to identify more with the pharisee than it is to identify with Christ.

Does all of this mean that critical race theory or cultural Marxism are exclusively bogeymen drummed up as the next red scare? Of course not. They are very real ideas that can be expressed in harmful extremes. But to use the terms as a line in the sand is to unnecessarily divide and forfeit an opportunity for productive dialogue.

Followers of Jesus would do well to be charitable in their dealings. It may just be the case that their apparent disagreements are only such to the degree that loaded terminology obfuscates dialogue. This is not to say that there is nothing on which they may disagree, but nuance is a greater companion than fog. As James Leo Garrett would often assert in his classroom, "Only when you can state your opponent's position so well that they themselves say, 'Yes, that's what I believe,' can you then begin to debate." To do otherwise is to simply speak past one another rather than engage, understand, and love.

Instead, the church ought to cultivate space where the application of Christian theology has room for nuance and charity. Where a humble orthodoxy guides candid and loving conversation around questions concerning systemic expressions of racism, responses to racial injustices and disparities, and the application of the spirit of Christ in everything. Where disagreements can walk away from a conversation without walking away from fellowship. Anything less is out of step with the kingdom of God. Maston writes at the end of *Segregation and Desegregation* that "freedom of discussion, private and public, must be maintained. There must not be pressure toward conformity, except the pressure that comes from truth itself."[17]

Conclusion

If integration is to be achieved, there is in some sense always more research to be done. This research is not necessarily into Maston or his framework, but would be any interaction that would further the ideals of integration. This will be along the lines of individual, academic, and ecclesial integration. Works which elucidate racial history and race relations, as well as works by racial minorities, only make clearer the steps that each level of integration can take from the individual to the SBC. T. B. Maston leveraged his gifts and capacities to make a distinct contribution to the field of racial ethics and the lives of the disinherited. He espoused a proper biblical theology in the face of segregation, made ardent steps to desegregation through a theologically

17. Maston, *Segregation and Desegregation*, 166.

coherent anthropology, and caused eventual change in race relations within the Southern Baptist Convention through his commitment to biblical ethics. His legacy still gives a blueprint for future racial reconciliation through integration in the church.

Appendix

A Case Study on the Question of Reparations

In December of 2018, my wife and I traveled the more than 1,200 miles from our home in Cleveland, Ohio back to our roots at Southwestern Seminary to receive my PhD. It was a peculiar feeling to be back on campus as I bustled from office to office to complete graduation clearance, constantly delayed by the friendly faces of professors and classmates I had not seen in several years. The longest of these welcomed detours came in a conversation with two professors discussing the recent report from Southern Seminary entitled, "Report on Slavery and Racism in the History of The Southern Baptist Theological Seminary."[1] Lauding the report and discussing my recently defended dissertation tracing, in part, race relations at Southwestern,[2] the discussion shifted to the many calls of social media for Southern to now respond with reparations. There was a distinct discomfort and tension in the air. Racism explored and studied as a discipline of history seemed all well and good, but to shift the application to consequences in the present seemed to threaten the school's mission. The first professor remarked that he had wrestled with reparations and found it difficult to draw boundaries on their implementation. The second responded, admittedly not having read the report yet, something to the effect that wouldn't it be enough to just love people and Jesus? The loving response from the first professor to his colleague was that, no, that isn't enough.

The very history in question is one in which men and women, passionate about equipping ministers to love people and Jesus, were at the same time "deeply involved in slavery and deeply complicit in the defense of slavery."[3]

1. https://www.sbts.edu/southern-project/.
2. Adapted herein.
3. Mohler, "Letter from the President," introducing the report.

This is not to say that either professor was in the end at odds with the other. In fact, it is conversations like these that move the conversation forward. These two friends and colleagues arguably reflect the SBC in which there is an agreed desire for reconciliation and commitment to the principles of the gospel and at the same time ambiguity and discord on what steps should be taken. Admittedly, in my initial dissertation, I relegated reparations to a footnote. "A full discussion of reparations for the sins of previous generations is impossible in a paper of this length. It is then better to consider how the present church can respond to injustice and division within the context of ministry today."[4] While my proposed actions of integration included the individual, the academy, the church, and the SBC,[5] I know that more could have been said in a development of biblical reparations. I hope to do so here, at least in part. The task is admittedly a difficult one, but difficulty should never resign the believer to inaction.

It would first be most helpful to define the term before moving to a discussion of it biblically. Reparations can be understood as compensation for a wrong endured made by the guilty party. In one sense, reparations are a consequence of repentance. One of the clearest examples of reparations seen in Scripture comes in the familiar account of Zacchaeus, recorded in Luke 19:1–10. While this is by no means the only example of a distinct call for actionable justice in Scripture (e.g., Amos), it does offer possibly the most succinct example of it. After receiving Christ's self-invitation into his home, the crowd began to complain that Jesus would lodge with such a wicked man. The chief tax collector, Zacchaeus, had a reputation of corruption and legalized robbery. This track record is not dissimilar to the legalized sins of the men and women who formed the SBC. Yet, in a picture of grace and submission to the gospel, Zacchaeus responds, "Behold, Lord, half of my possessions I will give to the poor, and if I have defrauded anyone of anything, I will give back four times as much" (Luke 19:8). While this passage is not inherently prescriptive, the Zacchaeus Principle, as we will call it, demonstrates the clear regard for acts of repentance by persons in Christ. While the details and application of this principle will be explored below, a case must first be made to view the SBC as possessing personhood and, consequently, the ability and need for acts of repentance.

It should be noted that corporate personhood is a solidly biblical concept. From the earliest pages of Scripture, God speaks collectively of the actions of cities, nations, and mankind as a whole. Israel becomes the most obvious of these examples in the Old Testament. Consider the Shema in

4. Morrison, "Segregation, Desegregation, and Integration," 12n30.
5. See ch. 9.

Deut 6, one of the most significant passages for Israel. "Hear, O Israel! The Lord is our God, the Lord is one! You shall love the Lord your God with all your heart and with all your soul and with all your might. These words, which I am commanding you today, shall be on your heart" (Deut 6: 4–6). Each verb and command assigned to Israel is singular, speaking both to the individual Israelites but also to something bigger: a single corporate person.[6] This is the same person that the prophets indict, God would consign to exile, and Christ would come to redeem. Individual actions are expressed in corporate being and the required repentance of which comes together in a unified spirit.

The New Testament further speaks in terms of personhood to both the church local and universal. As Paul points out the beautiful dichotomy of individuals making up a corporate person in 1 Cor 12:27 saying, "Now you are Christ's body, and individually members of it." The SBC, as a legal corporation with which local churches affiliate, exists between the church local and universal and maintains a similar corporate personhood. Just as Christ describes the church as a body and person, speaking to the whole beyond its individual parts, so the SBC operates as a corporate person and with that comes corporate culpability. Corporate repentance and reconciliation are seen throughout Scripture as the prophets call Israel and the nations to repentance just as Christ calls the seven churches to do in the book of Revelation. Lest we too soon dismiss the corporate, we should also note the generational nature of blessings and curses and that often in Scripture there is a repentance for the sins of those before us (Neh 9:2). The SBC is both capable and culpable in remedying the sins of its past. To do so requires direction and precision, both of which are seen in Zacchaeus.

Having considered the ability and need for corporate repentance, let us now move on to the direction of this action. The direction explored here is a patterning of one of Scripture's most laconic pictures of reparations in the words of Zacchaeus, "Behold, Lord, half of my possessions I will give to the poor, and if I have defrauded anyone of anything, I will give back four times as much." (Luke 19:8). The Zacchaeus Principle offers clear steps towards reconciliation for the SBC and its institutions. Dividing the Principle then into the two parts of its action, Zacchaeus makes two promises. In the former he vows to give half of his possessions to the poor, and in the latter to pay back those whom he has defrauded four times what he had taken. Zacchaeus weighs both the direct harm of his own actions as well as the indirect benefit that he enjoyed because of them. In theory, determining

6. For a deeper exploration of the concept of corporate personhood, including use of the term corporate person as opposed to other terms like objective spirit, see Morrison, "Won't You Be My Neighbor?"

the direct harm would be an easy task for Zacchaeus. The chief tax collector would surely have clear records of both his own assets as well the receipts of those he robbed. But the ease of its theory does not equate to painlessness in its application.

Zacchaeus's repentance came at great cost to himself and, at the same time, his actions were undoubtedly like the former possessions of the man who sold all that he had to purchase the field in which he found a greater treasure (Matt 13:44). Zacchaeus recognized the action of repentance demonstrated in reparations as well worth the sacrifice for the sake of the gospel and the kingdom. However, in the present discussion, reparations are not as simple. As thorough as the Report is and as detailed as my own research could be, the fullness of present racial disparity is impossible to quantify, at least on this side of heaven. The SBC, like the United States at large, failed to give proper restitution at the start. What then is to be done? For some, the call must be for financial reparations such as free tuition and boarding for all African Americans. For others, the report itself is unnecessary and just digging up the past. To be sure, many will read this appendix and find it, ironically, either too progressive or too dismissive. Such could be said of critiques against the SBC at large. In between the extremes, there is a balance to be struck informed by the Zacchaeus Principle. Examining the exchange more closely there seems to be three steps to the Principle.

The first step is in recognizing the need to act. Zacchaeus' words came as a response to the disheartened cries for justice by the crowd. Repentance is never satisfied by lip service. The word repentance portrays turning back and a change through course of action. This recognition and resolve to act should be seen from the individual to the corporate level. Vocal repentance, such as the 1995 "Resolution on Racial Reconciliation on the 150th Anniversary of the Southern Baptist Convention,"[7] have been made and ought not be dismissed, but actions in line with the next two steps are few and far between.

The second step is a general sacrifice, acknowledging the benefits made at the cost of subjugating others. Like Zacchaeus, there must be a recognition that even beyond the profits made in direct and knowing harm, there exists also a need in the gospel to lift up the entire community of the oppressed using the gifts and capacities God has given or we have stolen. In all practical forms this could be seen in intentional efforts to diversify faculty and curriculum and to create far more scholarships for racial minorities

7. https://www.sbc.net/resource-library/resolutions/resolution-on-racial-reconciliation-on-the-150th-anniversary-of-the-southern-baptist-convention/.

and the impoverished. This step is where the majority of reparations will likely take place, and should be both costly and voluntary.

The third, and likely most difficult, step is to identify wronged parties and direct culpability. Southern's Report does this in part by identifying and lamenting publicly its role in the continuation of racism and partiality. This is something each SBC seminary could likely do, as I discovered quite quickly the depths of shame in Southwestern faculty being members of the Ku Klux Klan alongside its equipping of Black ministers in night classes in the 1930s. This step would include the forgiveness of debts as well as additional restitution to identified wronged parties. As most of those directly harmed by the SBC in its formation and prominence during slavery and segregation have now passed, the work here must be done either posthumously or in benefit to the lasting effects to the children and grandchildren of the wronged parties. Regrettably, there are some direct wrongs which simply will not stand resolved on this side of heaven. But there is still plenty of work which can be done. A promising example of this action rightly done came in 2004 when Eugene Florence, a Black minister who attended Southwestern's night classes from 1943 to 1951 but never received a degree, was awarded his Master of Divinity at the ripe age of a hundred years old, just eight years before his death.[8] Florence had been deprived of what he was due for fifty-three years, but as his daughter, Emma, remarked, "It doesn't matter whether they did it when it was supposed to be done, but it was done [when] God said it was supposed to be done . . . in the fullness of time."[9]

Repentance is a difficult thing. It forces the guilty to see their guilt, to turn from it, and to move in a new direction. This turning can feel as though the roots of life are being displaced and severed. It is painful. But the return is joyous and the new direction is glorious. The Zacchaeus Principle gives a clear pattern of this decision in the actions of binding the wounds of direct harm, where possible, and in sowing greater benefit from the indirect and unknown harms of power and affluence. Both actions require sacrifice. The kingdom of God is a treasure well worth the sacrifice, and while the best time to make that sacrifice is yesterday, the second best is today.[10]

8. https://swbts.edu/news/releases/florence-102-will-preach-chapel-feb-14-attended-negro-extension-center-eight-years/.

9. https://swbts.edu/news/releases/florence-102-will-preach-chapel-feb-14-attended-negro-extension-center-eight-years/.

10. For a more substantial treatment of reparations as it relates to the church, see Kwon and Thompson, *Reparations.*

Bibliography

Adams, John Quincy. "Washington, March 2, 1820." In *The Memoirs of John Quincy Adams, Comprising Portions of His Diary from 1795–1848*. New York: Scribner, 1951.

Alexander, Charles T. "An Evangelistic Conference for Negro Baptists." *The Baptist Standard* 50 (1938) 4.

Alexander, Michelle. *The New Jim Crow: Mass Incarceration in the Age of Colorblindness*. New York: The New, 2012.

Allen, William Loyd, and Larry L. McSwain. *Twentieth-Century Shapers of Baptist Social Ethics*. Macon, GA: Mercer University Press, 2008.

Anderson, Bernhard W. *Contours of Old Testament Theology*. Minneapolis: Fortress, 1999.

Aquinas, Thomas. *Summa Theologica*. Translated by John A. Oesterle. New York: Benziger, 1947.

———. *Treatise on the Virtues*. Translated by John A. Oesterle. Notre Dame, IN: University of Notre Dame Press, 1966.

Aristotle. *Aristotle's Nicomachean Ethics*. Translated by Hippocrates G. Apostle. Grinnell, IA: Peripatetic, 1984.

Atkinson, David J., et al. *New Dictionary of Christian Ethics and Pastoral Theology*. Downers Grove, IL: InterVarsity, 2013.

Augustine, Saint. *The City of God*. Translated by Gerald G. Walsh et al. Edited by Vernon J. Bourke. Garden City, NY: Image, 1958.

———. *Confessions of St. Augustine*. Translated by John K. Ryan. Garden City, NY: Doubleday, 1960.

———. *The Writings Against the Manicheans and Against the Donatists*. Translated by Philip Schaff. New York: Scribners, 1901.

Bailey, Wilma Ann. "The Way the World Is Meant to Be: An Interpretation of Genesis 1:26–29." *Vision (Winnipeg, Man.)* 9 (2008) 46–52.

Barclay, Oliver. "The Nature of Christian Morality." In *Law, Morality, and the Bible*, 125–50. Downers Grove, IL: InterVarsity, 1978.

Barnes, Albert. *The Acts of the Apostles*. London: Blackie, 1832.

Barth, Karl. *Church Dogmatics*. Edited by G. W. Bromiley and Thomas F. Torrance. London: T. & T. Clark, 2009.

Baumgarten, Albert I. "Myth and Midrash: Genesis 9:20–29." In *Christianity, Judaism and Other Greco-Roman Cults: Studies for Morton Smith at Sixty*, 55–71. Leiden: Brill, 1975.

Beach, Waldo, and H. Richard Niebuhr. *Christian Ethics: Sources for the Living Tradition.* New York: Ronald, 1955.

Beauchamp, Tom L., and James F. Childress. *Principles of Biomedical Ethics.* 6th ed. New York: Oxford University Press, 2008.

Bebbington, David W. *Evangelicalism in Modern Britain: A History from the 1730s to the 1980s.* London: Routledge, 2003.

Berdiaev, Nikolaï. *The Destiny of Man.* San Rafael, CA: Semantron, 2009.

Bergsma, John S., and Scott Hahn. "Noah's Nakedness and the Curse on Canaan (Genesis 9:20–27)." *Journal of Biblical Literature* 124 (2005) 25–40.

Berkouwer, G. C. *Man: The Image of God.* Grand Rapids: Eerdmans, 1962.

Bertrand, M., and S. Mullainathan. "Are Emily and Greg More Employable Than Lakisha and Jamal? A Field Experiment in Labor Market Discrimination." *The American Economic Review* 94 (2004) 991–1013.

Better, Shirley Jean. *Institutional Racism: A Primer on Theory and Strategies for Social Change.* 2nd ed. Lanham, MD: Rowman, 2008.

Bhopal, Kalwant, and Patrick Alan Danaher. *Identity and Pedagogy in Higher Education: International Comparisons.* New York: Bloomsbury Academic, 2013.

Birch, Bruce C., et al. *A Theological Introduction to the Old Testament: 2nd Edition.* Nashville: Abingdon, 2005.

"Black Baptist Rejects Apology by SBC." *Christian Century* 112 (1995) 879.

Blum, Edward J., and Paul Harvey. *The Color of Christ: The Son of God and the Saga of Race in America.* Chapel Hill, NC: The University of North Carolina Press, 2012.

Bradley, Anthony B. *Black and Tired: Essays on Race, Politics, Culture, and International Development.* Eugene, OR: Wipf & Stock, 2011.

———. *Ending Overcriminalization and Mass Incarceration: Hope from Civil Society.* Cambridge: Cambridge University Press, 2018.

Bradley, Anthony B., and Carl F. Ellis. *Aliens in the Promised Land: Why Minority Leadership Is Overlooked in White Christian Churches and Institutions.* Phillipsburg, NJ: P&R, 2013.

Bradley, L. Richard. "Curse of Canaan and the American Negro." *Concordia Theological Monthly* 42 (1971) 100–110.

Braidfoot, Larry. "T. B. Maston on Race Relations." *The California Southern Baptist* (1982) 14–15.

Brister, C. W., and James Leo Garrett. *The Legacy of Southwestern: Writings that Shaped a Tradition.* North Richland Hills, TX: Smithfield, 2002.

Broad, C. D. *Five Types of Ethical Theory.* London: Routledge & K. Paul, 1930.

Brown-Glaude, Winnifred R. *Doing Diversity in Higher Education: Faculty Leaders Share Challenges and Strategies.* New Brunswick, NJ: Rutgers University Press, 2009.

Brunner, Emil. *The Christian Doctrine of Creation and Redemption.* Translated by Olive Wyon. Eugene, OR: Wipf & Stock, 2014.

———. *Man in Revolt: A Christian Anthropology.* Translated by Olive Wyon. Cambridge: Lutterworth, 2002.

Bulger, Jeffrey W. "Principlism." *Teaching Ethics* 8.1 (2007) 81–100.

Byron, Gay L. "Race, Ethnicity, and the Bible: Pedagogical Challenges and Curricular Opportunities." *Teaching Theology and Religion* 15 (2012) 105–12.

Cairns, David. *The Image of God in Man.* London: SCM, 1953.

Calvin, John. *Calvin: Institutes of the Christian Religion*. Translated by Ford Lewis Battles. Edited by John T. McNeill. Louisville, KY: Westminster John Knox, 2011.

Cameron, David J. "'Pluck This Thorn from Our Collective Sides': Texas Baptists and Race Relations." PhD diss., University of Houston-Clear Lake, 2012.

Carter, Christopher. "The Imago Dei as the Mind of Jesus Christ." *Zygon: Journal of Religion and Science* 49 (2014) 752–60.

Cassuto, Umberto. *A Commentary on the Book of Genesis*. Jerusalem: Magnes, Hebrew University, 1961.

Chappell, David L. *A Stone of Hope: Prophetic Religion and the Death of Jim Crow*. Chapel Hill, NC: University of North Carolina Press, 2004.

Chismark, Stacie R., M. S. and Kayla Mandel, M. S. Sheets. "Race." In *Salem Press Encyclopedia of Health*. Hackensack, NJ: Salem, 2014.

Chrisman, David Keith. "The Price of Moderation: Texas Baptists and Racial Integration, 1948–1968." PhD diss., Texas A&M University, 2001.

Clardy, Brian K. "Deconstructing a Theology of Defiance: Black Preaching and the Politics of Racial Identity." *Journal of Church and State* 53 (2011) 203–21.

Clark, David K., and Robert V. Rakestraw, eds. *Readings in Christian Ethics, Volume 2: Issues and Applications*. Grand Rapids: Baker, 1996.

Clement. *Christ the Educator*. Translated by Simon P. Wood. New York: Fathers of the Church, 1954.

Clines, David J. A. "The Image of God in Man." *Tyndale Bulletin* 19 (1968) 53–103.

Cochran, Gregory C. "Remembering the Father in Fatherhood: Biblical Foundations and Practical Implications of the Doctrine of the Fatherhood of God." *The Journal of Family Ministry* 1 (2011) 14–24.

Coffey, John. *Exodus and Liberation: Deliverance Politics from John Calvin to Martin Luther King, Jr.* Oxford: Oxford University Press, 2013.

Cohen, H. Hirsch. *The Drunkenness of Noah*. Tuscaloosa, AL: University of Alabama Press, 1974.

Cone, James H. *A Black Theology of Liberation*. Maryknoll, NY: Orbis, 1990.

———. *God of the Oppressed*. Maryknoll, NY: Orbis, 1997.

———. "God Our Father, Christ Our Redeemer, Man Our Brother: A Theological Interpretation of the AME Church." *The Journal of The Interdenominational Theological Center* 4 (1976) 25–33.

Cook, James Graham. *The Segregationists*. New York: Appleton-Century-Crofts, 1962.

Copeland, Luther. *The Southern Baptist Convention and the Judgment of History: The Taint of an Original Sin*. Lanham, MD: University Press of America, 1995.

Crouch, Andy. *Culture Making: Recovering Our Creative Calling*. Downers Grove, IL: InterVarsity, 2008.

Crouse, Stephen Gary. "A Missiological Evaluation of Southern Baptist Multiethnic Churches in the United States." PhD diss., The Southern Baptist Theological Seminary, 2014.

Cruz, Helen, and Yves Maeseneer. "The Imago Dei: Evolutionary and Theological Perspectives." *Zygon: Journal of Religion and Science* 49 (2014) 95–100.

Culver, Robert Duncan. *Anthropomorphism, Analogy and Impassibility of God*. Portland, OR: TREN, 1996.

Dailey, Jane. "Sex, Segregation, and the Sacred after Brown." *Journal of American History* 91 (2004) 119–144.

Dake, Finis. "30 Reasons for Segregation of Races." In *Dake's Annotated Reference Bible: The New Testament (with Daniel, Psalms and Proverbs)*, 159. Grand Rapids: Zondervan, 1961.

"Dallas Pastor Stirs Controversy with Statements on Integration." *The Baptist Message*, March 1, 1956.

Darwin, Charles. *The Descent of Man*. New York: American Home Library, 1902.

Davis, John Jefferson. *Evangelical Ethics: Issues Facing the Church Today*. 3rd ed. Phillipsburg, NJ: Presbyterian and Reformed, 2004.

Davis, Joseph J. "Embracing Equality: Texas Baptists, Social Christianity, and Civil Rights in the Twentieth Century." PhD diss., University of North Texas, 2013.

Delgado, Richard, and Jean Stefancic. *Critical Race Theory: An Introduction*. 2nd ed. New York: New York University Press, 2012.

Deslippe, Dennis. *Protesting Affirmative Action: The Struggle Over Equality after the Civil Rights Revolution*. Baltimore: Johns Hopkins University Press, 2012.

DeWolf, L. Harold. *A Theology of the Living Church*. New York: Harper, 1953.

Dickerson, Dennis C. "African American Religious Intellectuals and the Theological Foundations of the Civil Rights Movement, 1930–55." *Church History* 74 (2005) 217–35.

Dickey, Christina Robinson. *The Bible and Segregation*. Merrimac, MA: Destiny, 1958.

Diggles, Kimberly. "Addressing Racial Awareness and Color-Blindness in Higher Education." *New Directions for Teaching and Learning* 140 (2014) 31–44.

Dockery, David S. *Renewing Minds*. Rev ed. Nashville: B&H Academic, 2007.

Driver, S. R. *The Book of Genesis*. London: Methuen, 1904.

Du Bois, W. E. B. *The Souls of Black Folk*. Oxford: Oxford University Press. 2007.

Dueck, Gil. "Reuniting Relationship and Vocation: Reflection on the Divine Image." *Direction* 45 (2016) 149–56.

Dupont, Carolyn Renée. *Mississippi Praying: Southern White Evangelicals and the Civil Rights Movement, 1945–1975*. New York: New York University Press, 2016.

Eckes, Suzanne E. "Diversity in Higher Education: The Consideration of Race in Hiring University Faculty." *Brigham Young University Education and Law Journal* 1 (2005) 33–51.

Eighmy, John L. "Religious Liberalism in the South During the Progressive Era." *Church History* 3 (1969) 359–72.

Elias, John L. "Inter-Cultural Education and Religious Education, 1940–1960." *Religious Education* 103 (2008) 427–39.

Elliger, K., and W. Rudolph. *Biblia Hebraica Stuttgartensia*. Stuttgart: Gesamtherstellun Biblia-Druck, 1977.

Emerson, Michael O., and Christian Smith. *Divided by Faith: Evangelical Religion and the Problem of Race in America*. Oxford: Oxford University Press, 2000.

Epstein, Isidore. *The Babylonian Talmud*. London: Soncino, 1935.

Erickson, Millard J. *Christian Theology*. Grand Rapids: Baker Academic, 1983.

Eskridge, William N., Jr. "Noah's Curse: How Religion Often Conflates Status, Belief, and Conduct to Resist Antidiscrimination Norms." *Georgia Law Review* 45 (2011) 657–720.

Evans, David, and Tobin Miller Shearer. "A Principled Pedagogy for Religious Educators." *Religious Education* 112 (2017) 7–18.

Ezell, Humphrey K. *The Christian Problem of Racial Segregation*. New York: Greenwich, 1959.

Farley, Gary E. "T. B. Maston: Advocate for Living God's Word in the Marketplace." *Baptist History and Heritage* 31 (1996) 31–39.

Farmer, J. S. "Our Colored People." *The Biblical Recorder* 98 (1933) 6.

Feagin, J. R. *Systemic Racism: A Theory of Oppression.* New York: Routledge, 2006.

Feldmeier, Reinhard, and Hermann Spieckermann. *God of the Living: A Biblical Theology.* Waco, TX: Baylor University Press, 2011.

Fergeson, Joel. "History of Christian Teaching on Slavery." Unpublished research paper, Southwestern Baptist Theological Seminary, 1948.

Fergusson, David. "Humans Created According to the 'Imago Dei': An Alternative Proposal." *Zygon: Journal of Religion and Science* 48 (2013) 439–53.

Finkelstein, Martin J., et al. *The Faculty Factor: Reassessing the American Academy in a Turbulent Era.* Baltimore: Johns Hopkins University Press, 2016.

Fletcher, Joseph F. *Situation Ethics: The New Morality.* Louisville, KY: Westminster John Knox, 2000.

Földy, Reginald, and Tamara R. Buckley. *The Color Bind: Talking (and Not Talking) About Race at Work.* New York: Russell Sage, 2014.

Fong, Bruce W. "Addressing the Issue of Racial Reconciliation According to the Principles of Eph. 2:11–22." *Journal of the Evangelical Theological Society* 38 (1995) 565–80.

Fotiou, Satvros S. "Diversity and Unity: The Vision of Christian Education in an Age of Globalization." *Greek Orthodox Theological Review* 49 (2004) 269–78.

Frankena, William K. *Ethics.* New Delhi: Prentice-Hall of India, 2005.

Freeman, Curtis W. "'Never Had I Been So Blind': W. A. Criswell's 'Change' on Racial Segregation." *The Journal of Southern Religion* 10 (2007) 1–12.

Fullinwider, Robert. "Affirmative Action." In *The Stanford Encyclopedia of Philosophy*, edited by Edward N. Zalta. Fairfax, VA: George Mason University, 2013. https://plato.stanford.edu/archives/sum2018/entries/affirmative-action/.

Gagnon, Robert A. J. *The Bible and Homosexual Practice: Texts and Hermeneutics.* Nashville: Abingdon, 2001.

Gallegos Ordorica, Sergio A. "Prospects of a Dusselian Ethics of Liberation among US Minorities: The Case of Affirmative Action in Higher Education." *Inter-American Journal of Philosophy* 6 (2015) 1–15.

García, Justin D. "Ethnicity." In *Salem Press Encyclopedia.* Pasadena, CA: Salem, 2014.

Gardner, David M. "Racial Rabble Rousers." *The Baptist Standard* 57 (1945) 3.

Garr, W. Randall. *In His Own Image and Likeness: Humanity, Divinity, and Monotheism.* Leiden: Brill, 2003.

George, Timothy. "Southern Baptists' Long Journey." *First Things* 226 (2012) 16–18.

Gilbert, Pierre. "The Missional Relevance of Genesis 1–3." *Direction* 43 (2014) 49–64.

Gill, John. *An Exposition of the First Book of Moses Called Genesis.* Springfield, MO: Particular Baptist, 2010.

Gillespie, G. T. *A Christian View on Segregation.* Greenwood, MS: Educational Fund of the Citizens' Councils, 1954.

Gillette, William. *Retreat from Reconstruction: 1869-1879.* Baton Rouge, LA: Louisiana State University Press, 1990.

Gin Lum, Kathryn, and Paul Harvey. *The Oxford Handbook of Religion and Race in American History.* New York: Oxford University Press, 2018.

Godwin, Colin, and Saphano Riak Chol. "'God Gave This Land to Us': A Biblical Perspective on the Tension in South Sudan between Tribal Lands, Ethnic Identity and the Breadth of Christian Salvation." *Mission Studies* 30 (2013) 208–19.

Goldberg, David Theo. "A Political Theology of Race." *Cultural Studies* 23 (2009) 513–37.

Goldsworthy, Graeme. *Christ-Centered Biblical Theology: Hermeneutical Foundations and Principles*. Downers Grove, IL: IVP Academic, 2012.

Goto, Courtney T. "Beyond the Black-White Binary of U.S. Race Relations: A Next Step in Religious Education." *Religious Education* 112 (2017) 33–45.

Graves, Robert, and Raphael Patai. *Hebrew Myths; The Book of Genesis*. Garden City, NY: Doubleday, 1964.

Grenz, Stanley J. *The Social God and the Relational Self: A Trinitarian Theology of the Imago Dei*. Louisville, KY: Westminster John Knox, 2001.

Gritz, Sharon Hodgin. "T. B. Maston: A Principlist Approach to Christian Ethics." Unpublished research paper, Southwestern Baptist Theological Seminary, 1981.

Groves, Harry E. "Separate but Equal—The Doctrine of Plessy v. Ferguson." *Phylon* 12 (1951) 66–72.

Gwaltney, L. L. "The Race Problem." *The Alabama Baptist*, July 4, 1957.

Hall, Douglas John. *Imaging God: Dominion as Stewardship*. Grand Rapids: Eerdmans, 1986.

Hardon, John A. S. J. "Meaning of Virtue in Thomas Aquinas." *Great Catholic Books Newsletter* 2 (1995) 1.

Harris, Harriet A. *Fundamentalism and Evangelicals*. Oxford: Clarendon, 2008.

Harris, Peter. "A Whole Gospel for a Whole World." *Crux* 42 (2006) 43–49.

Hartocollis, Anemona. "Does Harvard Admissions Discriminate? The Lawsuit on Affirmative Action, Explained." *The New York Times*, October 15, 2018. https://www.nytimes.com/2018/10/15/us/harvard-affirmative-action-asian-americans.html.

Hauerwas, Stanley, and Charles Pinches. *Christians Among the Virtues: Theological Conversations with Ancient and Modern Ethics*. Notre Dame, IN: University of Notre Dame Press, 1997.

Haynes, Stephen R. *The Last Segregated Hour: The Memphis Kneel-Ins and the Campaign for Southern Church Desegregation*. New York: Oxford University Press, 2013.

Hays, J. Daniel. "Applying the Old Testament Law Today." *Bibliotheca Sacra* 158 (2001) 21–35.

———. *From Every People and Nation: A Biblical Theology of Race*. Downers Grove, IL: InterVarsity, 2003.

Hecht, Susan M. "A Biblical-Theological Analysis of the Description of God as Creator of Heaven and Earth." *Trinity Journal* 35 (2014) 120.

Hill, Kenneth H. *Religious Education in the African American Tradition: A Comprehensive Introduction*. St. Louis, MO: Chalice Press-Christian Board, 2007.

Hodges, Louis Wendell. "A Christian Analysis of Selected Contemporary Theories of Racial Prejudice." PhD diss., Duke University, 1960.

Hoffman, Louis, et al. "Diversity and the God Image: Examining Ethic Differences in the Experience of God for a College-Age Population." *Journal of Psychology and Theology* (2008) 26–41.

Holder, John. "The Issue of Race: A Search for a Biblical/Theological Perspective." *The Journal of Religious Thought* 49 (1992) 44–59.

Hollinger, Dennis P. *Choosing the Good: Christian Ethics in a Complex World*. Grand Rapids: Baker Academic, 2002.

Holmes, Arthur F., et al. *New Dictionary of Christian Ethics and Pastoral Theology*. Downers Grove, IL: InterVarsity, 2013.

Hursthouse, Rosalind. *On Virtue Ethics*. Oxford: Oxford University Press, 1999.

Ibarra, Robert A. *Beyond Affirmative Action: Reframing the Context of Higher Education*. Madison: University of Wisconsin Press, 2001.

JBHE Research Department. "Black Faculty in Higher Education: Still Only a Drop in the Bucket." *The Journal of Blacks in Higher Education* 55 (2007) 67–70.

Jennings, Willie James. *The Christian Imagination: Theology and the Origins of Race*. New Haven, CT: Yale University Press, 2010.

Jipp, Joshua W. "Paul's Areopagus Speech of Acts 17:16–34 as Both Critique and Propaganda." *Journal of Biblical Literature* 131 (2012) 567–88.

Johnson, Olatunde C. A. "Legislating Racial Fairness in Criminal Justice." *Columbia Human Rights Law Review* 39 (2007) 233.

Jones, A. Jase. "T. B. Maston: The Man, His Family, and His Ministry." Speech at Logsdon School of Theology, Hardin-Simmons University, Abilene, TX, March 27, 1999.

Jones-Armstrong, Amaryah. "The Spirit and the Subprime: Race, Risk, and Our Common Dispossession." *Anglican Theological Review* 98 (2016) 51–69.

Jones, David W. *An Introduction to Biblical Ethics*. Nashville: B&H Academic, 2013.

Jones, Jim. "A Seminary Issue in Black and White." *The Star Telegram*, March 21, 1987.

Jordan, Winthrop D. *The White Man's Burden: Historical Origins of Racism in the United States*. New York: Oxford University Press, 1974.

Joshee, Reva, and Lauri Johnson. *Multicultural Education Policies in Canada and the United States*. Vancouver: UBC, 2007.

Joustra, Jessica. "An Embodied Imago Dei: How Herman Bavinck's Understanding of the Image of God Can Help Inform Conversations on Race." *Journal of Reformed Theology* 11 (2017) 9–23.

Kaiser, Walter C., Jr. "New Approaches to Old Testament Ethics." *Journal of the Evangelical Theological Society* 35 (1992) 289–97.

———. "A Principlizing Model." In *Four Views on Moving Beyond the Bible to Theology*, 19–50. Grand Rapids: Zondervan, 2009.

Kant, Immanuel. *The Metaphysics of Morals*. Translated by Mary J. Gregor. Cambridge; New York: Cambridge University Press, 1996.

Kaplan, Jeffrey. "Christian Identity." In *Encyclopedia of White Power*, 50–53. Walnut Creek, CA: Altamira, 2000.

Kaplan, Jonathan. "Race, IQ, and the Search for Statistical Signals Associated with So-Called 'X'-Factors: Environments, Racism, and the 'Hereditarian Hypothesis.'" *Biology and Philosophy* 30 (2015) 1–17.

Katchanovski, Ivan, et al. "Race, Gender, and Affirmative Action Attitudes in American and Canadian Universities." *Canadian Journal of Higher Education* 45 (2015) 18–41.

Kean, Melissa. *Desegregating Private Higher Education in the South: Duke, Emory, Rice, Tulane, and Vanderbilt*. Baton Rouge, LA: Louisiana State University Press, 2008.

Keil, Carl Friedrich, and Franz Delitzsch. *Commentary on the Old Testament*. Translated by James Martin. Peabody, MA: Hendrickson, 2011.

Kelly, Hilton. "'Just Something Gone, But Nothing Missing': Booker T. Washington, Nannie Helen Burroughs, and the Social Significance of Black Teachers Theorizing Across Two Centuries." *Educational Studies* 48 (2012) 215–19.

Kelsey, George D. *Social Ethics Among Southern Baptists, 1917–1969.* Metuchen, NJ: Scarecrow, 1972.

Kendi, Ibram X. *Stamped from the Beginning: The Definitive History of Racist Ideas in America.* New York: Bold Type, 2017.

Kidner, Derek. *Genesis: An Introduction and Commentary.* Chicago: InterVarsity, 1967.

Kierkegaard, Søren. *Works of Love.* Translated by Edna H. Hong and Howard V. Hong. Princeton: Princeton University Press, 1995.

Killingsworth, Blake. "Here I Am, Stuck in the Middle with You: The Baptist Standard, Texas Baptist Leadership, and School Desegregation, 1954 to 1956." *Baptist History and Heritage* 41 (2006) 78–92.

King, Martin Luther, Jr. *A Testament of Hope: The Essential Writings and Speeches of Martin Luther King, Jr.* Edited by James Melvin Washington. San Francisco: Harper San Francisco, 1991.

———. "The Un-Christian Christian." *Ebony Magazine* 20 (1965) 76–80.

Kirkpatrick, Vance Crawford. "The Ethical Thought of T. B. Maston." ThD diss., Southwestern Baptist Theological Seminary, 1972.

Klink, Edward W., and Darian R. Lockett. *Understanding Biblical Theology: A Comparison of Theory and Practice.* Grand Rapids: Zondervan, 2012.

Kohlberg, Lawrence. *Essays on Moral Development.* San Francisco: Harper & Row, 1981.

Kotva, Joseph J., Jr. *The Christian Case for Virtue Ethics.* Washington, DC: Georgetown University Press, 1996.

Kow, David. "The (Un)compelling Interest for Underrepresented Minority Students: Enhancing the Education of White Students Underexposed to Racial Diversity." *Berkeley La Raza Law Journal* 20 (2010) 157–90.

Krause, Deborah. "Keeping It Real: The Image of God in the New Testament." *Interpretation* 59 (2005) 358–68.

Krause, Neal, and R. David Hayward. "Race, Religion, and Virtues." *International Journal for The Psychology of Religion* 25 (2015) 152–69.

Kreeft, Peter. *Back to Virtue: Traditional Moral Wisdom for Modern Moral Confusion.* San Francisco: Ignatius, 1986.

Kugel, James L. *Traditions of the Bible: A Guide to the Bible As It Was at the Start of the Common Era.* Cambridge, MA: Harvard University Press, 1998.

Kuhlman, Martin. "Direct Action in Texas: The Stand-In Campaign." *Journal of South Texas* 28 (2015) 46–59.

Kujawa-Holbrook, S. "Beyond Diversity: Cultural Competence, White Racism Awareness, and European-American Theology Students." *Teaching Theology and Religion* 5 (2002) 141–48.

Kwon, Duke L., and Gregory Thompson. *Reparations: A Christian Call for Repentance and Repair.* Grand Rapids: Brazos, 2021.

Kwon, Hyuck Bong. "An Evaluation of the Contributions of T. B. Maston to Christian Ethics." ThM thesis, Southeastern Baptist Theological Seminary, 1982.

LaPointe, Eleanor A. "Tokenism." In *Salem Press Encyclopedia.* Pasadena, CA: Salem, 2014.

Larkin, William J., et al. *Acts.* Downers Grove, IL: InterVarsity, 1995.

Lawler, Peter Augustine. "Higher Education vs. Competency and Diversity: An Afterword." *Modern Age* 59 (2017) 73–79.

LeBar, Mark and Michael Slote. "Justice as a Virtue." *The Stanford Encyclopedia of Philosophy* (2016) 1.

Lee, Boyung. "Broadening the Boundary of 'Textbooks' for Intercultural Communication in Religious Education." *Religious Education* 105 (2010) 249–52.

Lemke, Steve W. "Article XII: Education." In *Baptist Faith and Message 2000*, edited by Douglas K. Blount and Joseph D. Wooddell, 121–35. Lanham, MD: Rowman & Littlefield, 2007.

———. "The Uneasy Conscience of Southern Baptists: Support for Slavery among the Founders of the Southern Baptist Convention." *American Baptist Quarterly* 34 (2015) 254–70.

Leonard, Bill J. *Baptists in America*. New York: Columbia University Press, 2005.

———. *God's Last and Only Hope: The Fragmentation of the Southern Baptist Convention*. Grand Rapids: Eerdmans, 1990.

Lewis-Giggetts, Tracey M. *The Integrated Church: Authentic Multicultural Ministry*. Kansas City, MO: Nazarene, 2011.

Liederbach, Mark, and Alvin L. Reid. *The Convergent Church: Missional Worshipers in an Emerging Culture*. Grand Rapids: Kregel, 2009.

Liederbach, Mark, and Evan Lenow. *Ethics As Worship: The Pursuit of Moral Discipleship*. Phillipsburg, NJ: P&R Publishing, 2021.

Lietz, Megan E. "Hope for Reconciliation or Agent of the Status Quo: Multiracial Congregations, their Theological Foundations and Power Dynamics." PhD diss., Boston University, 2015.

Lipsey, P. I. "The Anti-Lynching Bill." *The Baptist Record* 24 (1922) 4.

Lloyd, Vincent William. "Paradox and Tradition in Black Theology." *Black Theology: An International Journal* 9 (2011) 265–86.

Lucas, C. B. "T. B. Maston." *Home Missions Magazine*, November 1973.

Luther, Martin. *The Disputation Concerning Man*. Translated by William R. Russell. N.p.: n.p., 1536.

MacIntyre, Alasdair. *After Virtue: A Study in Moral Theory*, Notre Dame, IN: University of Notre Dame Press, 1981.

Maldonado-Torres, Nelson. "Race, Religion, and Ethics in the Modern/Colonial World." *Journal of Religious Ethics* 42 (2014) 691–711.

Manis, Andrew Michael. *Southern Civil Religions in Conflict: Black and White Baptists and Civil Rights, 1947–1957*. Athens, GA: University Press of Georgia, 1987.

Marlow, Edward K., and Kendrith M. Rowland. "Affirmative Action: Federal Support, Supreme Court Decisions, and Human Resource Management." *Human Resource Management* 28 (1989) 541–56.

Marsden, George M. *The Outrageous Idea of Christian Scholarship*. Oxford: Oxford University Press, 1998.

Marsh, Charles. *The Beloved Community: How Faith Shapes Social Justice, From the Civil Rights Movement to Today*. New York: Basic, 2005.

Marshall, I. Howard. *Acts: An Introduction and Commentary*. Downers Grove, IL: IVP Academic, 2008.

Martin, Earl R. *Passport to Servanthood: The Life and Missionary Influence of T. B. Maston*. Nashville: Broadman, 1988.

Martyr, Justin. *Dialogue with Trypho*. Translated by A. Lukyn Williams. Washington, DC: Catholic University of America Press, 2003.

"Maston Presented Award for Distinguished Service." *Baptist Press*, March 9, 1966.

Maston, T. B. "Alternatives and Paradoxes." *"Both/And" Series, Baptist Standard,* October 15, 1980.

———. "Baptists, Social Christianity, and American Culture." *Review and Expositor* 61 (1964) 521–31.

———. *The Bible and Race*. Nashville: Broadman, 1959.

———. "The Bible and Racial Distinctions." The T. B. Maston Collection. Fort Worth, TX: Southwestern Baptist Theological Seminary, 1961.

———. "'Bible Nuggets' Baptist Standard Series." *The T. B. Maston Collection*. Fort Worth, TX: Southwestern Baptist Theological Seminary, 1972–1973.

———. "Biblical Basis for Social Concern." *Southwestern Journal of Theology* 7 (1965) 5–16.

———. "Biblical Concepts and Race Relations." The T. B. Maston Collection. Fort Worth, TX: Southwestern Baptist Theological Seminary, 1959.

———. *Biblical Ethics: A Biblical Survey*. Cleveland: World, 1967.

———. "Biblical Teachings and Race Relations." *Review and Expositor* 56 (1959) 233–42.

———. "'Both/And' Baptist Standard Series." The T. B. Maston Collection. Fort Worth, TX: Southwestern Baptist Theological Seminary, 1980–1981.

———. *The Christian and Race Relations*. Memphis, TN: Brotherhood Commission, Southern Baptist Convention, 1950.

———. *The Christian, the Church, and Contemporary Problems*. Waco, TX: Word, 1968.

———. *The Christian in the Modern World*. Nashville: Broadman, 1952.

———. *Christianity and World Issues*. New York: Macmillan, 1957.

———. "The Church, the State, and the Christian Ethic." *Journal of Church and State* 1 (1960) 26–36.

———. *The Conscience of a Christian*. Waco, TX: Word, 1971.

———. "Constructive Christian Tension." *Southwestern Journal of Theology* 1 (1958) 21–29.

———. "Continuing Concerns." The T. B. Maston Collection. Fort Worth, TX: Southwestern Baptist Theological Seminary, 1983.

———. "Ethical Content of Job." *Southwestern Journal of Theology* 14 (1971) 43–56.

———. "Ethical Dimensions of James." *Southwestern Journal of Theology* 12 (1969) 23–39.

———. *The Ethic of the Christian Life: Third Course Christian Ethics*. El Paso, TX: Carib Baptist, 1981.

———. *God Speaks Through Suffering*. Waco, TX: Word, 1977.

———. *God's Will and Your Life*. Nashville: Broadman, 1964.

———. *Integration*. Nashville: Christian Life Commission of the Southern Baptist Convention, 1956.

———. "Integration." Unpublished paper presented to the Advisory Council of Southern Baptists for Work with Negroes. Nashville: 1977.

———. "Interconvention Committee on Negro Ministerial Education." The T. B. Maston Collection. Fort Worth, TX: Southwestern Baptist Theological Seminary, 1960.

———. *Interracial Marriage*. Nashville: Christian Life Commission of the Southern Baptist Convention, 1963.

———. "Law, Order, and Justice." *Review and Expositor* 66 (1969) 89–100.

———. "Man: His Dignity and Worth." *Review and Expositor* 51 (1954) 299–311.

———. *Next Steps in the South: Answers to Current Questions*. Atlanta: Southern Regional Council, 1956.

———. "Notes on the Characteristics of Christian Ethics." The T. B. Maston Collection. Fort Worth, TX: Southwestern Baptist Theological Seminary, n.d.

———. "Of One": *A Study of Christian Principles and Race Relations*. Atlanta: Home Mission Board, Southern Baptist Convention, 1946.

———. "Personal and Social Morality." *Baptist Standard*, February 18, 1969.

———. "Principles of Christian Social Concern and Action." Unpublished paper presented to the Christian Life Commission of the Southern Baptist Convention. Nashville: 1977.

———. "'Problems of the Christian Life' Baptist Standard Series." The T. B. Maston Collection. Fort Worth, TX: Southwestern Baptist Theological Seminary, 1968–1970.

———. "Problems of the Christian Life: Race and the Nature of the Church." *Baptist Standard*, June 4, 1969.

———. "Problems of the Christian Life: The Association, the Convention, and Race." *Baptist Standard*, September 24, 1969.

———. "Problems of the Christian Life: To Sign or Not to Sign." *Baptist Standard*, July 30, 1969.

———. "Profiles: Dr. T. B. Maston." Fort Worth, TX: The Maston's Home, 1984. http://www.tbmaston.org/Videos/1984_Profiles_Interview/Video_1984_Interview.html.

———. "Race and Race Relations." Unpublished interview. Nashville: Christian Life Commission of the Southern Baptist Convention, n.d.

———. *Racial Revelations*. Birmingham, AL: Women's Missionary Union Literature Department, Sunday School Board of the Southern Baptist Convention, 1927.

———. *Right or Wrong?* Nashville: Broadman, 1955.

———. *Segregation and Desegregation: A Christian Approach*. New York: Macmillan, 1959.

———. "Some Ideas for Religious Education." The T. B. Maston Collection. Fort Worth, TX: Southwestern Baptist Theological Seminary, 1963.

———. "Southern Baptists and the Education of Negro Ministers." The T. B. Maston Collection. Fort Worth, TX: Southwestern Baptist Theological Seminary, 1953.

———. *Suffering: A Personal Perspective*. Nashville: Broadman, 1967.

———. "Theologians: Conservative/Liberal." *"Both/And" Series, Baptist Standard*, May 27, 1981.

———. "Theology and Ethics in Ephesians." *Southwestern Journal of Theology* 6 (1963) 60–70

———. *To Walk as He Walked*. Nashville: Broadman, 1985.

———. *Treasures from Holy Scripture*. Nashville: Broadman, 1987.

———. "'Trends to Watch' Baptist Standard Series." The T. B. Maston Collection. Fort Worth, TX: Southwestern Baptist Theological Seminary, 1968–1970.

———. "Where Are We in Race Relations? An Overview." The T. B. Maston Collection. Fort Worth, TX: Southwestern Baptist Theological Seminary, 1973.

————. "Who Is the Good Christian?" *Baptist Standard*, February 6, 1969.

————. *Why Live the Christian Life?* Nashville: Broadman, 1974.

————. *Words of Wisdom*. Nashville: Broadman, 1984.

————. *A World in Travail: A Study of the Contemporary World Crisis*. Nashville: Broadman, 1954.

Maston, T. B., and William M. Tillman. *The Bible and Family Relations*. Nashville: Broadman, 1983.

Maston, T. B., et al. *Both-And: A Maston Reader; Selected Readings from the Writings of T. B. Maston*. Dallas, TX: T. B. Maston Foundation, 2011.

Maston, T. B., et al. *Perspectives on Applied Christianity: Essays, in Honor of Thomas Buford Maston*. Macon, GA: Mercer University Press, 1986.

"[Maston, Thomas Buford] Bibliography." *Perspectives in Religious Studies* 12 (1985) 7–8.

Matthes, Erich Hatala. "Cultural Appropriation Without Cultural Essentialism?" *Social Theory and Practice* 42 (2016) 343–66.

Mattison, William C. *Introducing Moral Theology: True Happiness and the Virtues*. Grand Rapids: Brazos, 2008.

Maxwell, Joe. "Black Southern Baptists." *Christianity Today* 39 (1995) 26–31.

McBeth, Leon. "Origin of the Christian Life Commission." *Baptist History and Heritage* 1 (1966) 29–36.

McCabe, Herbert, and Brian Davies. "God and Creation." *New Blackfriars* 94 (2013) 385–95.

McCullough, Charles Franklin. "An Evaluation of the Biblical Hermeneutic of T. B. Maston." PhD diss., Southwestern Baptist Theological Seminary, 1987.

McDowell, Catherine L. *The Image of God in the Garden of Eden: The Creation of Humankind in Genesis 2:5–3:24 in Light of the Mīs Pî Pīt Pî and Wpt-r Rituals of Mesopotamia and Ancient Egypt*. Winona Lake, IN: Eisenbrauns, 2015.

McGee, Timothy. "God's Life in and as Opening: James Cone, Divine Self-Determination, and the Trinitarian Politics of Sovereignty." *Modern Theology* 32 (2016) 100–117.

McKinney, Larry J. "Evangelical Theological Higher Education: Past Commitments, Present Realities, and Future Considerations." *Christian Higher Education* 3 (2004) 147–69.

Mead, James K. *Biblical Theology: Issues, Methods, and Themes*. Louisville, KY: Westminster John Knox, 2007.

Meilaender, Gilbert C. *The Theory and Practice of Virtue*. Notre Dame, IN: University of Notre Dame Press, 1984.

Miller, Francis Pickens. "Christians in Racial Crisis: A Study of the Little Rock Ministry/ Segregation and Desegregation a Christian Approach/A Southern Moderate Speaks." *New Republic* 141 (1959) 17.

Moore, William T. *His Heart Is Black*. Atlanta: Home Mission Board, 1978.

Morrison, Paul. "Segregation, Desegregation, and Integration: The Legacy of Thomas Buford Maston on Race Relations," PhD diss., Southwestern Baptist Theological Seminary, 2018.

————. "Race and Virtue: The Virtuous Mean as Vehicle for the Integrated Church." *Bulletin for Ecclesial Theology* 9 (Forthcoming, 2022).

————. "Won't You Be My Neighbor? The Ecclesial Task of Virtue Formation." *Bulletin for Ecclesial Theology* 9 (Forthcoming, 2022).

Mouw, Richard J. *The God Who Commands*. Notre Dame, IN: University of Notre Dame Press, 1990.

Naidoo, M. "Liberative Black Theology: A Case Study of Race in Theological Education." *Acta Theologica* 36 (2016) 157.

Nelson, Jimmie. "Southern Baptists and the Issue of Slavery: 1835–1850." Unpublished research paper, Southwestern Baptist Theological Seminary, 1954.

Nestle, Eberhard, et al., eds. *Novum Testamentum Graece, Greek-English New Testament*. Stuttgart: Deutsche Bibelgesellschaft, 2013.

Newman, Mark. *Getting Right with God: Southern Baptists and Desegregation, 1945–1995*. Tuscaloosa, AL: University of Alabama Press, 2001.

Niebuhr, H. Richard. *Christ and Culture*. San Francisco: Harper, 2001.

———. *The Responsible Self: An Essay in Christian Moral Philosophy*. Louisville, KY: Westminster John Knox, 1999.

———. *The Social Sources of Denominationalism*. Cleveland: World, 1965.

Niebuhr, Reinhold. *Moral Man and Immoral Society: A Study in Ethics and Politics*. Louisville, KY: Westminster John Knox, 2013.

———. *The Nature and Destiny of Man: A Christian Interpretation*. New York: Scribner's, 1949.

Nussbaum, Martha C. "Virtue Ethics: A Misleading Category?" *The Journal of Ethics* 3 (1999) 163–201.

Odhiambo, Nicholas. "The Nature of Ham's Sin." *Bibliotheca Sacra* 170 (2013) 154–65.

"On Renouncing the Doctrine of the Curse of Ham as a Justification for Racism." http://www.sbc.net/resolutions/2287/resolution-4--on-renouncing-the-doctrine-of-the-curse-of-ham-as-a-justification-for-racism.

"Oral History Collection: T. B. Maston." In *Oral History Collection*, no. 228. Denton, TX: North Texas State University, 1974.

Orr, James. *God's Image in Man: And Its Defacement in the Light of Modern Denials*. London: Hodder & Stoughton, 1908.

Parham, Robert. "A. C. Miller: The Bible Speaks on Race." *Baptist History and Heritage* 27 (1992) 32–43.

Paris, Peter J. "The Ethics of African American Religious Scholarship." *Journal of The American Academy of Religion* 64 (1996) 483–97.

Park, Julie, and Nida Denson. "When Race and Class Both Matter: The Relationship between Socioeconomic Diversity, Racial Diversity, and Student Reports of Cross-Class Interaction." *Research in Higher Education* 54 (2013) 725–45.

"Pastor Should Play Key Integration Role, Dr. T. B. Maston Contends." *Biblical Recorder*, March 18, 1961.

Pennington, Kimberly Lynn. "Blueprint for Change: A History of Efforts by Southern Baptist Leaders to Reform Southern Baptist Culture on Race Relations." PhD diss., Southwestern Baptist Theological Seminary, 2016.

Pero, Albert. "The Nature and Function of God as Interpreted by the Church in a World Divided by Poverty and Plenty." *Currents in Theology and Mission* 40 (2013) 24–32.

Perry, Destiny. "The Colorblind Ideal in a Race-Conscious Reality: The Case for a New Legal Ideal for Race Relations." *Northwestern Journal of Law and Social Policy* 6 (2011) 473–95.

Phillips, Justin Randall. "Lord, When Did We See You? The Ethical Vision of White, Progressive Baptists in the South During the Civil Rights Movement." PhD diss., Fuller Theological Seminary, Center for Advanced Theological Study, 2013.

Pink, Arthur Walkington. *Gleanings in Genesis*. Chicago: Moody, 1981.

Pinson, William M. *An Approach to Christian Ethics: The Life, Contribution, and Thought of T. B. Maston*. Nashville: Broadman, 1979.

———. "Texas Baptist Contributions to Ethics: The Life and Influence of T. B. Maston." *Baptist History and Heritage* 33 (1998) 7–20.

Plato. *A Plato Reader: Eight Essential Dialogues*. Edited by C. D. C. Reeve. Indianapolis: Hackett, 2012.

Poinsett, Alex. "What the Bible Really Says About Segregation." *Ebony* 17 (1962) 73–76.

Pope, Liston. *The Kingdom Beyond Caste*. New York: Friendship, 1957.

Porter, Lee. "Southern Baptists and Race Relations, 1948–1963." ThD diss., Southwestern Baptist Theological Seminary, 1965.

Poythress, Vern S. *Logic: A God-Centered Approach to the Foundation of Western Thought*. Wheaton, IL: Crossway, 2013.

Priest, Josiah. *Bible Defence of Slavery: Or, The Origin, History, and Fortunes of the Negro Race, As Deduced from History, Both Sacred and Profane, Their Natural Relations–Moral, Mental, and Physical–to the Other Races of Mankind, Compared and Illustrated–Their Future Destiny Predicted, Etc.* Louisville, KY: Printed and published by J. F. Brennan for W. A. Bush, 1976.

"Protest Pamphlet on Integration." *The Baptist Message*, August 8, 1957.

Rai, Kul B., and John W. Critzer. *Affirmative Action and the University: Race, Ethnicity, and Gender in Higher Education Employment*. Lincoln, NE: University of Nebraska Press, 2000.

Rajagopalan, Kumar. "What Is the Defining Divide? False Post-Racial Dogmas and the Biblical Affirmation of 'Race.'" *Black Theology: An International Journal* 13 (2015) 166–88.

Ramsay, Nancy. "Intersectionality: A Model for Addressing the Complexity of Oppression and Privilege." *Pastoral Psychology* 63 (2014) 453–69.

Ramsey, Paul. *Basic Christian Ethics*. New York: Scribner, 1950.

Rawls, John. *Justice as Fairness: A Restatement*. Cambridge, MA: Harvard University Press, 2003.

Reed, John Shelton. "How Southerners Gave Up Jim Crow." *New Perspectives* 17 (1985) 15–19.

Rees, Thomas, et al. *The Racovian Catechism: With Notes and Illustrations, Translated from the Latin; To Which is Prefixed a Sketch of the History of Unitarianism in Poland and the Adjacent Countries*. Lexington, KY: American Theological Library Association, 1962.

Reichard, Joshua D. "Racial Diversity, Student Religiosity, and School Choice: An Empirical Case Study of Multi-Racial Religious Education." *Religious Education* 109 (2014) 81–92.

Reiss, Moshe. "Adam: Created in the Image and Likeness of God." *Jewish Bible Quarterly* 39 (2011) 181–86.

Reitman, Jason, dir. *The Office*. Season 5, episode 8, "Frame Toby." Aired November 20, 2008, on NBC.

"Resolution on Racial Reconciliation on the 150th Anniversary of the Southern Baptist Convention." http://www.sbc.net/resolutions/899/resolution-on-racial-reconciliation-on-the-150th-anniversary-of-the-southern-baptist-convention.

Roach, David. "Civil Rights Act Tore Down Walls, Expanded Reconciliation Efforts." *Baptist Press,* May 20, 2014.

———. "The Southern Baptist Convention and Civil Rights, 1954–1995." PhD diss., The Southern Baptist Theological Seminary, 2009.

Roberts, Jason P. "'Fill and Subdue'? Imaging God in New Social and Ecological Contexts." *Zygon: Journal of Religion and Science* 50 (2015) 42–63.

Roberts, Laura Schmidt. "Toward a Theological Anthropology: A Study of Genesis 1—3." *Direction* 45 (2016) 136–48.

Robertson, O. Palmer. "Current Critical Questions Concerning the 'Curse of Ham' (Gen 9:20–27)." *Journal of The Evangelical Theological Society* 41 (1998) 177–88.

Robiglio, Andrea A., and Hans Christian Günther. *The European Image of God and Man: A Contribution to the Debate on Human Rights*. Leiden: Brill, 2010.

Rothstein, Richard. *The Color of Law: A Forgotten History of How Our Government Segregated America*. New York: Liveright, 2017.

Rouse, John E. "Role of Segregation in Southern Baptist Polity." *The Journal of Religious Thought* 29 (1972) 19–38.

Rubio, Philip F. *A History of Affirmative Action, 1619–2000*. Jackson, MS: University Press of Mississippi, 2001.

Rutledge, Arthur B. "The Biblical Teaching on Slavery." Unpublished research paper, Southwestern Baptist Theological Seminary, 1941.

Ryle, Herbert E. *The Book of Genesis*. Cambridge: Cambridge University Press, 1921.

Sanders, Cheryl J. "Afrocentricity and Theological Education." *Journal of Religious Thought* 50 (1993) 11–26.

Sands, Paul. "The Imago Dei as Vocation." *Evangelical Quarterly* 82 (2010) 28–41.

Schleitwiler, Vincent J. "Into a Burning House: Representing Segregation's Death." *African American Review* 42 (2008) 149–62.

Schnabel, Eckhard J. "Contextualising Paul in Athens: The Proclamation of the Gospel Before Pagan Audiences in the Graeco-Roman World." *Religion and Theology* 12 (2005) 172–90.

Schüle, Andreas. "Made in the 'Image of God': The Concepts of Divine Images in Gen 1–3." *Zeitschrift Für Die Alttestamentliche Wissenschaft* 117 (2005) 1–20.

Schumacher, Lydia. "A Problem with Method in Theological Anthropology: Towards an All-Inclusive Theology." *Expository Times* 127 (2016) 375–89.

Sebastian, J. Jayakiran. "Engaging Multiculturalism as Public Theologians." *International Journal of Public Theology* 8 (2014) 335–43.

"Selma Association Adopts Resolution on Integration." *The Alabama Baptist*, April 17, 1958.

Shakespeare, William. *Oxford Shakespeare: The Merchant of Venice*. Edited by Jay L. Halio. Cary: Oxford University Press, 1993.

Sherman, Cecil E. "The Protestant Clergy and American Negro Slavery." Unpublished research paper, Southwestern Baptist Theological Seminary, 1956.

Shin, Patrick S. "Diversity v. Colorblindness." *Brigham Young University Law Review* 5 (2009) 1175–220.

Simmons, Paul D., and Bob Adams. *Issues in Christian Ethics*. Nashville: Broadman, 1980.

Simpson, Cuthbert A. *Interpreter's Bible*. Vol. 1. New York: Abingdon-Cokesbury, 1952.

Skinner, John. *A Critical and Exegetical Commentary on Genesis*. Edinburgh: T. & T. Clark, 1930.

Smith, Blake. "Southern Baptist Churches: Convention of Autonomous Bodies Faces Crisis: World Evangelism or Segregation?" *Christianity And Crisis* 18 (1958) 22–24.

Smith, Clint. "A Place of Their Own." *National Geographic* 233 (2018) 118–41.

Smith, H. Shelton. *In His Image, But . . . : Racism in Southern Religion, 1780–1910.* Durham, NC: Duke University Press, 1972.

Smith, Mitzi J. *The Literary Construction of the Other in the Acts of the Apostles: Charismatics, the Jews, and Women.* Cambridge: Clarke, 2012.

Snodgrass, Klyne. *Ephesians.* Grand Rapids: Zondervan, 1996.

Southern Baptist Convention. "2018 CP Ministry Reports." Advisory Council. http://www.sbc.net/advisoryCouncilReports.

———. "2018 CP Ministry Reports." Council of Seminary Presidents. http://www.sbc.net/cp/ministryreports/2018/presidents.asp.

———. "2018 CP Ministry Reports." Ethics and Religious Liberty Commission. http://www.sbc.net/cp/ministryreports/2018/erlc.asp.

———. "2018 CP Ministry Reports." Gateway Seminary of the Southern Baptist Convention. http://www.sbc.net/cp/ministryreports/2018/gs.asp.

———. "2018 CP Ministry Reports." Lifeway Christian Resources. http://www.sbc.net/cp/ministryreports/2018/lifeway.asp.

———. "2018 CP Ministry Reports." Midwestern Baptist Theological Seminary. http://www.sbc.net/cp/ministryreports/2018/mbts.asp.

———. "2018 CP Ministry Reports." New Orleans Baptist Theological Seminary. http://www.sbc.net/cp/ministryreports/2018/nobts.asp.

———. "2018 CP Ministry Reports." North American Mission Board. http://www.sbc.net/cp/ministryreports/2018/namb.asp.

———. "2018 CP Ministry Reports." Southeastern Baptist Theological Seminary. http://www.sbc.net/cp/ministryreports/2018/sebts.asp.

———. "2018 CP Ministry Reports" The Southern Baptist Theological Seminary. http://www.sbc.net/cp/ministryreports/2018/sbts.asp.

———. "2018 CP Ministry Reports." Southwestern Baptist Theological Seminary. http://www.sbc.net/cp/ministryreports/2018/swbts.asp.

———. "African American Taskforce Report." Advisory Council, 2012. http://www.sbc.net/advisoryCouncilReports.

———. "Multi-Ethnic Advisory Council Report." Advisory Council, 2016. http://www.sbc.net/advisoryCouncilReports.

"Southern Baptist Convention." *Biblical Recorder,* June 16, 1956.

Southern Baptist Historical Library and Archives. *1845 Proceedings of the Southern Baptist Convention,* Southern Baptist Convention, Richmond, VA: 12–18. http://www.sbhla.org/sbc_annuals.

Spain, Rufus B. *At Ease in Zion: Social History of Southern Baptists, 1865–1900.* Tuscaloosa, AL: University of Alabama Press, 2003.

———. "Oral Memoirs of T. B. Maston." Waco, TX: Baylor University Institute of Oral History, 1973.

Spencer, Aída Besançon. "Father-Ruler: The Meaning of the Metaphor 'Father' for God in the Bible." *Journal of The Evangelical Theological Society* 39 (1996) 433–42.

Stassen, Glen H., and David P. Gushee. *Kingdom Ethics: Following Jesus in Contemporary Context.* Downers Grove, IL: InterVarsity, 2003.

Stern, David. "*Imitatio Hominis*: Anthropomorphism and the Character(s) of God in Rabbinic Literature." *Prooftexts* 2 (1992) 151–74.

Storey, John W. "Thomas Buford Maston and the Growth of Social Christianity Among Texas Baptists." *East Texas Historical Journal* 19 (1981) 27–42.

Strickland, Walter R., II. "Liberation and Black Theological Method: A Historical Analysis." PhD diss., University of Aberdeen, 2017.

Stricklin, David. *A Genealogy of Dissent: Southern Baptist Protest in the Twentieth Century*. Lexington, KY: The University Press of Kentucky, 2015.

Sullivan, H. T. "The Christian Concept of Race Relations." *The Baptist Message*, October 10, 1957.

Swift, Donald Charles. *Religion and the American Experience: A Social and Cultural History, 1765–1997*. Armonk, NY: M. E. Sharpe, 1998.

Swinton, John. "Who Is the God We Worship? Theologies of Disability; Challenges and New Possibilities." *International Journal of Practical Theology* 14 (2011) 273–307.

Tatum, Beverly Daniel. *"Why Are All the Black Kids Sitting Together in the Cafeteria?": And Other Conversations About Race*. New York: Basic, 2017.

T. B. Maston Collection. A. Webb Roberts Library. Southwestern Baptist Theological Seminary, Fort Worth, TX.

"T. B. Maston: Retired Professor's Emphasis has been Applying the Gospel to Life." *Baptist Courier*, February 13, 1986.

"Thomas Buford Maston: A Chronology." *Perspectives in Religious Studies* 12 (1985) 5–6.

Thomas Buford Maston Collection. Southern Baptist Historical Library and Archives. Nashville, TN.

Thomas, Gerald L. "Achieving Racial Reconciliation in the Twenty-First Century: The Real Test for the Christian Church." *Review and Expositor* 108 (2011) 559–73.

Tillman, William M. "Barnette and Maston: We Need Them More than Ever." *Baptist History and Heritage* 38 (2003) 28–34.

———. "T. B. Maston (1897–1988): Mentor to Southern Baptist Prophets." In *Twentieth-Century Shapers of Baptist Social Ethics*. Macon, GA: Mercer University Press, 2008.

———. "T. B. Maston: The Conscience of Texas Baptists." *Texas Baptist History* 20 (2000) 71–85.

———. *Understanding Christian Ethics*. Nashville: Broadman, 1988.

Tillman, William M., Jr., and W. Andrew Tillman. "Martin, Maston, and Millard: 3 M Baptists and Social Justice." *Baptist History and Heritage* 44 (2009) 70–80.

———. "The Rise, Decline, and Fall of Christian Life Commission Entities and Voices." *Baptist History and Heritage* 41 (2006) 21–34.

Tilson, Everett. *Segregation and the Bible*. New York: Abingdon, 1958.

Timmermann, Jens. "V-What's Wrong with 'Deontology'?" *Proceedings of the Aristotelian Society* 115 (2015) 75–92.

Timmons, Mark. *Moral Theory: An Introduction*. Lanham, MD: Rowman & Littlefield, 2012.

Tisby, Jemar. *Color of Compromise: The Truth About the American Church's Complicity in Racism*. Grand Rapids: Zondervan, 2020.

Tse, Justin K. H. "Grounded Theologies: 'Religion' and the 'Secular' in Human Geography." *Progress in Human Geography* 38 (2014) 201–20.

Turpin, Katherine. "Christian Education, White Supremacy, and Humility in Formational Agendas." *Religious Education* 112 (2017) 407–17.

Turretin, Francis. *Institutes of Elenctic Theology; v 1: First through Tenth Topics, v 1.* Translated by George Musgrave Giger and James T. Dennison. N.p.: n.p., 1992.

Tutt, Daniel. "The Notion of Authority by Alexander Kojève. Trans. Hager Weslati." *Philosophy Now* 106 (2015) 43–45.

Valentine, Foy. "Baptist Polity and Social Pronouncements." *Baptist History and Heritage* 14 (1979) 52–61.

———. "General Social Problems of the American Negro." Unpublished research paper, Southwestern Baptist Theological Seminary, 1946.

———. "A Historical Study of Southern Baptists and Race Relations, 1917–1947." ThD diss., Southwestern Baptist Theological Seminary, 1949.

———. "Negro Institutions and Institutional Life." Unpublished research paper, Southwestern Baptist Theological Seminary, 1946.

———. "The Negro's Place in the American Way of Life." Unpublished research paper, Southwestern Baptist Theological Seminary, 1946.

———. "Programs for the Solution of Race Problems." Unpublished research paper, Southwestern Baptist Theological Seminary, 1946.

———. "T. B. Maston: A Conscience for Southern Baptists." *Southwestern Journal of Theology* 25 (1983) 89–103.

Wadell, Paul J. *Primacy of Love: An Introduction to the Ethics of Thomas Aquinas.* Eugene, OR: Wipf & Stock, 2009.

Ward, James D., and Mario Antonio Rivera. *Institutional Racism, Organizations and Public Policy.* New York: Peter Lang, 2014.

Weatherford, Willis D. *American Churches and the Negro: An Historical Study from Early Slave Days to the Present.* Boston: Christopher, 1957.

Weatherspoon, H. H. "Christ and Human Brotherhood." *The Biblical Recorder* 110 (1944) 10.

Weaver, Aaron Douglass. "Impact of Social Progressive T. B. Maston Upon Southern Baptist Life in the Twentieth-Century." https://web.archive.org/web/20110106101433/http://www.thebigdaddyweave.com/BDWFiles/Maston.pdf.

Webster, John. "'Love Is Also a Lover of Life': 'Creatio Ex Nihilo' and Creaturely Goodness." *Modern Theology* 29 (2013) 156–71.

Wenham, Gordon J., et al. *Genesis 1–15.* Grand Rapids: Zondervan, 2014.

Wesberry, James Pickett. "Georgia Baptists Hold Convention: Delegates Reject Proposal to Endorse Supreme Court Decision— Plan Segregation Campaign." *The Christian Century* 74 (1957) 54.

Westermann, Claus. *Creation.* Philadelphia: Fortress, 1974.

Wheeler, Edward L. "An Overview of Black Southern Baptist Involvements." *Baptist History and Heritage* 16 (1981) 3–11, 40.

"Who Loves the Negro?" *The Baptist Record* 30 (1928) 2.

Wiggan, Greg A. *Education for the New Frontier: Race, Education and Triumph in Jim Crow America (1867–1945).* Hauppauge, NY: Nova Science, 2011.

Willard, Dallas. *Renovation of the Heart: Putting on the Character of Christ.* Colorado Springs, CO: NavPress, 2002.

Williams, Jarvis J., and Kevin M. Jones. *Removing the Stain of Racism from the Southern Baptist Convention: Diverse African American and White Perspectives*. Nashville: B&H Academic, 2017.

Williams, Michael D. "Made for Mission: A New Orientation for Anthropology." *Presbyterion* 42 (2016) 36–53.

Williams, Michael E. "Thomas Buford Maston (1897–1988) Southern Baptist Pioneer in Race Relations." In *Witnesses to the Baptist Heritage: Thirty Baptists Every Christian Should Know*, 183–88. Macon, GA: Mercer University Press, 2015.

Williamson, Joel. *The Crucible of Race: Black-White Relations in the American South Since Emancipation*. New York: Oxford University Press, 1984.

———. *A Rage for Order: Black-White Relations in the American South Since Emancipation*. New York: Oxford University Press, 1986.

Willis, Alan Scot. *All According to God's Plan: Southern Baptist Missions and Race, 1945–1970*. Lexington, KY: The University Press of Kentucky, 2005.

Willoughby, Karen L. "Historic: Fred Luter Elected SBC President." *Baptist Press*, June 19, 2012.

Wilkens, Steve. *Beyond Bumper Sticker Ethics: An Introduction to Theories of Right and Wrong*. Downers Grove, IL: IVP Academic, 2011.

Wise, Tim J. *Affirmative Action: Racial Preference in Black and White*. New York: Routledge, 2005.

Wold, Donald J. *Out of Order: Homosexuality in the Bible and the Ancient Near East*. Grand Rapids: Baker, 1998.

Wood, James E., Jr. "Maston, Thomas Buford, 1898–1988." *Journal of Church and State* 30 (1988) 430.

Wood, John A. "Black America: From Bad News to Good News-Bad News." *Perspectives in Religious Studies* 12 (1985) 67–81.

Wood, Thomas E., and Malcolm J. Sherman. "Is Campus Racial Diversity Correlated with Educational Benefits?" *Academic Questions* 14 (2001) 72–88.

Woods, James R. "Authority and Controversial Policy: The Churches and Civil Rights." *American Sociological Review* 35 (1970) 1057–69.

Wray, Matt. *Not Quite White: White Trash and the Boundaries of Whiteness*. Durham, NC: Duke University Press, 2008.

Wright, Almeda M. "Mis-Education: A Recurring Theme? Transforming Black Religious and Theological Education." *Religious Education* 112 (2017) 66–79.

Wright, G. Ernest. *The Biblical Doctrine of Man in Society*. London: Published for the Study Department, World Council of Churches by SCM, 1975.

Wright, Richard, et al. "Patterns of Racial Diversity and Segregation in the United States: 1990–2010." *Professional Geographer* 66 (2014) 173–82.

Yancy, George. *Black Bodies, White Gazes: The Continuing Significance of Race in America*. Lanham, KY: Lexington, 2008.

———. *White Self-Criticality Beyond Anti-Racism: How Does It Feel to Be a White Problem?* Lanham, KY: Lexington, 2015.

Young, James O. *Cultural Appropriation and the Arts*. Malden, MA: Wiley-Blackwell, 2010.

Zamani-Gallaher, Eboni M. *The Case for Affirmative Action on Campus: Concepts of Equity, Considerations for Practice*. Sterling, VA: Stylus, 2009.

Subject Index